To Graham and !

Thanking you for
and trusting you will find this book
stimulating.

FALTERING PURPOSE:

A Tale of High Security Mental Hospitals

With Kind Regards,

Stephen .

J. Burke .

About the Author

Stephen Burrow was born in Surrey and flourished in all the pursuits offered by the Grammar School which he attended, until the very final hurdles of school life. He eventually settled to a varied professional career in the public sector which commenced with a Registered Mental Nurse training in 1973 in a traditional mental hospital; then a Registered General Nurse training at St Thomas Hospital in London; a Teacher Training Certificate; and a Practitioner training in Cognitive Analytic Therapy, also at St Thomas Hospital. Professional roles and positions ranged over middle management, research, teaching and lecturing, professional development, and therapeutic practice. Other professional development was derived from Honorary Lecturer and Honorary Researcher positions at the Institute of Psychiatry, London. His academic credentials include a first degree in Sociology at the London School of Economics, London University, and a Masters Degree in Crime, Deviance and Social Policy from Lancaster University. Much of his career focused on the specialism of forensic mental health nursing, spending varying periods in medium security facilities, high security hospitals (notably Broadmoor and Ashworth), and Prison Service health care. In the area of professional publication he has acted as an Editorial Board Advisor to two professional journals and has published a number of editorials, journal articles, book chapters, and original research. His long-term interest in writing culminated in the publication, in 2010, of his first professional memoir *Buddleia Dance on the Asylum: a Nurse's Journey through a Mental Hospital*. He is now writing his third book. Taking early retirement in 2005, he moved to the pastoral heart of Dorset to pursue his lifelong enthusiasm for the countryside but really longs to settle in France. He has two daughters to whom he is devoted.

Stephen Burrow
M.A., B.Sc(Hons)., RMN., RGN., RNT., Cert.Ed.
Practitioner in Cognitive Analytic Therapy.

Published Work:

The Treatment And Security Needs Of Special Hospital Patients (1995) by Maden, Curle, Meux, Burrow and Gunn
Whurr publishers

Buddleia Dance on the Asylum: a Nurse's Journey Through a Mental Hospital (2010)
Melrose Books

FALTERING PURPOSE:

A Tale of High Security Mental Hospitals

Stephen Burrow

FALTERING PURPOSE:

A Tale of High Security Mental Hospitals

Olympia Publishers

www.olympiapublishers.com
OLYMPIA PAPERBACK EDITION

ISBN: 978-1-84897-107-3

First Published in 2010

Olympia Publishers part of Ashwell Publishing Ltd
60 Cannon Street
London
EC4N 6NP

Printed in Great Britain

Disclaimer

Much of the material in this book necessarily identifies named individuals because it is available in the public domain. Where it has been possible I have endeavoured to protect the identities of all other patients and members of staff.

Dedication

This book is dedicated to my two daughters,
Rachel and Heather.

Abstracts

'The way of peace they know not; and there is no judgement in their goings: they have made them crooked paths: whosoever goeth therein shall not know peace'. (Isaiah, 59: 8).

'The evil that men do lives after them; the good is oft interred with their bones;' (William Shakespeare. *Julius Caesar*, Act 3, Scene 2).

'The fact of the matter is that the organisations such as schools and hospitals will, like dragons, eat the hero innovator for breakfast,' (Giorgiades and Phillmore, 1980).

'Kindness and forbearance are first principles in the care and management of persons of unsound mind; few such persons are beyond their influence. The mischievous will become somewhat less troublesome, the dirty less careless; the irritable and violent often render most essential service to the Attendants who treat them firmly, justly, and kindly.' (Rules for the Guidance of Officers, Attendants, and Servants. Broadmoor Asylum, 1866).

Chapters

Preface

Understandably, I have met precious few people during normal social contact who have any more than the vaguest comprehension of the concepts of forensic psychiatry, or forensic nursing, or forensic mental health care, though some may take an intelligent stab (so to speak) at that of the mentally disordered offender. As a rule, reference to any of these will require an immediate explication of the professional field, its objectives and parameters. Therefore, it may be useful to give a brief introduction for the benefit of anyone finding such terminology to obfuscate what many consider to be a truly absorbing area of life as well as for others who, at the very least, would admit to it stirring their morbid curiosity.

The culprit, of course, is the presumption behind the term "forensic". Most people will have a passing association with forensic science, and forensic pathology, and the application of scientific method, tests and technology to search for and establish incontrovertible evidence which is used to secure either the release or the conviction of a defendant charged with a criminal offence. Hence, the *forensic examination* will subject the defendant/s, and/or their alleged victims, and/or the background circumstances, to investigative procedures such as fingerprinting, DNA profiling, and a diverse range of other scientific analysis. The trick in the box is that the derivation of "forensic" is not just the scientific evidence, per se, but that the presentation of such findings materialise within the context of a *court*. The term "forensic" is rooted in the Latin "forensis" which described the legal disputes which took place in the physical place of the Roman open public forum. The contemporary legal forum for administering legal disputes and justice is that of the court: the Magistrates' Court, the Crown Court, the Divorce Court, the High Court, and the Appeal Court. Clearly, this means that "forensic" is not confined to the notion of *forensic space* but also implies a "forensic process" which, again, people will be more familiar with than they realise. A *forensic frame of reference* requires a body of law to define the alleged illegal actions and intentions of individuals or groups within a wider society, as well as facilitating and legitimising the progress and legal status of the defendant/s, and the adjudication of the contested events within the court by the adversarial parties. The judgement will elaborate on the court's deliberations, determine a verdict that appropriately reflects the available evidence, and determine the disposal options which may include a full acquittal, a conditional discharge, a suspended sentence, a probation order, a community service order, a prison sentence, or other judicial outcome. Operationalising this legal frame of reference requires *forensic agency* whereby the various adjudicating bodies, and adversarial parties acting on behalf of, or against, the defendant/s may have the means to contribute their parts. This provides for the police service, police surgeons, coroners, the Crown Prosecution Service, Judges, Juries, Defence and Prosecution Lawyers, Probation Officers, and any other professional groups to present their expertise for the scrutiny of the court.

Police Officers, Judges, the Crown Prosecution Service, and Probation Officers, and suchlike, whose occupational function is specifically related to criminal matters, are examples of groups who do not require the forensic prefix to denote a specialist adjunct to their main professional focus. So, there is no requirement to refer to a forensic Police Officer, or coroner, or Probation Officer. Conversely, the forensic world has such a considerable application in today's affairs that it represents a specialist split from a core professional body. It can be prefixed to any and every occupation or profession where there is a need to develop a subsidiary expertise in that field to take account of crime related events, or criminal deviations, arising out of its operations. Such fields as forensic dentistry, forensic anthropology, forensic computer technology, forensic accountancy, and the criminal investigation of injury and death by forensic medicine, to name but a few, work within similar parameters to the forensic pathologist in that they have to bring their expert witness to the court. This requires any forensic specialist from any occupational field to function at an interface between their occupational field and that of the court, weaving the search for illegal behaviour through the machinations of their industry and presenting their conclusions for legal scrutiny.

Similarly, the forensic psychiatrist, in the capacity of an expert witness, contributes to the modern forensic process by presenting their medical findings and psychiatric opinion, on a client whom they have examined and possibly treated, to the court. It is then the court's task to weigh this medical evidence along with all the other contributors in the trial and to determine a defendant's overall "responsibility" for the criminal actions for which they have been charged. A successful psychiatric defence would mean that an accused did not have the necessary mental capacity, or criminal motivation, or intent, for the criminal transgression they committed, even though they did actually commit the act, because *at the time of committing that offence* they were suffering from a mental disorder. In other words, the responsibility of the accused was substantially diminished as a result of the mental disorder. The nature of that disorder will, routinely, have been specifically diagnosed to give credence to the professional opinion that the defendant should not be held responsible for their transgression, whatever it may be, however serious. Consequently, even though guilty of the criminal act itself, the conventional route of conviction, sentence, and imprisonment would not be considered appropriate. Of the many outcomes available to the court at this stage, one would most certainly be the "diversion" of the defendant to a secure hospital for treatment, under a psychiatrist's jurisdiction, of the exhibited mental disorder. This will be effected by the court's use of the Mental Health Acts in operation at that particular point in time which will facilitate the lawful disposal of a defendant into the jurisdiction of psychiatry until there is sufficient evidence that the client, in most instances, no longer represents a high risk to the rest of society.

Forensic psychiatry is a professional enterprise with a commitment toward the normal psychiatric trajectory of diagnosing, treating, and managing clients' mental disorder. But there is an inclusive requirement to take account of, manage, and treat any seriously antisocial, dangerous, and law-breaking behaviour that derives from, or is associated with, that disorder. This has created a conventional definition of forensic psychiatry as that branch of psychiatry which deals with mentally disordered clients at a medico-legal interface. Consequently, forensic psychiatry has a unique operational jurisdiction that predominantly hospitalises the mentally disordered offender in a mutant environment spanning mental health care and secure custody. Hospitalisation may range from high security forensic facilities where security and control are maximised, through to medium and low facilities which optimise secure custody, and which is augmented by a community service which will monitor any discharged clients. But evolving debates about what should constitute the limits of forensic mental health care has extended its focus to include not only the patients as perpetrators of mentally disordered crime, but as victims in their own right, along with the victims of their crimes. In the USA this later area is a veritable industry in its own right! It has been argued that most patients have been past victims of a range of adversity, in some cases of a "multiple victimisation", whether of circumstantial trauma, or dysfunctional family dynamics, or other socially derived adversity. Therefore, the rationale for an inclusive victim-centred approach that recognises that mentally disordered clients, and their victims, have the potential to suffer acute or chronic disorder as a result of their experiences, amounts to a preventative medicine. Such protagonists argue for an alternative definition that proposes that forensic psychiatry is the prevention, amelioration and treatment of victimisation which is associated with mental disease (Gunn and Taylor: *Forensic Psychiatry. Clinical, Legal and Ethical Issues.* Butterworth-Heinemann Ltd, 1993).

000

So what, if anything, is the link between mental disorder and offending behaviour that could justify the use of forensic psychiatry? Clearly, if mental disorder was absolutely determinate of offending behaviour then all those with such difficulties would be falling foul of the law on a regular, if not continuous, basis. Because this is most certainly not the case, offending behaviour is not generally characteristic of mental disorder per se. Neither is any specific psychiatric disorder invariably linked with antisocial, dangerous or violent behaviour. This is not to suggest that mental disorder cannot be criminogenic. There is an accumulating body of evidence which reveals fairly strong correlations between specific psychiatric symptoms, along with one or two exceptional diagnoses, and a related offending outcome. However, there are far too many caveats to the rule to consider listing and explicating these symptoms and diagnoses here. There is a danger of being over-prescriptive, and over-simplistic, about symptom-generated offending.

What must be said is that a person experiencing the exceptionally disturbed symptoms of a mental disorder may lose the capacity to negotiate and abide by more conventional social expectations. When these symptoms are of an exceptionally disturbing nature such persons may be unable to resist the psychological urge to commit deviant, antisocial, dangerous, or violent acts which they would not normally entertain so that they cannot be held wholly responsible for their offending outcomes, no matter how severe they were. It is this fundamental premise that informs the entire forensic process in relation to the mentally disordered offender: the court decision to

22

"divert" a defendant to a hospital for treatment of mental disorder; the provision of a professional platform of mental health disciplines, led by forensic psychiatry, to treat the criminogenic aspects of a mental disorder and to develop adaptive mental health; and to permit mentally disordered offenders the right to continued citizenship whether detained in secure conditions or residing in the community. Indeed, the non-judgemental belief that every reasonable opportunity should be afforded to a forensic client to be returned to mental health, and to the community, however extreme the criminal transgression that has been perpetrated, is the only ethical position that can be assumed by mental health workers in this field, and the rest of society.

Chapter 1

Substantiation

Of the many impressions the place made upon me over a number of years the most concerted was that the conventional world was to be kept as distant as its inhabitants were to be kept close, and that the surrounding deciduous and conifer forest far from wrapped a shepherding arm around the sequestered hospital site that had gouged a hole in its side. All this to contain what was perceived as the preternatural proceedings operating within. Viewed from the concealed road to its rear the continuous line of red-bricked, hospital buildings and glinting windows, embedded into the crest of the slope, could have passed for a Napoleonic fortification. An inner wall, as high as any protective rampart, banked away through the kitchen gardens to a perimeter wall that flanked the entire ground to the rear. From here on, the imagination induced various vantage points from which could have protruded the rude threat of canons, or the assembled bristle of muskets and bayonets, and that the whole imposing and intimidating scene was nothing, if not defensive. On the adjoining margins of the outside moor, the acquired sheep and cattle fields encroached as much as they dare while crowing roosts fidgeted in the high trees that overlooked the estate wall. Also spread beyond the back wall was the remaining neglect of the former hospital farm. Over the many preceding decades it had, like an attached placenta, supplied a virtually self-sufficient provision of meat and dairy products to its marooned dependents. But, superseded by commercially contracted food deliveries, the replenishing chord had been tied off and the farm expelled from the body of the estate. Now, the decaying organ hosted little more than a metal sprawl of obsolete machinery, wracked brick farmhouse and piggeries, and shelled corrugations. Yet, this defunct wasteland still accommodated the secluded public footpath that ran like a vital, bloody thread through beads of buddleia bushes, foxglove groves, long-grassed mounds, matted sheep, and diverse birdsong.

From within the perimeter walls, a quite different perspective was offered while standing on any of the upper floors of the several residential blocks. From this vantage the interested party could trace the long slope sweeping through the productive patchwork of kitchen gardens which, again, would have yielded a past independent supply of fruit and vegetables. Beyond these the expansive, but generally vacant, sports field extended to the rear wall. Up on this residential ridge, parting the inner wall and the male patients' blocks, lay the Terrace which could have adorned any grand house. Its immaculate lawn of green was laced around its edges with a broad grey walkway and, when the sun was so positioned, an archaic clutch of yew trees cast a variegated, dark shade across it. Aesthetics aside, this was the hospital's superior equivalent of a prison exercise yard and had borne the preoccupations of its male inmates and their countless perambulations for over a century and a half. With the advantage of these several scenes the ambiance of the past, the pastoral calm, and the more relaxed but active regime, was easily evoked. Abutting the female wards, but containing its own arboreal seclusion, was what would have been the original residence of the Medical Superintendent, replete with family. From this proximate position the Medical Superintendent would have had to give account for everything that happened across the site: the building stock, the entire treatment and security regime, the welfare of patients, his staff, and their relatives, as well as bearing the personal brunt for any calamities. Gathered round him was a tight circle of Deputy Superintendent, Assistant Medical Officer, Chaplain, Steward, Storekeeper, Matron, Clerk of Works, Bailiff, and Gardener, and from this sparking node, he conducted an imperial and steadying rhythm throughout every organ and channel of the hospital body. And to this routine beat, the institution's diverse cacophony was orchestrated: the bashing, sawing and nailing from the workshops' tools as patients learned the trades of the carpenter, upholsterer, bookbinder, cobbler and tinsmith; the percussion of clashing utensils in the bakery, kitchen and milking parlour; the women pummelling and gliding in the laundry, and picking and weaving the thready strings of the sewing rooms. And in the dimming recreational hours the dancing feet, rehearsing dramas, asylum band and choir, soothed the fading, jarring day with more voluntary rhythms. Released from the wards, half the community would mill about the bunting-sprayed sports field on Sports Day, and visiting teams compete across the bowling green and soccer pitch. And there, would thrive the working party tilling at the kitchen-garden soil and enjoying the airy tea breaks with the staff. And there, the very trusted souls who manned the general stores. Beyond the hospital precinct, other working parties of escorted patients in the hospital uniform tramping to their farming tasks, or tidying and mending the estate, or trimming the gardens of the staff quarters, like casual chain-gangs. Recreational parties would be rambling, and scuffing through the meandering trails of the woods. But parading through the village shops and thoroughfares under the dubious, and ambivalent, gaze of the local populace would have been a more self-conscious trial. For, in their sceptical eyes, these trailing forays of criminals and their wardens were trespassing from the gates of a prison no less.

They would not have been party to, or entertained, the stories of the inmates who had their own remarkable tales to tell. Such a one would have been that elderly gent with the beard and long tunic, seated beneath his window, with the light slashing across the opened tomes on his desk who came to be the longest serving of all the inmates up until that point in time, incarcerated behind those walls for twenty years. William Chester Minor, a commissioned Assistant Surgeon in the American Army, had discharged himself from that service and spent some time in an American asylum for a very obsessional form of paranoia before arriving on British shores with his paranoid ideation still intact. His psychological burden was an incapacity to shake off the belief that he was being pursued by Fenians – Irish Republicans – who were trying every conceivable way of penetrating his privacy in order to kill him. These delusions were fatally activated one night in 1872 when, in the Borough of Lambeth, he mistakenly identified a stranger as one of the said Fenians and shot him dead with the pistol he carried. While at his subsequent trial the jury took due regard for the fact that Minor had committed a murder, because of the clear evidence of his deluded thinking, it found him *not guilty on grounds of insanity*. Therefore, instead of a prison disposal he was "detained in safe custody... until Her Majesty's pleasure be known" – Her Majesty being Queen Victoria – effectively, to spend the rest of his life in custody until she declared his discharge appropriate. And from the moment he woke every day in his hospital rooms he would still attest to the haunting delusions that a host of individuals intended to do him harm. Yet it did not prevent him from exercising his native intellect which he applied to his sketching and painting, to thumbing those numerous tomes, or that obsessive reading and study, as he sat there throughout the long, long years. Anonymously residing behind those asylum walls he became one of the most notable of the volunteer contributors to the compilation of the *New English Dictionary* – later to become the *Oxford English*

Dictionary. Minor acquired his own library of books for the purpose, which the hospital permitted to be stored in an adjoining room to that which was assigned as his sitting room! And while the ensuing years were spent in a scholarly contribution to the compilation of the dictionary, and the incidental acclaim that accompanied the enterprise, he was never deemed fit for release and died behind the walls. What a transformation on the local community's prejudices there might have been if his story had been known! To all but those privy to the occupants of this walled, esoteric confine – even to the dictionary's editor – he was "persona non grata". Obscurity indeed!

Of the building, itself, you could not doubt that you stood in the presence of a living monument to history and that this was one of the original and most durable of this genre of psychiatric establishments. Its stature as a notable building in its own right was unquestionable. Erected in red brick throughout, but trimmed with the artistry of artistic beige, the Victorian penchant for expansive construction sprawled across the site. These were the several, three-storey blocks of wards, the chapel, the hall, the administrative offices, and the main gate. Within the blocks the same grandeur was expressed in the generously proportioned, high-ceilinged, multiple-windowed, airy dayrooms and sleeping dormitories, and the side rooms that regularly punctuated the elongated corridors.

The main gate, alone, suggested a stockade and its brick bowers darkened the passage from freedom for any who passed beneath it. Yet, even here, the contrasting impressions projecting from the imagination perfectly symbolised the countervailing purposes of the institution. Ostensibly, it was nothing more than a stocky portal, modelled on prisons and, to a very large extent, fitted for the same purpose. The great arched wooden doors gave every indication of imposing impenetrability. Like iron ligaments, their clasping hinges stretched them open, then closed again. The doors were flexed like a male's pectorals between the muscular biceps of the double towers that brandished their barred windows like tattoos. But, closer scrutiny also yielded the exquisite form and creativity of the piece. For the workmanship had constructed something that could be likened to a massive cuckoo clock. From this stance, the towers protectively cosseted the intricate centrepiece of masonic colonnades, in-set alcoves, curved vaulting, and chiselled foliage which, in turn, embroidered the iron, Roman-numeralled clockface. And casting a succinct light over all, the iron and glass lamp perched at the very centre lay ready to illuminate any human form or vehicle that appeared at the sprung doors beneath. And, with some regularity, the patients and staff peeked out from behind their shuttered seclusion onto the world beyond before being retrieved, again, according to the institution's schedule. But, instead of the accompanying piping of a bird, on the hour, every hour, the air was rent with the weekly, screaming rehearsals of the hospital's sirens that foretold of escapes, taunted the peace of the forest, and sent the deer crashing through the disturbed undergrowth. The demand for the installation of hospital sirens had derived from a succession of hospital escapes one year. As events transpired, the first few proved to be apocalyptic, for the last ended catastrophically, fatally. In a planned operation, culminating in climbing what was only a ten foot wall at that time, a patient had gained a brief excursion through the proximate garden alleys, and into the fields and nearby villages. Following his recapture alongside an army base, there came the discovery of a strangled young girl deposited alongside her bicycle in a nearby secluded hamlet. Concerted action from the local Parish Council, and the Hospital Inquiry Committee, resulted in the siren installation which would alert the local population for miles of similar escapes. From then on, when the alert was implemented, the siren whirred and wound into an airy crescendo, and settled into a steady, two-tone clarion *alarm* that contrived to give voice to the piercing, wailing appeals of the little, flailing girl and her struggles for life. Her fading will and breath were captured by the succeeding winding down of the alarm, then the gasp of a pause and, finally, the sustained single note of the *all-clear* that hummed like one last protracted resigned breath. As if in a conclusive act of registering her death the siren droned down to a morbid stunned silence. The rare alerts, and weekly practice runs, only ratcheted up the ominous imagery, the contained dread of, and the muted awe toward, the place. The place was variously ascribed the titles of a "Special Hospital", and a high security hospital, having been relieved of the spectral name it once held of Broadmoor Criminal Lunatic Asylum.

000

'Sometimes, I think to myself, female patients must have been born on another planet.' So said the Acting Senior Nurse who had been leading me across the courtyard. While her remark could have been ruminative, and was presented without any hint of perplexity, I construed it was intended to take soundings of my personal opinions about our "Special Hospital" patients. An appropriately relaxed response on my part, I presumed, would then free her up for a more private and open commentary without it being considered unprofessional. We had, by then, approached the ground floor doorway at the very corner of a far-flung residential block of the hospital. The door was made diminutive set, as it was, against into the right-angle of two adjoining walls to the three-storey buildings. But before she could register any such readings, as if antagonised by our approach, a flurry of muted shrieks, intermingled with insults, rose like a two-fingered reprimand from within the building. I feigned an easy nonchalance with regard to both the disturbance, and her comment, for I surmised that every facet of my behaviour would be scrutinised by my escort during our acquaintance, however brief, and reported on to her colleagues. This was not so fanciful as it might seem for it most certainly applied to the hospital where I had recently achieved a managerial position and acquired the curious status of an "outsider" into the bargain. Throughout the early contact with my new colleagues, I had just hoped to give an authoritative impression of having forensic mental health credentials, and of an industrious and challenging leadership. Such credentials had proven to be naïvely misplaced as I came under the worldly scrutiny of my fellow staff who examined every nuance of my managerial and personal conduct in a calculation of my tribal loyalty, alone. A calculation that determined whether I could be counted to side, incontrovertibly, with the nursing staff or whether I was deemed a liability by being partial towards the patients' interests. Never before had quite such a staff/patient divide been so revealed to me. Whereby an interest in patient therapy and well-being was considered, ipso facto, a treacherous compromise of staff interests. A stance, I have to say, for which I would pay heavily in the not too distant future.

It was then that it dawned on me that her sounding of me about the patients' origins, as she had configured it, had been her very first reference to the hospital residents during our short time together. That it captured, in a solitary quip, the general orientation she must have owned about her work. It was such a distancing remark, not so related to defamation, I fancied, but more indicative of her own alienation from them. The remark lay before me like an ideational temptress. She had already admitted that she was looking to develop herself beyond the limitations of a ward environment and the routine functions of a Ward Sister. Allied to this, it was clearly her bold intention to attend as many professional development courses as were on offer, paid for by the hospital training budget, and pertinent to furthering her promotional potential. This was probably a rationalisation of an ongoing requirement for new challenges that might, in turn, fix some superimposed destination onto her life's uncertain passage. So that, with each new training course, she was stimulated to trim her drooping sails and chart a path away from the doldrums of her generally unsatisfactory working and personal life and head for an ever-changing horizon. Such impositions as the wards and their occupants which clearly so discomforted her had not dissuaded her the eminent pleasure, if I was any judge, of escorting me to the wards. While a reply from me was irresistible I hauled up the plummeting line she had cast at me and threw it back at her in an effort to further gauge her occupational proclivities.

'I'm wondering how much you meant that?' I posed, with an amused attention.

'What, about patients being born on another planet?' she said, promptly, stopping to face me with a barely concealed smile. Those large brown eyes studied my disposition while I returned a reassuring equanimity. She continued, equally assertively.

'Well they sure didn't come out of the same pods as you or I!'

'Do you mean in what they've done?' I had assumed she had given voice to an otherwise populist demonising of the transgressions of mentally abnormal offenders – criminal lunatics, as once was – and, no doubt, an implicit sense of personal impotence in the face of their daunting presentations and histories. I could only guess.

'Partly, but it's more that, once here, they seem to want to make their lives so complicated that they can't really be trying to get out! They're either fighting each other, fighting the staff, or harming themselves, without any realisation of how it will queer their pitch! So it's hard for us to work well with them and get any sense of achievement when they're forever going backwards and making so little progress. I was not too shocked by this having not so long, previously, been disposed to the view that so many patients seemed so unmotivated to want to demonstrate their capacity to return to the community once they had been accustomed to a long spell in in-patient care. But then I had benefited from a recent spell in an exceptional, relatively new, medium security unit, where the contemporary practices of a bright bunch of staff had a lot to prove to the more traditional, sceptical, hospital community in which they were embedded. There, there was an acceptance that among patients subject to extended hospitalisation one of the many detrimental effects was

31

that of "learned helplessness". This self-explanatory re-appraisal deflected the blame for de-motivation away from the patients themselves and focused on incentivising them to "unlearn" this and re-establish their motivational viability.

'You don't have much faith in getting them back out there, then?'

'Let's say I don't believe in miracles.'

'I don't say *I* believe in miracles *either*, but…' and then I trailed off for she had given voice to something for which I tried to avoid giving too serious consideration. What, exactly, did I have faith in? Curing, rehabilitating, our seriously transgressing mentally abnormal offenders? Naturally it featured in the professional vocabulary like the specious pledges of any commercial enterprise but was it backed by any belief? A curative rehabilitation implied something transformed, restored, as in a completed, indistinguishable state. Surely, the past was so indelibly distinguishable in so many seriously mentally disordered offender cases that we health professionals dare not hope beyond the platitudes of reducing the risk of further dangerousness, and of diminishing relapse of the accompanying mental disorder? As for her, my candid companion, better that she obliterated her cynicism from consciousness, preserve her own integrity, and find consolation in the diverse stimulation of education and professional development. It was a strategy that we all adopted from time to time.

Over an extended coffee in the office in which she had temporarily taken up residence, this lady and I had already spent an agreeably informal prelude prior to our departure to the wards. During this time we were completely undisturbed by the affairs of state, telephone calls, visitations or emergences, as if the hospital was in a state of dormancy.

'So, you're visiting us as part of your orientation programme, you say? My, my, things are getting grand!' This enquiry was an amicable introduction by this Acting Nurse Manager to whom I had been allocated for the next couple of hours. The pallid face, tight brunette curls, and dark brown eyes projected themselves above an imposing uniform dress of cornflower blue, belted in navy-blue. And the continuous, artless smile suggested that this was no chore and, possibly, an opportunistic flirtation. 'Pleased to meet you, I'm Sally.'

'Hi, Sally, I'm Steve. Pleased to meet you too.' She paused and inclined her head with a measured assurance while I extended my hand to shake hers not knowing whether I was overdoing the courtesy bit. But her bright reception and handshake seemed to contain aspects of both muted surprise and flattery. 'That's right. I've just come into the "Special Hospital" fold, as you've probably guessed, and been given the chance to look over one of the other sites so as to get a feel for the whole system. I chose yours, you lucky things!' I said with a hint of mock derision which my playful escort was quick to appreciate with a roll of her eyes. And escort was exactly what she was as no visitor was entitled to wander around the grounds of a "Special Hospital" unattended even if they were colleagues from a sister site.

'So, you're a new Nurse Manager from Moss Side Hospital. I didn't know that your place accepted outsiders for senior promotions. Thought it was only jobs for the boys! Working so close to the wards!

'You're correct. I'm the first outsider to be appointed to a Nurse Manager role working close to the wards, but they've accepted outsiders for the two posts above me.'

'OK, the office-wallers and such-like, shifting paper far away from the coalface. Congratulations for being a first, then! It's got a reputation for being a bit behind the times, that place. It's got a reputation, full-stop!' she emphasised with a side-long glance of mock disapproval, and a sceptical cackle, which I found less than reassuring. Her derision did not stop there. 'How've you found the staff, anyway? Thought it was just jobs for the boys when working so close to the wards. If they haven't, and you are, they soon will.' Another sceptical cackle. 'Mark my words, these places are all more or less the same.' What she gleaned from my protracted silence I couldn't judge but, sure as hell, I was none too thrilled by these insights. I was some minutes in conjuring a light-hearted retort.

'You really believe that? I mean, that despite being hundreds of miles apart you're all of a likeness? I suppose when I think of it, I trained in a County hospital and, though we virtually never had any formal professional contact with each other, when you made a visit to any one of them every hospital operated along such similar lines we could all have been pressed through a single template. Or is it *that* fundamental that if you whisk one group of more powerful people in with another more powerless group, and throw the lot into a mix of closed buildings, you simply wait for the institutional mould to set? Like it's a social recipe for conformity,' I proffered with some alacrity.

'Oh very eloquent!' Meanwhile my erstwhile guide rose from behind the office desk, with a display of wanting to get on with the tour of the female hospital grounds that she had put together for me.

'Had much exposure to mentally abnormal offenders, have we?'

she continued, and revealing a certain persistence in fathoming my background.

'Trained in a traditional "bin" then in a number of small units. Forensic-wise, I've been in two medium secure units – the last one just outside Manchester. The Manchester place was quite something – new unit, very sharp managers, very bright staff, loads of them with therapy training. I'd never been anywhere like that. So does medium security experience give me any credibility?' I jibed, knowing that it did whether she cared for it, or not.

'Oh, that's a *world* away from us. And you've obviously moved around in your career and kept yourself updated? I don't know whether either of those will prepare you for the "Specials" – it'll be a shock to your system. That's if the staff here are anything to go by.'

'Go on,' I urge.

'Most of our people originally trained here and don't have any intention of moving around the health service to better themselves. And the outsiders, once they've arrived, will generally spend all their working lives in these places and won't intend to go anywhere else, either. Once you're in, you're in for life. It's such a safe number. Which is why they'll resent the likes of you coming in to take their manager's promotion from them because that's what they've been hanging on for, of course,' she added, wryly, but in a continuing vein of acceptance toward me, it appeared.

'Understandable as far as it goes,' I replied with some small equivocation, having experienced, during my training years in a County asylum, all manner of home bred people who had been promoted to senior positions seemingly having been rewarded for their stalwart propensity to maintain the status quo rather than to model an enthusiasm for generating new ideas and practices. There again it was, perhaps, a little too easy to defame such folk when it may have been qualities such as their inimitable humour, sociability and years of solid experience which enhanced staff respect and reinforced working relationships.

'So, what's your poison, in the professional stakes, of course, Sally, if you don't mind my asking?' I had asked.

'What's my what?' she had replied, her brown eyes flaring with intrigue.

'What area of the work takes your fancy most? I'm assuming you have a special interest, something you're aiming for.'

'Oh, I see. Curious way of asking! Well, I'm involved in security issues, mostly, along with "control and restraint". I wouldn't mind being a "C and R" instructor but I couldn't work alongside the crew that teach it! Have you done the "C and R" course because you'll have to if you haven't.'

'Yeah, already done it in the medium secure units,' I replied, gratefully, thinking that that would enhance my credibility. At the "Special Hospital" at which I was now employed, Control and Restraint was the one and only course that every member of the nursing staff wanted to be signed up for. During my short time there I had received not a single request from my staff to do anything else. Control and Restraint had been around for a couple of years, now, thanks to the inexpert handling of disturbed people in the Prison Service, the "Special Hospitals", and elsewhere. The inexpert handling was a euphemism for what, in the absence of any particular training, was the understandable, free for all, physical suppression of aggressive and violent prisoners and patients. Indeed, one Consultant Psychiatrist of my acquaintance often referred to his observations of this past procedure as watching a version of the *Keystone Cops* in action! These informal practices had resulted in untold numbers of injuries to staff, prisoners and patients and, in some instances, some deaths among the latter two groups. The management of violence had now been formalised into a practical course which prepared staff to act in concert, as a team. By so doing, there would be a much reduced likelihood of causing, or sustaining, injury and the interpersonal outcome for all parties was likely to be of a more positive tenor because of the more professional approach to disturbances.

'On top of that I'm involved in the search teams.'

'Search teams?' I said, with unconcealed surprise.

'Yeah, we've dedicated staff who turn over a patient's room or a whole ward if we have to if we suspect a hidden weapon, or drugs, that sort of thing. It's a pretty filthy job going under floorboards and delving into every imaginable crevice.'

'What on earth do you get out of that!'

'Oh, I love it!' she said, with a responsive smile to my astonishment.

'Did you volunteer for that or were you drafted in?'

'Volunteered. Right up my street! Suits me just fine. I enjoy turning up the unexpected. I'm the only female, as it happens!'

'A feminist!'

'Not me! You don't have to be a feminist to get what you want – just box clever. Besides, I can't stand working with female patients – far too erratic for my liking – so, I can't be a feminist.' Whether she was concealing a feminist position, or not, I imagined it would have been an insurmountable stance to assume amongst the masculinist culture of a "Special Hospital" and the sexist taunts and recriminations it would have engendered. My inclination was that Sally had consciously developed an occupational stance which incorporated into her femininity a desire to be counted among the men, doing men's work, and that the message she was sending out was that there was nothing they could do that she could not match and she was not to be underestimated in anything. Added to which, the security practices, the "C and R", and the "search teams", were entirely practical modes of working, something to get your proverbial teeth into. It was then that a related image came to mind, between her frequent shrills of laughter and the flaring brown irises, that she was also happy to give off lusty signals of her competitive, amorous intent. Toward me, perhaps!

'Ask anything you want on the wards. I'm sure no one will mind. And if they do, I'll have something to say. And I'd be interested in your impressions of us. That'll be interesting!' she exclaimed. I had to say, I looked forward to more of the colourful candour with which she had impressed me so far.

In truth, I itched to get my hands on a sample of the care plans ascribed to individual patients by the nurses who worked closest to them. This was no idle curiosity but derived from a long held conviction that these formal records of nurse-prescribed care were the most illuminating single factor about ward organisation and leadership. Only working physically alongside the staff, and watching their behaviour, would reveal as much. It was not that these records necessarily spoke of the *quality of patient care* but that it was one of the most incisive indicators of the *quality of the staff* who composed them. I had sufficient awareness to know that this was more than just professional curiosity, of gauging my colleagues' organisational, intellectual and emotional capacities as they translated into their care strategies. That it was also informed by an agenda of sheer, personal competitiveness on my part because of the repeated finding that planning was carried out with such perplexing paucity, brevity and inconclusiveness. Of course, individualised care plans were deemed contentious with traditionally orientated staff since they cut across the easier to manage, generalised, task-orientated care which dominated the ward organisation. But, I'd no desire to appear overly intrusive, or enthusiastic, and would present myself in a casual low-key persona even though I was more like an eager but restrained collie, intuitively, observantly, herding in the panoramic detail about me. And, that was the state of things when entering the female block.

From the black leather pouch hanging from the belt on her hips my guide drew out the super-sized Home Office key that had enabled our passage through a number of gates and doors since she had collected me from the expansive reception area. Now it was to facilitate our entry to the female block and the several wards, therein. The first door closed, and locked, we briefly found ourselves in the so-called *airlock*. What technically described a safety chamber separating two areas of differing pressures, in this case, represented a precautionary space dividing an internal area of high volatility from an external one of relatively normal social conditions. In plain terms, it was intended to provide a measure of assurance that, in the event of a patient absconding through the internal door, he or she would be prevented from passing through the outer door for on no occasion would both doors be unlocked simultaneously. The second of the doors opened into a well-lit gallery – for that was what it was called – extending to the left. Along the wall backing onto the courtyard a line of reinforced doors were regularly spaced, which with the spartan absence of any other artefacts or furniture, for all the world, gave an impression of a row of cells on a prison segregation unit. And, the impression would have been pretty accurate. Each room was set aside for a single occupant, with no separate sanitation, with merely a mattress on a reinforced, rubber plinth. The windows were crossed with metal bars. High along the gallery's opposite wall, the intermittent windows hung with the stained glass of the sun's brilliance streaming through the bars of metal that prevented escape. The remainder of the gallery was an ocean of space, listing on a reflective sea of linoleum, with not a single picture on the ward horizon. From within one of the seclusion rooms there issued the verbal graffiti that had accompanied our arrival.

'I'll fucking kill myself if I want to. It's my life. Just fucking leave me alone, do you bleeding understand? *Comprendez*, you dozy twats!'

'Oops, that's dear old Cheryl again! Sweet isn't she? In seclusion because she's been *cutting up* again, I do not doubt.'

'I don't want no fucking medication. How many times do I have to bleeding tell you, you *FUUUUUCKS*,' she emphasised in a protracted scream.

'Regular occurrence, that, with Cheryl. I'd best introduce you to the person in charge, the Ward Sister's not on duty today, though. Got to respect etiquette.' In point of fact, this rather confused me. I couldn't decipher whether she agreed with this type of formality or not since she didn't seem to have much regard for traditional rituals.

'Umm, she's quite expressive! Are the staff OK about language like that, because I know where I come from that would be an issue for them?' I asked, provocatively.

'Don't think it's not an issue for us, either! You don't know what a handful she can be sometimes! When she's in that mood, and you just can't reason with her, you have to let it go. *And,* she's a rather big girl. That doesn't mean we turn a blind eye, though, or allow patients to be abusive, because things could easily get out of control.' One of the nearer doors announced the ward office into which I, and my purpose, was introduced to a short, slightly stocky, sensitive-looking, young woman who held the post of Staff Nurse and was charged with managing the morning shift. Sally truncated the introductions, for which I was relieved.

'You're expecting us, I hope. This is Mr. Burrow, recently appointed as a Nurse Manager at one of our illustrious neighbours, Moss Side. Could you give him a general idea what we do here on the intensive care unit?'

Perfectly respectfully, the cherub-faced Staff Nurse rose from her desk chair to acknowledge me and introduce herself in a somewhat hushed and guarded manner .

'Good morning, I'm Verity Hughes. I'm in charge, for my sins,' she said in an engagingly coy fashion, accompanied with a nervy giggle. The hair was un-fussed, and an arch of acne lay across the nose and cheeks. 'So, you're a novice for this neck of the woods, so to speak! No offence meant. Makes a pleasant change to have a fresh face, if only for a fleeting visit.' The exchange was delivered through lips that were tightly drawn even as she smiled so that it was not quite clear what emotional contours she conveyed. Similarly, the face had a certain mask-like quality – not because of any incapacity to smile – but, as if the apparent inflexibility mirrored an emotional rigidity or covered up a fragility. 'Did you want to have a quick look around the ward, Mr. Burrow? We could talk on the way. Feel free to ask anything you want.' I could not but notice the keen gaze I felt had settled on me which, together with her remark, gave further impetus to my conjecture that here was another staff member who seemed to approve of different people in their midst, as if they were cut off from the wider world.

'I'd appreciate that very much, thanks. Can I call you Verity?'
She manoeuvred her way from behind her desk, squeezed between me
and Sally, and exited the office while the latter locked it behind us.

'Better do. Can't stand too much formality myself,' she said with
a stiff grin. She proceeded to guide me along the gallery with the dark
seclusions on one side and the bright light of the windows on the
other. 'This gallery is where we have all our seclusion rooms, as you
can see... and hear, no doubt!' Indeed, the close strains of the irate
patient issued from one of these doors, at which three of the female
staff were fused in vigilant and impatient attendance. They were
levelling with her in uncompromising terms.

'Right, first of all, I've had just about enough of your swearing,
young lady. Cut it out, we're not here to be spoken to like that. Either
pack it in, now, or you can say goodbye to any privileges. Got that?
Now, this medication. You can suit yourself, Cheryl. You can have it
the easy way, or the hard way. It's your choice. The Doctor's
prescribed it to calm you down so that you don't hurt yourself. So do
yourself a favour, will you?'

'And us,' moaned one of the others.

'Exactly. Now, hurry up, we've got other people to see too
besides you. That's more like it.' Obviously, Cheryl had given some
unspoken sign of recanting for, without any of us hearing any sound
from Cheryl, the three of them shunted into the room, the last cradling
a plastic kidney dish containing, what I presumed was, a prepared
injection. As we sauntered by I could just catch sight of a heavily
built, dishevelled female in her thirties, sitting at the side of her bed,
and that the cardboard chamber pot on the floor was the only other
object in the room. Depriving though this might appear it was not, in
itself, contrary to any other hospital policy concerning the seclusion of
a patient who needed to be kept safe from harming themselves, or
others. The staff, seemingly, had dealt with the task in a peremptory
manner and were already vacating the room. The need to repeat this
exercise so regularly had, presumably, blunted the social niceties.
'Right, that'll settle you down, then we'll think about some time out of
your room. It's up to you, young lady'. And, with that the door was
slammed and the lock turned with the Home Office key but not before
the rank odour of the room had hit me. This was not unusual in itself;
when rooms are used for disturbed patients, often for long periods,
urine and faeces become a permeating by-product that is not easily
extinguished. The staff passed me with hardly an acknowledgement,
one returning to the clinic room, the others to chatter their

unconcerned route back along the gallery. I imagined that, dressed as I was in my suit, they merely regarded me as another nuisance manager for whose encroachments they had very little time. They considered themselves to be the shop floor workers, carrying the can, and managers could steer a wide berth until it was felt they might be put to some useful purpose. I discovered that no less than four of the seclusion rooms were currently being occupied which seemed a lot to me, or would have done should I say, had I not become acclimatised to the same phenomena in the sister hospital in which I had recently been employed.

'You have four disturbed patients this morning!' I said, hoping to open up their perspective on the issue.

'That's pretty regular for this ward being it's *for* our disturbed patients. Well, you know there are various types of disturbance. We're quiet compared with some days.' By the time we had turned at the end of the gallery was long enough for me to be informed that the greatest single reason for seclusion on the female blocks was the patients' *cutting up.* Again, I had encountered *cutting up* in unbelievably high numbers at my own hospital. I confirmed the fact.

'We have the very same problem where I'm based. It's unprecedented in my past experience, even though I worked in an Accident and Emergency Department for almost a year and a half,' I offered, quite honestly, and hinting that this state of affairs was simply unconscionable. My stance was predicated on the premise that it must be the hospital regime, and the quality of the staff-patient relations, as much as the predispositions of the patients themselves, which was responsible for this perpetuating debacle.

'It's always been part of our experience, anyway,' retaliated Verity with no great venom though I sensed she'd gleaned my inference. 'Since the first day on a female ward in this hospital I remember self-harm being the main nursing problem. You wouldn't really expect that in most mental hospitals, from what I've heard?' she quizzed.

'I don't believe so, no. So, why should the "Specials" have this problem on such a massive scale when nobody else does?' I posed, in an insinuating tone.

'Don't forget the prisons! Same situation applies.' interjected Sally who had remained in close attendance. To my mind, this merely bolstered the view that the cause was institutional pathology rather than individual perversity. 'I suppose it just goes to show that we deal with the hard core of psychiatric patients with the most difficult histories and the greatest level of disturbance.'

'And if they're capable of harming other people – otherwise they wouldn't be here – it stands to reason they're as capable of inflicting harm upon themselves,' Verity added, turning toward me with a studied intensity.

We had returned to the entrance lobby. Verity approached an open door and stood aside, with her arm extended before her, as if lighting our way across the threshold, and we entered into the ward dayroom that slouched in a depressingly dull shade. The several armchairs tended in the direction of the reinforced and immoveable TV and female patients, in motley civvies, sprawled in disinterested poses, seemingly preoccupied and distant. By contrast, taking up a consecutive row of chairs abutting one wall, close to the door, a line of recumbent, chattering female staff, with their blue tunics and belts toned down by the gloomy hue, stretched like a garrulous throng of starlings dotted along a telegraph wire. But our appearance did not startle the little things and, unabated, they remained ensconced in their own smoke and the ward newspapers without even the curiosity of idleness. The lifeless atmosphere was broken only by the twittering staff until a clutch of three patients, like plump little chaffinches, in low reverential chirrups, congregated before their black squawking monitors for permission to relieve themselves as it was now the time for a scheduled toilet run. As per routine, one of the monitors rose from her seat and left the room to invigilate the lavatory area while another called after her with "*threes out*", whereupon the three patients were allowed to pass out of the dayroom to attend to their toilet. After a few minutes of Verity's commentary about the day's ward routine there seemed no point in remaining longer. Judging that there was no great enthusiasm from the staff assembly that I should approach them I turned toward the door in a purposeful show of receding. Verity led the way back across the dank threshold and, in re-entering the bright light of the gallery, seemed momentarily illuminated so that I captured a semblance of Holman Hunt's painting *The Light of the World* and Christ holding his brilliant lantern aloft.

I had, by now, noticed that her gait was of a bustling kind and this she employed to lead us across to another door which was ajar, and opening into the corridor.

'I don't know how much you've learned about our way of doing things in the "Specials" but you'll notice all doors open outwards, not inwards, yes? That's to ensure no patients can barricade themselves into their rooms so that we can put out fires quickly, if necessary, or minimise self-harm or hostage-taking. All learned from past experience. If they opened inwards, life becomes very difficult. Anyway, this is the occupational therapy room where those ladies who are fit enough can spend their time usefully. It's not terribly stimulating but it gives them a change of aspect, and activity, at the very least. Our ladies are not allowed to attend the hospital workshops or other facilities because they need too much supervision. It's a shame, really, because they don't get off the ward much. Otherwise, it's the dayroom or access to the exercise area, provided things are quiet enough.'

'Do they receive any other input: psychology, therapy, and the like?'

'Oh, the multi-disciplinary team are here, all right, but there's no real therapy to speak of.'

'They're not here for therapy if you consider that they've had to be removed from the admissions or rehab wards because they're too disturbed to remain amongst stable patients. It's our job to contain them, settle them, and return them to where they originated. First, they earn their places back on their wards then they can get the therapy,' blurted Sally with some extravagance. I'm not sure whether Verity had the intuition to sense my scepticism at this but her reply could have suggested it.

'That's *about* right,' continued Verity. 'With most of our problems being self-harm and cutting up perhaps the ladies are considered too complicated for therapy,' she drawled with a short titter and a cynical shift of the eyes. 'Maybe I'm being harsh towards our illustrious therapists. Though there's some sense to it when you think about it. If you're disturbed enough to be cutting up, or head-banging, or self-injuring in other ways, you're not exactly in the frame of mind to examine your thinking and feelings. As I see it, if your internal frustrations are building up to the point of being unbearable you can channel them onto the surface which gives you another outlet and a measure of control, perhaps? No, it's we nurses that have to hold the fort down here. But, you have to be careful you don't get too blasé about the self-harm when it's a daily occurrence because you get drawn into the same external game, become distracted by dealing with the body, because it's easier, rather than appreciating the difficult feelings and thoughts that produce them. We all get so waylaid that we avoid focusing on all the psychological stuff as if the ladies have succeeded in distracting our attention away from having to examine their feelings.' Verity was proving to be a well spoken, thoughtful and articulate soul and I could imagine her having had a fair education to be so considerately conveying the psychological texture of her patients. She smiled intermittently, yet, there was more sadness than joy lurking around the creases of her mouth and eyes so that they foretold of an inner struggle – an anguish, intimately personal, professional, maybe both. She was becoming more enigmatic by the minute because I could see that these patients could be seen to remind her of, to symbolise, to be partly blamed for, her own angst, and the difficulty she must have had in balancing the competing tenets of empathy and exasperation.

'Threes in,' came the raucous call from the nurse who had been standing by the dayroom door awaiting the return of the three toileting patients. Presumably, the toilet doors were now to be locked again.

'So, can I ask the dirty question – do you like working in this area, Verity?' I found myself asking with genuine interest. Again, the studied gaze that seemed to penetrate, earnestly searching for clues about my opinion of her, or even how I viewed the state of play here, perhaps?

'Oh, I wouldn't want to work anywhere else,' she replied almost plaintively and I had a sense that, maybe, she needed to be here among these desperate souls, as if it reflected her own inner quandary. She could be substantial and steadfast at times, I could see that, but I was certain she could feel empty and yielding, with equal resolution. 'Let's face it, women get a pretty raw deal in the world, on the whole and, maybe, these ladies are the product of the worst of all deals.'

'Oh God, she's getting all philosophical on us!' interjected Sally. 'Put it away, Verity, for heaven's sake girl! Right, I think we've seen enough so we'll push off upstairs.' This was a timely distraction, whether for Verity's benefit or Sally's, I wasn't sure, but it was becoming clearer that Verity was straining under the work. Probably, because she did have a regard for her ladies, and of the inability to prevent their interminable self-lacerating, attempted hangings, swallowing of foreign objects, head banging, and other means of self-harm, and of the necessity of reporting this day in and day out, which left her decidedly confused, impotent and consequently depleted both as a nurse and as an individual. Now I became aware of the abiding weariness that listed about her presence competing, simultaneously, with a vigilant edginess that informed her observations of the ward and its potential catastrophes. Both combined to drain her of her resources. I proposed to squeeze just a little more from the encounter and held her attention.

'At our place, the males rarely self-harm. It's mainly a female issue there, also, so maybe you're making the point that it's sociological, then?' I suggested, glancing between the pair of them.

'That's as good a way of putting it as any, I suppose,' Verity replied with a dubious giggle, suitably impressed by the scientific-sounding jargon. She surveyed me with those plaintive, blue eyes again and queried, 'how do you mean, *exactly*?'

'Well, that women, as a group, learn certain ways of dealing with their conflicting social circumstances, family cultures and pressures, school and work place expectations, that sort of thing. That's what you're getting at, isn't it?'

'Exactly, only I couldn't have put it like that. It's the way they're treated as women, and working class women, especially! Something else has been emerging recently from going into the ladies' histories. Something you blokes are either unaware of, underestimate, or choose to ignore, frankly.' Verity fixed me with a half-challenging stare. 'Abuse: emotional, physical, sexual; harassment, stalking, and rape. I think that says it all! The sort of life events which dog women rather than men. Is that sociological or psychological – I don't know! Does it damn well matter for all that?' This edged between a sardonic smile and something of a release. Then, for the moment, I was overtaken by the discomforting realisation that I must represent a discredited and culpable predator of the male species and it scrabbled about my conscience like an accusing claw. Returning to my thesis, things were not looking good. How much mileage remained for the notion that it was institutional pathology that predisposed a captive population to its self-harming excesses? Especially taking into account the inverse position of male patients, relative to their female counterparts. But, I was not done yet.

'If the cause is either sociological, or psychological for that matter, you would expect the self-harming to have commenced prior to their coming into a Special Hospital,' I posed, rhetorically.

'That's something which I don't have the answer too,' Verity admitted, looking to Sally, questioningly, but who, in turn, shrugged undecided. 'Guess you'd have to research that.'

'So, you really don't have a clear picture of whether the self-harm existed prior to admission or actually started when they came into the hospital?' I suggested, sticking to my case. Sally intervened.

'Hm, impossible to say. These ladies – most of them, I'd say – have been in all sorts of institutions all their lives. Children's homes, prisons, mental hospitals – not seen much of family life. It could be because they've been institutionalised *all* their lives, you see? Who knows?'

'But the same applies to the men, presumably,' I added, now uncertain of any safe ground in my argument but willing to air my views. With a disarming simplicity Sally found the devastating rejoinder.

'Perhaps the women are just a more extreme, sicker group than the men, the hard core of mentally ill women, and we know that's the case, anyway?'

'Or that, as women, they have more severe problems to deal with than men?' was Verity's calculated challenge.

While Verity had fashioned this conclusion, I surmised by her narrowing, glazed eyes – with what vitality they contained threatening to abandon her – that this summation was a cut too deep. What hope was there for her patients, for her care of them, for the hospital's efforts? Herself even? I was amazed by what I felt was the palpable collapse in her mood, the droop of the shoulders, the flattening of the face, the suspension of her contact, as if she had silently receded into an inner space. What I could only perceive as a companionable self-consciousness came over me at this moment and it occurred to me that I was rather reluctant to be leaving the area. Sally, the Acting Nurse Manager, meanwhile, guided me toward a hitherto unopened door. In doing so, she punctured the prevailing uncertain atmosphere with a mischievous and resounding laugh, 'so, sort that little lot out.' Verity rallied with her own distracting quip.

'Well, who are we to worry ourselves about these things when nobody else seems to have worked it all out? We're only nurses after all?' she delivered, but with such heavy irony that it was deliberately intended not to convey any real sense of conviction. Then, Sally unlocked what would prove to be the entrance to the ward above – the acute admission ward - while I carried an uncomfortable belief in having stirred Verity's grudging preoccupations and responsibilities.

'She *was* in good form and you appeared to enjoy that,' Sally offered, returning to her role as a beaming companion, as we ascended the unprepossessing stairwell to the first floor of the female block. 'She's a bit of a thinker, that one. Don't know whether it's altogether healthy, mind you.'

I refrained from being drawn on this but couldn't help commenting on the organisation of the ward, though I anticipated the situation, full well. I asked 'do the staff regularly take up that position in the day area, Sally. They appeared to be lodged there?'

'Oh, ongoing problem, that! We're trying to change old habits and encourage more interaction with the patients instead of facilitating a gossip shop but, when all's said and done, it's just easier to monitor the comings and goings of the patients if the staff are close to the door.'

'Yes, I noticed that patients were either in the dayroom or the O.T. room. Presumably they're not allowed to wander freely about the ward?' This was a little disingenuous since I fully realised that the same standard operated at my own hospital on the vast majority of the wards.

'That's ward policy. Can't afford to allow them the opportunity of harming themselves, or each other, or staff, so we do tend to keep a tight reign on their movements. Whether it's the right thing I couldn't say.' Again, this was said in such a carefree tone that it was impossible to decipher her personal stance, and whether she cared about the matter, or not. I managed to trip on the stairs and was drawn to the decades of bare, worn stonework before we rounded the last right angle and arrived at the ward entrance. This turned out to be a straightforward door, without an airlock this time, that opened directly onto the residential area. The environment was not altogether different, perhaps less barren, but palpably lighter in atmosphere. Perhaps more carpeting, a few covered tables, but no hanging pictures along the galleries, no tablecloths or vases of flowers. There was no significant improvement in colour, or activity, or movement that I could judge. Colour began with the long-limbed Ward Sister Tracy whose gold wedding ring reflected the strawberry blond strands of her neatly cut hair all set against the cornflower blue uniform dress. Sister Tracey drew, elegantly, on a cigarette held in her prematurely arthritic fingers and scrutinised me with a calculating interest. In charge of this morning's shift on the female admission ward she cut a very fine, feminine image indeed and shared with us her longing to be removed from the female area altogether.

'I can't be dealing with all these hysterical women day in, and day out,' she exhaled through her cigarette smoke, pleasantly enough. 'You need a break from all this.' 'All this' turned out to be the daily grind of facing bitter, thankless patients who reeked havoc as the fancy took them and, even when they could be moved on they were merely replaced with more of the same. '"Admissions" is just a conveyor belt of bloody mischief!'

'Where else in the place would you want to be, Tracey, if you had a choice?' interjected Sally.

'Give me anything! On second thoughts, anything but females!'

000

'By the time you've viewed this next ward you'll have had an insight into the whole spread of our female patient areas,' was Sally's concise introduction to the third ward that we visited. 'And now for something completely different, as the saying goes,' and she preceded me into a little sanctuary of veritable quaintness relative to what I'd seen so far. The dayroom, with the exception of the barred windows, much more resembled a conventional, if extended, sitting room adorned with comfortable armchairs, sofas, tableclothed side furniture with vased flowers, framed wall pictures, carpets and wallpaper. A ward radio played in a lighter, more harmonious tone than the blaring over-ride it had been on the disturbed ward, or the insistent distraction of the admission area. A near-retirement Ward Sister was the single member of staff on duty. Doubtless relieved of the frenetic storms of her earlier, acute, career she was now holidaying in the becalmed waters of this residential cove and only too pleased to advertise this hospital's rehabilitative showpiece to all-comers. In a deliberate and rehearsed tour we were the beneficiaries of her guidance on this relaxed regimen, the open ward entrance, the homely décor, the patients' individualised rooms, the kitchen facilities, the bathroom suites, all of which the patients had unrestricted access to through the day. Nevertheless, trust remained an issue as patients were locked into their individual quarters at night, like everyone else in the hospital, and the ward entrance, too. So, what, really, was being achieved in this pre-discharge haven? I guessed not very much. For the hospital had had too much adverse occurrences during its lifetime to dare to extend itself to such a risk. And the ward would be locked for sure. We were also informed of the ladies' *parole* status, the highest status to which patients could aspire within the hospital hierarchy. Parole has many nuances – in today's terms, an early release from penal servitude or a current prison sentence, or probationary supervision – but originates from the release of war prisoners who would, in return, give their word to abide by the restrictions imposed upon them. The principle is exemplified in the *Adventures of Don Quixote* where the main protagonist, himself, is considered for release from the cage in which Sancho has confined him "if he will give his parole of honour". In practice, this sanction gave the patients official approval to access prescribed areas of the internal hospital grounds unsupervised by staff.

Their whereabouts and time outside of the ward – but within the hospital grounds – would need to be known and accounted for, nonetheless, so that the degree of liberty was the very minimal possible. To be permitted parole, the staff would have measured their risk levels to be very low indeed as well as being the best possible achievement for calibrating the patients' discharge prospects.

And of the patients? Well, strangely subdued! While casting about the ward I reflected on the vagaries of the aims of this elderly female holding pen that had systematically inoculated its elderly residents from the everyday hazards of normal life? They were mobile, of course, pottering here and there, but with no apparent goals to make this environment any more purposeful than anywhere else in the hospital. So, as much as I favoured the relaxed regime, what impressed itself upon me more was that these maturing women – some quite elderly – had been so cowered by the unrelenting conformity over the long years of their confinement that this submissive state was just about the optimum state that was acceptable. I would have been surprised if there was any realistic possibility of a return to the outside world following such institutional processing. It would seem to be little more than a necessary retirement home for the too-old-to-move, and "gate-fevered". Gate-fever, in these circumstances, was a perfectly credible status. It described one who, having been subjected to institutional routines over an extended period which, necessarily, proscribed most efforts at personal initiative, produced a person who had more or less lost all motivation and volition for the external world so that they resigned themselves to the restrictive cloister to which they were accustomed rather than risk the uncertainty of being rehabilitated, discharged or released. In the 1950s a British psychiatrist by the name of Barton had reified this phenomena to the status of a disease which he called "institutional neurosis". The overriding characteristic was the resigned acceptance of the present with no sign of future planning or initiative. Indeed, the Ward Sister almost admitted as much only it was presented under the guise that it was unkind to expect these souls to manage a change of environment after having become so used to a life spent on this one site. It was a notion that most institutional staff, whether they be psychiatric, prison or children's care home, were well acquainted. This being the case, and faced with these all but dispirited women, what was the purpose of utilising a person such as herself, with all the seniority and expertise forged over her career, when her role merely amounted to an institutional supervisor.

'I thought you might be interested in meeting with Alec Robinson who's part of the security team in the hospital. He's a Charge Nurse and a great talker when he gets going and I think he'll be right up your street.'

'What makes you think I'd want to trawl through the same security routines as we have?' mildly bating her. I had had some considerable contact with the security team at my own sister institution but, though a convivial lot, with their own air of expertise, they gave no indication of any therapeutic interest in their work which was my prime concern.

'Ah, but Alec is something special,' she added with an indicative glint in her eye. 'It'll be this way, then!' she said, leading off with a playful and chuckling finality without awaiting my agreement. Alec revealed himself to be a heavily rotund, slow-moving character with a fleshy, pale complexion, who carried his arms loosely by his sides, hands in pockets, and who spoke with an earthy and resonant Scottish drawl. Despite his proportions his immediate contact was somewhat feathery and mellow – a limp handshake, a short nod of the head, a gentle grunt of welcome, a replacing of the hands in his pockets – as if he allowed himself only the briefest of reciprocating overtures. The outwardly dour persona that was draped around a precise and sceptical examination – which I suspected he retained for all newcomers – was levelled on me with the measured aim of a tank barrel. Yet his tone, that seemed to camouflage a voice that could boom across the firmament when it had the will, suggested a mixed sensitivity of stalwart conviction, on the one hand, and a receptivity, on the other. The spectacles that narrowed his eyes only added to his inscrutability and, as our encounter unravelled, he cut a rather intriguing presence. Perhaps Sally had got it right!

'So, from what you've just said you're a wee bit sceptical of the security measures we take in these places, Mr. Burrow?'

'Please, call me Steve, if you would.' I had, indeed, after an introductory preamble, shared with him my view that, at my own hospital, the greater part of nursing activity had more than accommodated what I could only describe as a policing role that predominated over every aspect of hospital life. As I had relayed this, Mr. Alec Robinson's head had all but flinched in the manner of sustaining an insulting blow. He answered with a gently patronising exasperation.

'A small piece of psychiatric history for you, then, er... Steve. This place was, as you know, a criminal lunatic asylum and I wonder whether there should have been given more consideration to what was being lost before dropping the term. I mean, a "Special Hospital"! It just doesn't do it for me, you know? What's it mean? It means nothing to anybody! It's meaningless!' He smiled, and grimaced, hunched his shoulders, and splayed his hands in benign exasperation so that this expressive deliberation honed toward me, unthreateningly. 'Come over here, I want to show you something.' It was noticeable that he was gradually assuming an altogether more assertive air as if the subject into which he was to launch was something about which he had an absolute conviction. He ambled across to the office window and with a sharp nod of his head I was referred to a metal construction with tannoys leering over the hospital wall. 'Recognise it? You've got something similar, of course. That is where our hospital alarm is erected and it is there for a very good reason. You could see at as a monument of a kind as relevant, today, as the day its original predecessor was built. You see, our most reputed resident, John Straffen, will always remain among the local annals and memories of the surrounding region because he was the perpetrator of a little girl's killing some ten miles, or so, away. Have you heard about him?' I had not, I informed him. 'You haven't? If I had my way, I would make his story part of everyone's induction who comes to work in one of these places.' So, he proceeded to unravel the tale of the patient's escape – as alluded to earlier – and then drew upon some concluding comments which he had obviously rehearsed over his career. 'His legacy was several-fold, you see: partly for the killing; partly for the installation of the hospital siren which you see over there; partly for the history that brought him here beforehand; and partly for the mistakes in managing him. Of course, with no forensic evidence, his culpability for the killing of the five-year-old was entirely circumstantial. In fact, when recaptured he not only protested his innocence, but no one had witnessed even seeing them in company together. But, along with his presence in the vicinity, Straffen's past history was the crucial clue.' Alec trailed off for a pregnant pause which, again, owed as much to a theatrical rendition before continuing his tale. 'Because, you see, he had originally been admitted to the asylum for the very same act that brought him here. In 1951, only the year previous to his escape, he had strangled two other girls, aged five and nine years old.' Another gloriously timed pause, magnifying the import of what he was to impart, and the hint of a wry grimace. 'As if that wasn't enough, his trial also threw up a history of certified mental deficiency and a mental age of ten so that the jury found him unfit to plead, and insane. So that's how he came to us, in the first place, for treatment, rather than being sent to prison, for punishment. Now, with that nice assortment, what the hell anybody expected us to do for him, God only knows! In the light of that story, alone, and all the rest I could tell you, what possible rationale would there be for just managing the place as a hospital without a total security programme? How can we not take security seriously? With all due respect, you might do yourself a service if you were to do a little research into some of our patient histories. Don't get me wrong, Mr. Burrows, I'm all in favour of whatever treatments you want to apply, any therapy, any rehabilitation. You'll find me backing you all the way. But,' and he lowered his voice to a somewhat effacing quietness, 'if we don't do our job and hold onto them, securely, other people who want to perform their therapy can't do their job. See what I mean?' He held me with a stiff stare as if to drill home his conviction on the matter. On this information I certainly could not have argued against the principle but the detail, I was still convinced, was up for debate. But assertions from both sides can be complicated by events on the ground.

'Your inference is that it's the nursing staff who secure the patients, the non-nursing staff that do therapy, is that right?' Alec smiled at the little dilemma facing him.

'It depends what you mean by therapy. If it's the general idea of treatment then nurses do their bit – nursing care, administering medication, counselling, building relationships, defusing violence, rehabilitation trips outside of the hospital, etc. But we don't aspire to any thing too... umm... what shall I say... too high-minded? We leave that to therapists, naturally.'

'Fair enough, but despite what you've said, all that you've described seems to be secondary to the security, as if that's the absolute priority, the baseline of care, if you will. You're policing them, in which case it has to undermine your *therapeutic* relationships with patients.'

'No doubt it does but what choice do we have?' From my peripheral vision I caught sight of Sally nodding in a steady assent. This was more her line, definitive, unequivocal, providing some pragmatic purchase on these unwieldy issues. 'To be sure, security is everybody's business, whatever their job, role or profession, and if one person makes a mistake the whole system collapses. But, I would suggest that it's the nurses who continuously pick up and carry the security baton, relaying it from one person to the next, one ward to another, one working shift to the next, linking one area of the hospital to another, each day merging into the following day with never a break in the chain. No one can choose to drop out of the team or we're up shitcreek. We all keep up our training and practice so that we're fit to meet any challenges. Nurses *are* the security and everyone else, including the therapists, can be thankful we do what we do, otherwise they couldn't do what they do.'

'Just one problem with your argument. Where in our professional training as nurses did it prescribe security as part of the syllabus or practical experience?'

'Well, there you have me,' Alec replied, with disarming ease. A brief pause for reflection before he regained his thread. 'All I can say is that when I was in training, I was learning my profession; when I'm in someone's employ, I have to abide by whatever the job demands. Working in a high security establishment probably compromises my professional training, as you imply, but, I say again, what choice do we have? Someone has to take responsibility for maintaining security otherwise it'll have no rigour. And, since nurses as a group are continuously on duty, it makes sense that we take on the task.'

'I suppose you're right. I'm being too much of a purist, perhaps, but there's also an argument for employing a detachment of security personnel, leaving the nursing staff to focus on care and therapeutics. Then you wouldn't be so compromised.'

'That's often been argued but, at the end of the day, what's the point, Mr. Burrow. It's reasonable to do both jobs. We know, we've been doing it like, forever, and I don't see why we shouldn't carry on as we are, frankly. Security is part of the care of these patients. If nurses are responsible for it within their professional role then they're far more likely to appreciate all the issues involved than the security guards you're suggesting.'

'I'm not so sure. I accept your argument, to a point, but there's so much security to be monitored in a "Special Hospital" that it no longer looks like a nursing or caring role. I think there should be a separation of powers,' I responded, without reserve.

'We'll have to agree to disagree, then.' Alec shrugged his shoulders with a casual, but not impolite, air before continuing. 'And if you believe treatment does the trick, I'd like to tell you of another of our residents who graced our little circle. Now when was it...?' He looked toward the window as if, smudged on the pane, some vestige of a clue was to be found. 'Yeah, about the 1960s it would be. Anyway, we had a young man named Graham Young admitted to these precincts at the age of fourteen, would you believe! It was all well before my time, naturally. In that same year, Young's stepmother had died from poisoning and been cremated. In hot pursuit, three further family members fell ill to poisoning – father, sister and friend. Suspicion fell on Young as the surviving family member. After he was arrested by the police, he appeared in Court and pleaded guilty to the attempted murder of the three aforementioned victims. The medical evidence in Court diagnosed that he was suffering from a Psychopathic Disorder so he was committed to this hospital. He was given a fifteen year tariff so that he was *supposed* to remain for at least that period.' The rising scepticism of his tone allied to the sardonic inflation of a grimace suggested that this was not how matters had transpired. 'In their infinite wisdom, the opinion of at least two of our own resident psychiatrists, bless them, begged to differ.' Another weighty pause while Alec seemed to gather himself to deliver the incredulous information that he was about to launch in my direction. 'After nine years of observing and treating Young they decided that he was entirely fit for discharge. OK, professional prerogative and all that jazz,' he said with a shrug of his heavy sloping shoulders, 'but the Home Secretary accepts the psychiatrists' recommendations, signs the release order, and lets the bugger go free.'

'It still happens, doesn't it?' I replied. 'I mean, it's not unknown for these bloody Mental Health Review Tribunals to let patients out before they're fully ready,' attempting to show some support though, by all accounts, the event was only partly well-founded. Unfortunately, since such rare errors as occurred had the most dire repercussions for the relevant victims they smeared the reputation of all decision-makers within the relevant bodies.

'Shouldn't happen. Anyway, in 1971, he's merrily practicing his dark arts at his workplace and the entire workforce become so ill they think they've contracted a virus which they're all passing round! Turns out,' a smirk creaks across his cheeks, 'that he's been poisoning them, too, ending in a few of them kicking the bucket! In other words, nothing had changed all through his treatment, all through his hospitalisation, all through our observations of him, and despite having been caught for the very same thing years beforehand! It shouldn't have happened. I'd argue that security should be ongoing, should never really stop, not until we're absolutely certain someone's safe. And that can't be guaranteed anyway.' What could I say to that?

'Am I beginning to make my case, Mr. Burrow?' I assumed he was reverting to my surname to maximise the import of his case which he didn't want diminished by the casual use of a Christian name with a stranger. 'Let me give you another example. My very own homeland, Scotland, sustained possibly the worst disaster in "Special Hospital" memory.' After I had returned a look of some equivocation, followed by his own polite pause, he pronounced, 'I see you're not entirely with me. I refer to The State Hospital, Carstairs, Scotland's very own equivalent of a "Special Hospital", if you will.'

When opportunity afforded itself a few years hence, I did visit Carstairs. Of truly gothic appearance, the original buildings, strung across abutting turrets, leered, ungraciously, over Carstairs Junction railway station, where it was situated. From this vantage, I could only presume, it conveyed the most daunting macabre images to the passengers passing through its vicinity. A newer development had been erected on the opposite side of the railway line which must have enhanced the sensibilities of the train passengers, no end, as they fantasised on the shorter-term, rehabilitative cases on one side of the tracks and the permanent incurables on the other! Alec parted his legs, widely, continued with his hands in his pockets, and leant back in a prelude to his admonishing tale.

'In its infinite wisdom, the Carstairs Hospital management decided to experiment with a more liberal treatment approach which included freer movement of patients around the estate – parole, as you know. For its sins, it also set up a drama therapy group. During one of the group's sessions, two patients used it to effect a long-planned escape. Only, they weren't acting, if you'll excuse the pun! Showing no qualms they killed the senior nurse in charge, and a fellow patient, and were away. Just along the road from the hospital, on the outside, they flagged down a car only to discover it was a police vehicle and the local village bobbie. They killed him and seriously injured another constable. And guess what was uncovered? What was uncovered was a degree of fore-planning that compromised nearly every part of the hospital. They'd developed a small armoury of weapons, some smuggled in, some produced in the workshops; gathered a whole range of physical disguises, moustaches, attendants' caps, and ropes; reproduced a set of hospital keys; and obtained road maps of the outlying area. Oh, and not forgetting the money! Everything they'd need. Can you believe that, Mr. Burrow?' Alec stood squarely before me, eyes narrowed with what is now a conceited conviction, clearly in his element. 'As I said, there should be an introductory talk given to all new staff on these characters so that, in my view, security is made the absolute priority it deserves. Quite simply, these patients cannot be trusted and the staff have to be safeguarded from them.' A restrained laugh introduces the corollary to this. 'And, as we all know, not even the patients themselves are safe from one another. What's the worst dealings you've had when it comes to patient-on-patient assault, Mr. Burrow?' It is surely no coincidence that the security Charge Nurse is reiterating my surname to emphasise the import of his case and a slight enlargement of his gall, at the audacity of my stance.

'Um...now you have got me. Do you know, I've dealt with various scuffles, and disturbances, but never come across what I would consider terribly serious patient-on-patient incidents. Nope, none springs to mind as overly significant. It's the staff that have been assaulted in my experience. See that nose,' pointing to my own, 'fractured by a straight punch when I was a third year student in training. And this hand,' raising my right one, 'broke that in the same incident. But, you're going to top that, obviously.' I had been seated for a while, aware of progressively slumping into a sort of ruminative doldrum, as each sorry tale unfolded, until speaking of my own injury, had stirred me.

'I agree,' Alec replied. 'For some reason, miraculous really, patients don't usually do each other a lot of damage.'

'Ha! You want to have a spell working on the female side - you'd sing a different tune, then!' Sally interjected with a real show of feeling. Both Alec and I laughed, appreciatively, accepting her word for it.

'Nevertheless, we have had another serious precedent in our history, here, for that, too, and that involved dangerous young men. This particular incident was orchestrated by one Robert Maudsley, who, by the time he came to the attention of psychiatric services as a teenager, he'd already been a rent-boy, a drug addict, suicidal, and eventually garrotted a male who approached him for sex. That would be about 1974. Sentenced to life imprisonment, with a recommendation that he should never be released, he came to us. Within three years he had perpetrated one of the most macabre acts and, I can tell you, since I learned about it, it's stuck in me all these years like a vicious nightmare. Along with a patient accomplice – strains of Carstairs, now I think of it – he took hostage a third patient who was a convicted paedophile, locked themselves into a sideroom, while they tortured him to death. When the ordeal was eventually terminated the hostage's skull had been cracked open and a spoon wedged into it. This is the really good bit. Part of his brain was depleted, presumed scooped out, and eaten, by Maudsley. For your edification I'll finish the story. This was his second killing, if you're keeping up, but Maudsley wasn't finished. Convicted of manslaughter for the hospital death he was transferred to the prison service where, the following year, he killed two more prisoners, one by garrotting and stabbing him, the other by stabbing and smashing and hacking at his head. By all accounts, he'd been trying to lure other prisoners into his cell, beforehand, presumably, with the same intention. So, you see, Mr. Burrow, each time some novel crisis comes to light with each patient attempting to beat the system, by whatever means at their disposal, it presents us with a duty of care to assume that it can reoccur. Then, we're duty bound to integrate another security contingency into our defensive armoury. In that particular case we had to liaise with the police and prison services to develop legal responses to hostage taking scenarios! That wasn't on our training remit, either!'

'That's going beyond the pale, surely! That's a criminal act which comes within a police jurisdiction. Surely, you'd call them in.' As Alec peered at me with the nearest he could muster to a disdainful, pitying frown, I feel I had a clear enough impression of the man who is sincerity and charm, personified, so that the earnest stance he adopted toward security matters was all the more persuasive.

'And we are supposed to do exactly what, prior to the police arrival, whilst the hostage taker is yelling at you from the other side of a door that, unless you show some immediate response to his grievance, he will cut off the hostage's finger? He just doesn't tell you this for a laugh,' Alec continued, with some vehemence, 'he starts cutting, and the screams are for all to hear! This is unadulterated torture, we're talking! Sorry, we're not waiting for the police.' If I was honest, I was now becoming mightily confused. Alec was not fitting neatly into the insensitive, anti-therapy, security camp but bestriding both security and an acute sensitivity toward a patient's interests. The two were not so mutually exclusive! It is a credit to his quality of almost unassuming insistence that I found myself speechless and stunned by the extent to which our patients were determined to upset the rules of engagement. Alec had not finished.

'Believe me, there's nothing like listening to someone's screams, putting yourself in that patient's predicament, and thinking about what's happening to him behind that door. The sheer bloody terror of imagining a knife cutting away at skin and vessels and bone. Let me tell you, it certainly sharpens up your act.'

'What, you've actually experienced a similar scenario?' I exclaimed, wanting to believe that such incidents were far too rare to warrant the procurement of a training package in readiness for such an unlikely predicament.

'No, I haven't, but I've enacted the situation in police role plays where I've been the hostage negotiator and learned how every solitary word, or grunt, or prevarication on your part can have immediate consequences for the patient. I tell you, it frightens the hell out of you!' His tone had plummeted to a deep and convicted sonority which was remarkably engaging. To regain my ground, I found myself shaking off the captivating atmosphere he'd wrought.

'But, how many times has a hostage situation recurred since Maudsley's time?' determined to play out my tune.

'You're right, it hasn't happened often here, at least, but we also had a certain Mr. Bronson as a patient and he most certainly took hostages while he was with us and when he was returned to the Prison Service. Oh, by the by, he also had a little engagement in a rooftop protest while he was with us and caused thousand of pounds worth of collateral damage as he pelted us with roof tiles.'

'OK, I understand your defensive approach but my point is that you seem to have adopted a hyper-alertness to the *possibility* of adverse security incidents when, in fact, their potential is very low.' The need to flail the matter to a satisfactory conclusion had still not deserted me.

'What about our duty of care to be prepared for any eventuality once a real life precedent has been set? Not a theoretical one, an actual one? We wouldn't have a leg to stand on if we were not seen to take precautions having sustained such a situation. And that's why a handful of us are trained hostage negotiators.' This was impressive but was this really necessary given minimal possibility of the event and continued to argue so.

'Well, I'm not convinced that we have to anticipate every conceivable eventuality, even if it has happened once, or that it's necessary to establish a dedicated training programme for its *possible* recurrence.'

'Fair comment, but our rationale is that we are increasingly accepting prison transfers and prisoners have a greater likelihood of doing these sort of things. They may well have seen it happen during their sentence, so that they carry the idea in their head, and, because their illness is more of a temporary incapacity, they may have a greater capacity to hatch such a plan than our usual patients, even recruiting other accomplices. We have to be prepared in these changing times.'

What was the more disconcerting, was that this security critique was more premised on dangerousness being a natural proclivity of the patient class rather than the extraordinary product of mental disorder. In other words, vigilance was paramount at all times, for every patient, because adversity was more or less inevitable. It was what so perplexed me as a newcomer to the high security field – that the staff and the establishment had less trust in the defensive safeguards of therapeutic insight-development, and relationship-building, than the offensive force of security. To my way of thinking this characterised the "worst contingency planning" of the "Special Hospitals" investment in security matters.

Alec, as if accomplishing his task, pursed his full lips and sunk his ample frame into a straight backed chair as if heralding a determined, but friendly, closure while courteously awaiting my departure. In truth, I had never heard any mention of these horrifying tales during my career, to date, and rather wondered how on earth I hadn't. Standing before two relatively senior members of staff steeped in the myths of the "Special Hospitals" what was there to say that would make a sensible defence of my sensibilities toward the overriding prioritisation of hospital security! I knew that the security protagonists would point to the concessions made to the Parole System which was a sufficiently liberal step, they would argue. But, the past contained the lessons for posterity and they were manifold. Such circumstances as Alec, the security Charge Nurse, had described, and their attendant mythologies, must necessarily prepare subsequent generations of staff into incorporating such material into their occupational awareness and to assume the obvious precautions deriving from them. Treating patients as individuals did not entirely evaporate but was subsumed beneath a blanket regime which prioritised patient, staff and public safety, and the integrity of the hospitals and politicians, alike.

Glancing toward my escort I received back the knowing raised eyebrows of one who was well satisfied with her colleague's performance. I extended a handshake, ambled toward the security office door huddling all this awkward information, looked back to him, and genuinely nodded my acknowledgement for he had done me a very great service.

000

When, at a later date, I pursued these catastrophic episodes further in my own investigative trawl it was to be acquainted not just with the various routes by which patients entered the "Special Hospitals" but also the comprehensive calamities and repercussions that pursued their admissions. There were, in the first instance, examples of a direct hospital admission from the Court, following an individual's trial, the Court verdict, and the pronounced hospital disposal. Into this category fell the aforementioned John Straffen, Graham Young, Robert Maudsley and the Carstairs patients.

All the chilling detail of the Graham Young case became available to the general public in a biography called the St. Alban's Poisoner. In this we learned that he had acquired an adolescent interest in toxic chemicals, Black Magic and Nazism, culminating in an experimental poisoning regime against those in close contact with him. When, under the Mental Health Act (1959), the Court verdict disposed of the defendant into a psychiatric hospital for treatment it meant that, owing to his mental disorder, he was excused from being held fully culpable for the poisoning of his family. There was an accompanying condition on Young's committal that he must not be released within fifteen years without the express authority of the Home Secretary. But, as Alec had relayed, owing to his psychiatrists' professional intervention and the Home Office release, he was given what was termed a Conditional Discharge which permitted some regulation of his return to the community. Within nine months of this Young was re-arrested and, at St. Alban's Crown Court in 1972, he was found guilty of three counts of murdering three workmates. Incredibly, when he had applied for a post in a photographic supplies store – thus, enabling him to access the desired toxics – his prospective employers were not informed of the applicant's poisoning proclivities by any authority. The fall-out from the case prompted the formation of the Aarvold Committee which performed the function of a special advisory board on a minority of special hospital patients who, based on past behaviour, were viewed as presenting an enhanced danger to the public on their release. I also discovered that John Straffen had also undergone a second trial following his hospital escape and the associated murder of the third little girl. The jury verdict was the death sentence – still available in law at the time – and a date for his execution was set. But, the Home Secretary's reprieve meant the death sentence was commuted to life imprisonment and John Straffen was ensconced for the next fifty-five years as the longest serving prisoner of the British prison system until his death in

2007.

Some have speculated that Robert Maudsley may have been the prototype for the literary and cinematic mythology that emerged into "Hannibal the Cannibal", and *The Silence of the Lambs*. But with competitors of the calibre of the USA's Jeffrey Dahmer, and Russia's Nikolai Dzurmongaliev and Andrei Chikato, Robert Maudsley was no more likely than any of these to have provided the real life persona that transmogrified a human being into the eponymous "Hannibal Lecter"!

Of the Carstairs incident, the damage to hospital reputation and detrimental reversal of liberalising policy were immediate casualties. For, more than any other single event in the collective history of British institutional mental health management, it displayed the calculating, indiscriminate and uncompromising potential of the smallest minority of mentally disordered patients who were diagnosed with Psychopathic Disorder. From then on, the potential for such single-minded ruthlessness to attain illicit bids for freedom would always be factored into every aspect of the organisation and the treatment planning of high security mental health care. All of these, along with the recommendations of the accompanying Independent Inquiry, translated into a rigorous reappraisal of the hospitals' regime which could only become ever more stringent following the unprecedented calamity. For starters, extra perimeter fencing and floodlighting should be installed; a radio communications network with a control room, linking all staff with two-way radios, to monitor all patient-escorted movements in the hospital – thereby, instituting the phonetic alphabet for radio communication such as was used in the Police, Prison and Military services; and that a button-operated alarm system be erected in each ward and centrally coordinated. The patients' access to occupational work, the work tools, materials, and waste products, should be better controlled; that nurses should assist in supervising these areas (as with the education centre); that there should be random searches of patients leaving such a department, as well as following outside visits; that patients' visitors be supervised for the passing of contraband; and that parole patients should be issued with their own card and photograph which should be carried on their person. The meticulous security overhaul fingered a path into practically everything that was connected to their operations within, and without, their precincts. The repercussions were so comprehensive that all operational matters within the "Specials" would conform to what a critical clinical psychologist would come to formulate as "worst contingency planning". That is, for every conceivable staff manoeuvre relating to patient management, security, rehabilitation, and therapy there was to be an assumption that, at any moment, the patients were capable of the most extreme infringement. In turn, the hospitals' security planning should prepare for the very worst of these contingencies. And assuming the very worst outcome was ritually adhered too and overshadowed any individual discretion or initiative to manage patients on a discriminating basis. Overnight the Carstairs incident and its Inquiry findings bought into sharp focus the image of the homicidal maniac and galvanised "Special Hospital" nursing into defensive control measures, while effectively relegating therapeutic strategies to a back burner. But, at least, I had an understanding of the causes for this custodial craft, and more than a little sympathy with its adherence.

Whilst the forensic system facilitated the departure of "Special Hospital" patients for the Prison Service, the Mental Health Acts also permitted an equally important admission route into these hospitals in the opposite direction, *via* the Prison Service. Prisoners who had been tried and convicted of crimes and disposed of with prison sentences might be found to have developed a mental disorder before the conclusion of their sentence. A person's mental health rights called for an entitlement to receive psychiatric treatment within the National Health Service if his or her mental status warranted it. Inmates were then found inpatient beds in psychiatric hospitals and transferred out of the prison service until they were returned to normal health, or their original sentence expired. In the case of prisoners who, it was deemed, gave rise to concerns about their potential for "grave and immediate danger", they could well find themselves transferred to a "Special Hospital" until their mental health recovered. In a few cases, this might transpire at the very end of a prisoner's sentence if it was felt that mental health treatment was necessary! Again, there were notorious examples which exemplified this particular category of patients whose deeds would always haunt the public imagination.

The inaugural criminal conviction which instigated Charles Bronson's custodial career was, like Robert Maudsley, enacted in the year 1974. Though this was nothing more than an inept armed robbery it was the commencement of an unmitigated tally of crimes ranging from robbery, conspiracy to rob, blackmail, threats to kill, criminal damage, wounding, wounding with intent, false imprisonment and grievous bodily harm, many of which were perpetrated from inside the prison system! Successive attacks on prison staff also figured amongst this litany but he was equally renowned for his recurrent hostage-taking of prisoners and staff. Eventually deemed to be in need of psychiatric treatment he was transferred from the Prison system to a "Special Hospital" and was an example of the second major route by which people entered the high security health care system. Again, like Robert Maudsley, he took patient hostages while a resident in Broadmoor hospital in 1983, but his reputation, whilst there, was also built on the excessive damages caused during a long roof-top demonstration. Like all the foregoing perpetrators, he was transferred out of the "Special Hospitals" and into the Prison Service for all his latter years. Together, both Charles Bronson (whose name he had acquired by deed poll from his birth-name, Michael Peterson), and Robert Maudsley remain detained as Category "A" prisoners, in solitary confinement, in a specialised unit within Wakefield High Security Prison.

Over subsequent decades, others of particular note have displayed an earlier, pre-morbid propensity for crime. "Pre-morbid" meaning the personality that existed prior to the onset of a mental pathology. In these cases, the offending history preceded the mental disorder that would eventually lead to their disposal to "Special Hospitals". A few have epitomised a life-long, criminal lifestyle long before a deteriorating mental state was diagnosed and causing them to become long-term "Special Hospital" residents. The late Ronnie Kray, twin to Reggie Kray, who with their other brother, Charlie, formed the London-based Kray gang, carried an inimitable reputation. The brothers' criminal reign lasted until 1968 when, at the Old Bailey Central Criminal Court, they were convicted of several murders, as well as grievous bodily harm, demanding money with menaces, and fraud, and sentenced to life imprisonment with a recommendation to serve a minimum of thirty years. At the time that Court proceedings prosecuted their criminal empire, culminating in a guilty verdict, it was not concluded *at the time of committing these serious offences* that Ronnie Kray had an accompanying mental disorder which might have had some bearing on, or excused to some extent, his actions. However, over the ensuing years of disruptive and violent behaviour during his prison sentence a psychiatric evaluation discovered Ronnie Kray to have developed a mental illness. It was at this point in his "stretch", in 1979, that Ronnie Kray was transferred to Broadmoor from Parkhurst Prison, where he remained until his death in 1995, sixteen years later.

In the same vein another individual with a pre-morbid past history of criminality who became a "Special Hospital" patient via the prison route was Ian Brady. Along with his infamous female accomplice, Myra Hindley, he was found guilty in 1966 of murder. In what were called the "Moors Murders", Ian Brady was convicted of three counts of murder – two of children and one teenager, all involving sexual sadism – and sentenced to three life sentences, while Myra Hindley received two verdicts of murder and one of being an accessory after the fact. In later years, Ian Brady confessed to the murder of two further children. The two accomplices had abducted their young victims, often through subterfuge, tortured and murdered them. Of the many gruesome features, some of them were buried in shallow graves on the Moors north of Manchester – hence, the "Moors Murders". At the time of the offences, during the time of their trial, and for the early part of his sentence no mental disorder was apparent. But, in Brady's case, he developed signs of mental disorder after nineteen years of his sentence, whilst at Parkhurst Prison, and was transferred to a "Special Hospital" in 1985. Ian Brady's route in was an indirect one, while serving a prison sentence, and until the disorder sufficiently improved to return the patient to prison. In his instance, he continues to be contained within Ashworth Hospital, the very latest high security hospital to be constructed. I have it on good account from a member of staff who had had close contact with him that he disdained the input of nursing staff, telling them to leave him be so that he could be allowed to "get on and do me bird".

The admission circumstances of another Broadmoor patient of prominent notoriety, namely Peter Sutcliffe, exemplified the dynamic connundrum of the forensic process. Peter Sutcliffe, who acquired the inimitable tag of the "Yorkshire Ripper" was, in 1981, found guilty by the jury of thirteen murders of women in Yorkshire towns. He confessed at the Central Criminal Court trial that he believed that he had a mission from God to remove all prostitutes and that he also believed that all his victims were prostitutes. Into the forensic pot was added the medical evidence of no less than three eminent Consultant Forensic Psychiatrists who provided a unanimous diagnosis of paranoid schizophrenia for the defendant Peter Sutcliffe. The expert medical evidence was only part of the body of evidence available to the court and certainly was no guarantee that it should be prioritised over the Prosecution's case. In this instance, the jury chose to downgrade the evidence that the defendant had believed he had been handed a mission from God to remove the prostitutes, and the additional evidence that this delusion was only one of several signs and symptoms of schizophrenia that he had displayed. The jury, despite having been given conclusive evidence in court that the defendant was mentally disordered *at the time of the killings and that this would have influenced his reasoning and mental competence*, chose to convict him on grounds that he should be held responsible for his actions. In sentencing him, the Judge's recommendation was that he serve at least thirty years imprisonment. In the event, having commenced a prison sentence, he had to be transferred to Broadmoor when his psychiatric symptoms became so severe as to make his continued detention in prison untenable and his psychiatric transfer unavoidable. It could be said that this was an example of a variant to entering a "Special Hospital" via the indirect, prison route. The forensic process recorded the defence of medical diagnosis at the trial; over-ruled it in favour of the Prosecution's case to find a guilty verdict; sentenced to imprisonment; effected a prison disposal; and reversed this with a necessary re-disposal for hospitalised, psychiatric treatment.

All these individuals had, in common, a patent capacity for committing the most severe crimes. Some deserved the reputation of criminals before acquiring a later mental disorder while others committed crimes with the caveat of having done so whilst mentally disordered at the time. For those whose crimes were influenced by their pathological mental state most were immediately granted what the law permitted as a degree of excusability. During the Court process, it was determined that they were not entirely responsible for their actions and, therefore, could not be held to account. Consequently, rather than criminal punishment, such individuals were given an immediate "Special Hospital" disposal.

Despite the collage of individual detail, all these representative examples of the patient community would share the common principle that seriously dangerous behaviour, almost invariably amounting to criminal conduct, often with fatal consequences for the victims, were but the extreme prerequisites for a "Special Hospital" admission. In this respect, the stories of John Straffen, Graham Young, Robert Maudsley, Charles Bronson, Ronnie Kray, Ian Brady, Peter Sutcliffe, and the Carstairs' incidents do not stand alone but are a representative gallery of the more exotic patients, past and present, whose exploits had brought them up the steps of the "Special Hospitals". At the very least, they provide an indication of the apparently inexplicable acts that some of the most disturbed mentally disordered offenders appeared to be capable and which informed the contact that the staff necessarily had with them. Patients whose extreme criminality generated the most stupefying revulsion so that it precipitated inferences about their devilish and evil motivation. The universal antipathy which this produced made it more or less unlikely that these elite few would ever be permitted to reclaim their citizenship and freedom. The clarion call for "life", in these instances, would probably mean *life*, effectively. For many, including mental health staff, some patients had defaulted on their purpose of fulfilling bona fide citizenship.

The litany of these notorious residents, for whom these "Special Hospitals" catered, would condemn both to an irredeemable infamy. Of particular note regarding many of this selected few was the disturbing reality that they had committed their worst acts either after their admission to hospital, or on escaping, or on transfer to the prison service, or on release from the hospitals! In such circumstances, their treatment options within National Health facilities were curtailed and the patients lived out their remaining lives in prison custody! Thus, an uncomfortable irony could not be avoided whereby the initial legal efforts to decriminalise these patients' acts were suddenly revoked in favour of a reclassified criminalisation. Were they no longer mentally disordered? Did they have greater capacity and responsibility for subsequent behaviour and crimes which they had not before? Consequently, for the general public, media, and professionals alike the foregoing constituency of patients and their preternatural deeds launched themselves like alien, shooting stars across the communal consciousness. To be taken into consideration, however, was the fact that the majority of "Special Hospital" patients, though quite exceptionally deviant at the time of their offence, lay on a sliding scale of relatively reduced dangerousness compared with the most extreme tier. This risk reduction could be causally associated with many disparate factors, not least, the patients' personal motivation and volition.

Quintessentially, the combination of prisoner transfers, along with high profile patient admissions and the subsequent calamities they perpetrated, dictated the organisational progress of the high security hospitals in the image of a swinging pendulum. At one point in time, a particular therapeutic era would veer the organisational pendulum toward the liberalising extreme until a catastrophe, which could be fairly blamed on that endeavour, ushered in a defensive clampdown and a veering toward the opposite, conservative extreme. In turn, that defensive era would yield its own accusations of undue authoritarianism and the hospital regime would swing back to its polar opposite. This was to happen time and again as, from one point of view, demands for procedural safety eventually spawned outcries of institutional abuse, whereas, the subsequent relaxation of controls left the organisation vulnerable to abuse by the patients themselves. Whichever position on the therapy-custody continuum the current organisational pendulum was set, the resulting adverse scenarios would guarantee a reactionary fallout against the staff and the hospital philosophies of the period.

000

Having left behind the female side of the hospital's residences I was handed over, for the afternoon, to a time-served Nurse Manager for a briefer excursion into the male patient side of the estate. It was "Special Hospital" policy, with the exception of one solitary ward, not to integrate the patient population. Mark, as he introduced himself, invited me to accompany him to the block of three wards for which he was responsible. Personable though he was, the most memorable aspect about him was the broad swell of his mouth and cheeks that rippled around his teeth and laughter. The patter with which he engaged me was on a jocular, social plain rather than professional, tending toward enquiries into individuals whom we might mutually know, and the state of industrial relations in our respective hospitals, but with not a mention of the clinical arena. It was mightily clear that he was not about to enthral me with engaging insights into the clinical regime that it was my intention to observe and take note of. For he was already displaying what I had come to expect among many senior nursing staff in the institutionalised mental health services: that they possessed a casually low expectation of their personal therapeutic accreditation; that holding a position of authority was their main occupational goal; that subordinate nursing staff could be as security attentive as they wished without the need to show much interest in clinical activity; and that their relationships with staff were most certainly a priority over relations with patients. On the brink of entering the ground floor ward he finally yielded some perspective on the destination to which I was to be taken. Security arrangements on this three ward block, I was informed, were quite low key with quite a lot of the patients having regular access to the Occupations Departments. Nevertheless, as we turned into the ground floor stairwell of this male block of three wards, a seated nurse, monitoring the entrance and departure of all personnel in the block, inscribed us onto his running ledger. This had been designated a nursing task, day in, day out.

The ground floor ward was what, in any psychiatric hospital in the country, would be instantly recognised as a run-of-the-mill facility for patients in for the long haul. It advertised itself as such in the abiding drabness of the environment and the complete absence of viable activity or stimulation. But always the snooker table straddling the dayroom like a recreational oasis among a plain of unprepossessing furniture, and always the TV facing the spread of chairs like an alter. Few patients were present and only the raucous jibes of the staff from the distant office spattered across the dead ward silence. Mark acknowledged the two members of staff who, lounging over the wall radiator at their appointed station, reluctantly observed the dayroom between idle chatter. Capturing my sense of being thoroughly unimpressed with all that was on show my guide quickly returned us to the broad stairwell that linked the three units.

'This ward I'm taking you to, now, has been a bit of an experiment in terms of the "Specials", to be honest. It's operated for a few years and been pretty innovative, and all that, but I'll let the staff do the talking.' Marlborough Ward, on the first floor, was cushioned between what we in the County hospitals would have called "back wards". This was a euphemism for "backward", owing to the lack of activity and innovation attached to such units. But, they were residences which were literally allocated toward the rear area of a hospital away from the busy optimism at the front where its admission wards rubbed shoulders with offices, therapeutic clinics, and the chapel. Opposing this, Marlborough Ward had, indeed, acquired a substantial reputation for its innovative practice in what it called its "approach". Impressions of activity and movement were evident the moment we stepped into the ward and, from my point of view, prospects were looking up.

We had the good fortune to be introduced to a Charge Nurse who proved to be a strong protagonist for the ward's raison d'etre. A bespectacled Tom, who had been present from its inception, possessed all the self-assurance of one who was well used to evangelising the ward's exceptional aims and activities. From the way in which he handled himself there was an immediate semblance of a nursing impresario.

'How are things, Tom, still holding it together in this cauldron of excellence?' the Nurse Manager quipped.

'Oh, we're keeping the blighters at bay!' was the Charge Nurse's artful deflection of his superior's sarcasm.

'Mr. Burrow is visiting us from one of our sister establishments and I thought he'd appreciate the low-down on what you do here. I've not queered your pitch any. Thought I'd leave it for you to do that, ha, ha, ha!' Mark continued, while sharing another of his sputtering peals. And, as he passed me over to the redoubtable Tom, he switched attention to the remaining staff in the office to continue his jocular banter. One of these, a young staff nurse, politely interjected with an enquiry as to whether we would all want tea, which only Tom and myself accepted. To my complete astonishment, the young man detached a microphone from the office wall, belted out an instruction that so-and-so – undoubtedly one of the patients – should bring two cups of tea to the office, before casually replacing it. I envisaged the public missive ricocheting up and down the length of the ward to the accustomed distraction of the ward population. The pronouncements, presumably, were routinely made, very public, and entirely non-negotiable. My surprise was noted.

'Don't you have this piece of equipment at your place?' asked Tom.

'What, a ward microphone and public address system? No, not to my knowledge. Our wards are quite compact, though. Wouldn't be any call for them.'

'That's the point. It's a God-send in these areas. Can't understand why they stretched these wards out so much when they built them! Did they think the exercise was good for us, or something! Any rate, saves us a lot of leg-work.' Remaining seated as he was, the bounding authoritative self-confidence, not to say slightly arrogant manner, seemed all the more imposing as he assumed immediate control of our encounter. It led me to wonder if this was what all of us who took charge of wards customarily did, wittingly or otherwise! Were we merely assuming a dominating role to suit the expectations made of us or was it more of an individual trait which only some needed to portray? (Irrespective of either consideration, I had little doubt that I'd portrayed the same dominating style!) Tom's stance was, also, interesting for one who would be professing a therapeutic commitment to his work. 'Well, I'll assume you're not au fait with who we are and what we're about so I may as well start at the very beginning. We have a capacity of twenty-nine beds and there's a waiting list of patients from the other wards waiting to come here. The staff assess each patient, individually, to see if they're ready for what we've got to offer. You've got to remember that many of them will say anything that gives them an advantage in getting discharged so we like to make sure they have a proper motivation for coming here. If we like what we see then we lay it on the line as to what they can expect. There's no point in giving them the false impression that it's going to be a bed of roses. The first thing to say about the Marlborough patients is that they are the most complicated in many ways. The vast majority suffer from psychopathic disorder – we tend to talk about *personality disorder* on this ward to keep up with the times. We're interested in all those difficulties which arise from personality – self-esteem, getting along with people, sexuality, managing anger, etc.'

'And their crimes?' I ask.

'Yes, and their crimes, you're quite right,' with a veiled patronising touch. 'Homicide, sex offences, arson, grievous bodily harm, you name it, they've done it, frankly! We aim to provide a wide range of therapies on Marlborough that you won't find on any other ward in the rest of the hospital. Matter of fact, I'd doubt there's a therapeutic unit in the entire "Specials" that we could be compared with. We have the best psychiatrist, with an international reputation, and a renowned psychotherapist – both smashing fellas, too. There's also a speech therapist, a psychologist, and a social worker attached to the ward. That means to work here you need to be highly motivated, and willing to learn, so everyone is hand-picked. Many of us nurses have done extra training and are allowed, and encouraged, to use our skills, here. Me, for instance, I've finished a counselling course.' You could not help but note from the sustained build up that this was an elite team he described. And for good reason if all this was true. What more was I about to hear? 'We offer two types of group-work as well as individual therapy. One set of groups are open and unstructured. These can be either supportive or confrontational depending what the aim is, and how able the patients are. The less able aren't up to being challenged so the supportive groups can give them self-confidence, to open up a little, where we can listen to their concerns, help them to take responsibility for their actions, encourage them to make suggestions about how the ward is run, etc. The idea's not to do everything for them, see, and it takes time to shake off that expectation! The more confrontational groups are for those who've the ability to move on, who have a degree of confidence, can tolerate being challenged without completely losing it, and are prepared to take a deeper look at themselves. The other closed groups are very structured and limited to addressing a particular issue such as social skills, assertiveness training, anger management, sex education, that sort of thing. Oh, mustn't forget, we're writing a multi-disciplinary article for publication at the moment, too. You look surprised, even impressed, if I may say?' I was, indeed, totally bloody amazed and didn't mind showing it, to be honest.

'Alcohol and drug abuse?' I asked, facetiously, thinking that there was not much else that had been left untouched.

'Blimey, hang on! What do you think we are – miracle workers!' Shame, just as I was beginning to believe the very same! 'No, the hospital's got a separate unit for that. They're seen as quite separate problems, though they may affect our own patients, naturally. Substance misuse would likely be tackled before being admitted to Marlborough. As I was saying, then, added to group-work we have the individual therapy which helps patients to come to terms with their offences, what led up to them, looking into the family background.' Effusing alongside his rendition of the unit's clinical protocol was the unmistakable presence of Tom's personal pride.

'And how much do the nursing staff get involved in all this?' I added, with huge reservation. 'You say that nurses have done extra training but I don't know of courses that tackle forensic mental health issues from a therapeutic perspective. So, where do you get the preparation?'

'Point taken. Well, as nurses we don't get asked into the psychotherapists' individual therapy work, obviously, but we can be involved in most of the remaining areas as co-therapists. We learn a lot on the job, quite frankly, but that's why you have to be highly motivated. And we also have our individual sessions with patients to try and sort out a lot of everyday issues that might not be covered elsewhere. And some of us will have ongoing counselling sessions with individual patients. There's a lot going on, believe me! On top of all that...' a pause for emphasis... 'we also have the responsibility of laying down the ward ground rules because, alongside all this intensive work, we're all in one living space and the patients have got to work alongside each other while eating together, sleeping in the same place, etc. Conflicts are bound to erupt and we have to maintain a safe environment, especially with the histories of some of them. At the end of the day, this is a "Special Hospital", not any old hospital, and security is part of their treatment – a very considerable part of it.

So, we nurses have a very important role in keeping the ship steady and if you don't possess very strong therapy skills there's plenty of valuable work to be done, besides. Anyway,' and he rose from his desk chair, 'let me show you round – give you an idea of how we fit all this into our ward space.' With that, having built up a head of aggrandising steam, he rose from behind his desk and led me out of the office to indicate the various consulting and therapy rooms, along with areas for general social and domestic usage, and the single rooms allocated to each and every patient. En route, the comments shared with available patients were probably designed to illustrate both his authority and skills, I surmised. While he finished walking me back to the office I reflected on the sheer clinical scope of the unit.

'This unit must make very high demands on you. I was wondering how much support the nurses receive?'

'Plenty, as you'd expect,' he said, with a shrug of self-approbation. 'With these patients it's vital that all the staff trust each other and have a forum for bringing everything into the open. We have a weekly staff group which includes all the therapists and nursing staff, where we get support from each other and supervision of any of the therapy. Added to that, we nurses provide informal support for one another as, and when, we need it. But, then, nurses have always done that.'

I could hardly believe what I was hearing! What was this – a therapeutic hotbed? It was almost unheard of for psychiatric nurses to receive such focused guidance in the clinical area, certainly within a large institution. I quickly convinced myself that the entire therapeutic initiative must have lain with the medical and psychotherapeutic leadership and so I wallowed in more than a little professional jealousy at this lucky bugger's opportunity to avail himself of such a notable experience, with such reputable colleagues, when such resources were far from the reach of the majority of us.

'Strikes me that you were in the right place at the right time,' I poked at him, with a pall of thoroughgoing envy lodged into the comment.

'No use denying that,' he replied. There was no doubting this man's abundant enthusiasm, integrity, and benign belief in what he was doing. Yet, I retained a healthy scepticism for his honorific appraisal of the nursing input into these exceptional conditions. It would be a skilled practitioner, indeed, that was able to conflate within this type of environment and residents the competing role of routinely controlling sentinels, on the one hand, with the requisite individualising demands of therapeutic endeavour, on the other. Seriously, just how integrated into the therapeutic work could the nursing staff manage to be when they were compelled to organise the minute by minute housekeeping and utilitarian aspects of this controlled residency? As if intuitively countering my discrepant reservations the Charge Nurse's air of scintillating self-satisfaction entertained no such piffling trifles! Rather, he apparently possessed an unshakable belief that not only counted him among the hospital's elite, but that this clinical enterprise conferred an aptitude for managing the disparate occupational dilemmas and contradictions.

While Tom resumed his place at the office desk with a cheery 'get the hell out of my chair, you idle bastard' to the staff nurse who had temporarily ensconced himself there, I finished my tea and interrupted the continuing banter between the young staff nurse and his regaling manager. He was an affable lad with an approachable disposition which invited personal contact. He noted that my attention was now set toward him and chirped in.

'Tom's been giving you the low-down on the ward, well, his version anyway. So just fire away and I'll put you straight!'

'Try this for size, then! I'd be interested to know your thoughts on whether the other disciplines really take the nursing staff seriously as co-therapists in all this therapeutic endeavour? Take yourself. As a junior member of staff, do you think you get a fair crack of the whip?' A conniving glance passed between himself and the Charge Nurse.

'Well, there's bit of history in that. For years, nursing staff have argued that they were left out of all the therapy because the other disciplines just viewed us as guards, really. We've had to fight our corner, like, but the team are pretty accepting of us I'd say. We still have to compete with trainee psychologists and social workers and the like which is a bit of a bummer. The other main hindrance is that we have to work a rotating shift system so that we're not always available on a regular basis when the groups are taking place between nine-to-five.'

'So why don't you work regular nine-to-five hours some of you – to ensure you're available?' A burst of spontaneous laughter all round.

'Well now that would be about money, of course!' Of course. Why should nurses give up the opportunity of extra payments for working antisocial hours?

'Understood,' I nodded. 'That would imply that if further training was made available to staff so that they were on a more level footing with other therapists you would still be disadvantaged by the shift work? Not always available during the therapy hours?'

'That's all been considered but who, in their right mind, is going to sacrifice a good part of their salary?'

'Fair enough, but let's say that extra training was put in place do you think staff would take it up?'

'Oh, without doubt because nurses want to be taken far more seriously than just dealing with security issues and everyday housekeeping.' And he, as an individual, seemed to mean it. But time would play a different tune. When I was to return to this hospital some four years later to instigate an innovative forensic programme for nurses from medium secure units, intensive care units, the Prison Service, and "Special Hospitals" – that is, those areas managing mentally disordered offenders – the latter group was extremely difficult to recruit from.

Tom's final comment before passing me back to the chattering Nurse Manager who, by now, was itching to be off was 'in a word, Mr. Burrows, Marlborough is a Therapeutic Community.' Then, discovering a patient's postal delivery lying on his desk he slipped, comfortably into his Charge Nurse role, deftly reached for the microphone and intoned, nonchalantly, 'Weston! Come to the office, please, and sign for this parcel.'

As we sauntered from the male block, crossed the open quadrangle en route to the hospital reception I offered my gratitude. 'That was very illuminating and totally unexpected, thanks Mark. That's an impressive unit and a sound man, that Charge Nurse, I have to say, and a great opportunity whether you're staff or a patient.'

'Sounds like therapeutic work, and such like, is up your street, then?'

'Times have changed from when I started out. Far more therapy is what is expected of us, now, not just locking people away.' This was a mischievous challenge as was my next enquiry which I already knew the answer too, I fancied.

'Do you get involved in any of the clinical work, at all, then Mark?'

'Do I what? Nah! Not my cup of tea, mate! I mean, all credit to the staff but there's too much arsing around with fancy ideas when there's no proof they work anyway. But, we don't all want the same things in the job, do we? Some of us are content to do our basic nursing care and keeping everyone safe. That's the bottom line and no mistake. In any case, the staff don't expect us managers to interfere in clinical stuff. Why would you? It's not our job when we get to our position!' I considered this a matter of personal opinion.

'Perhaps, we should be setting the example rather than there be some sort of dividing line between managers and ward staff?'

'I do what's expected of me. Come to the Clinical Team Meetings each week so's I can keep in the loop and offer advice when it's needed but it's just to keep an eye on things, really.' I was not too surprised. Senior staff in most mental hospitals with which I had had contact seemed to take it for granted that, ipso facto, they were entitled to disengage themselves from clinical work, and to make patient contact if and when they pleased. And, it had to be said that, on the basis of the apportioned division of labour, there was a strong argument as to why this should be the case. But, for myself, I never understood anyone who would not want to continue to avail themselves of some form of clinical connection despite their managerial promotion. After all, their profession was nursing, not general management. In short, I was mystified that senior staff would be prepared to settle for the arid tasks of management save, naturally, for the advantages of being able to exercise authority and the concomitant increase in salary.

'But, if you really wanted to work alongside patients and staff do you think you would be afforded the chance to do so?'

'I'm not sure I would be, actually. Other managers would wonder what the hell I was playing at and if anything went seriously wrong on the unit I reckon I'd be called to task for not devoting myself to managing. Besides, the staff would see me as interfering so I can't see the sense in complicating things! Are you sure you want to be a manager?' And so ended my day's succinct, multi-faceted, and agreeable orientation of Broadmoor.

Yet, as I walked away from the place I could not help but be hounded by an uncomfortable reverie which filtered through this orientation into the management of dangerousness. For, if my personal knowledge of one particular individual was anything to go by, contrasted to many of the foregoing "Special Hospital" roll-call, it must have also counted among its number some fairly innocuous cases. At the very time that I had commenced my own nursing career I was personally acquainted with the family of a young lad who had sustained a mild learning disability and an accompanying epileptic condition from birth. His needs demanded that he attended a specialised boarding facility for children away from his home. He had never been a violent lad but his physical condition affected his temperament to the extent that he could not help revealing his frustration in periodic outbursts of agitation. Otherwise he was a delightful, and agreeably sociable young man. Upon leaving his school at age fifteen he was provided with a sheltered work placement for people with mental and physical disabilities and performed very satisfactorily until one day when his debilities erupted into a single incident. His condition and confused frustration conspired to cause him to toss a metal object across the room in which he was employed, with the outcome that the facilitator sustained a serious gash to her head. The injurious act was accidental with no deliberate intent to harm anyone but the ensuing investigations and forensic calculation enforced a disposal into the highest security in the land – Broadmoor! And this was his allotted residence until it was confirmed that he represented no danger to society. What effect had the place had on him?

000

What effect did the place have on anyone? No one who had experienced the life of a high security hospital could remain immune to its profound and ranging contradictions that weighed ever more poignantly when given its intimate association with therapeutic endeavour. Assuming that some therapeutic endeavour was attempted! Many of these contradictions emanated from the earlier necessities of these hospitals' histories and how they came to clash, eventually, with the evolving political and social perspectives about mentally ill patients and what should be their proper management given the emerging transformation of wider mental health policy. These inevitable contradictions reverberated through the very nomenclature by which they were identified over time – initially criminal lunatic asylums, then "Special Hospitals", eventually, high security hospitals.

Contradictions characterised their very foundations. Broadmoor, the very first to be purpose-built, was an exclusive establishment which set it apart from the ordinary County asylums whose existence was validated under quite separate legislation. It had taken three years to build this monument to history, this edifice of psychiatry, this virtual prison, and it was a convict contingent who constructed the brick and mortar and a prison architect, Joshua Jebb, who devised it. The provision was special, bearing as it did, the unenviable status of a *criminal lunatic asylum*. Its residents were special, too, and as patients and virtual inmates they bore the very exceptional stamp of *criminal lunatics*. This very much reflected the social aggravations of the period, especially that of crime and contrived notions of the "criminal classes". In the immediate years around Broadmoor's construction and operational beginnings, a diverse range of criminal legislation was enacted, including Acts for whipping, garrotting, penal servitude, offences against the person, habitual criminals, prevention of crimes, and a Prison Act. A Criminal Lunatics Act sat very comfortably amongst this legislative onslaught.

Built within the immediate geographical locality of Broadmoor Hospital, both the Royal Military Academy Sandhurst, and the Wellington Public School (in honour of the Duke of Wellington), anyone could be forgiven for positing the calculated irony of positioning this dwelling of exclusive notoriety alongside these pinnacles of the Establishment. What could more epitomise the extremes of the social spectrum than setting alongside, what many would view as, the desirable educational and military elitism, the social inferiority of criminal insanity? Neither could there be any escaping the symbolism of the Victorian institutionalisation of discipline, privilege, virtue and entitlement versus that of undisciplined mental chaos and virtual statelessness. The institutionalisation of both social extremes would illuminate the crucial ingredients of standards, stability, and order, and the continuity of a certain breed of social hierarchy. Perhaps, there was also a political fantasy that the superior air emanating from the Sandhurst and Wellington estates would waft an exemplary draft through the insane vapours of Broadmoor?

Nothing better characterised Broadmoor's own perception of the need for discipline and control than when the non-medical staff affiliated themselves to the Prison Officers' Association at the latter's inauguration just after the start of the Second World War. This early association with the Prison Service was logical enough, at the time, and dictated the Broadmoor Attendants' orientation to the roles, and prescripts, of the prison officer. As such, the attendants became organically committed to what was, in essence, that of the *Discipline Officer*. With this included within the hospital's organisation the staff, as they saw it, managed a criminal class by *maintaining good order and discipline* through routine control, rule enforcement, and security practices.

The affiliation to the P.O.A. also entitled the staff to similar terms and conditions of service as the prison officers. Remuneratively, the benefits package aimed to partially compensate the staff for working within this demanding environment, with its proportionate degree of danger, and the geographical segregation from any metropolis. This negotiating advantage also enhanced the entitlements of the non-P.O.A. staff, thereby, making the benefits package a sizeable inducement to all job applications. The Attendants were granted a complete uniform entitlement from top to toe, of inner and outer clothing, gaberdine coats and leather gloves, all topped with peaked caps adorned with the crowned badge of the realm. In this garb, they mirrored that of the Prison Officer in practically every detail. Thus, they periodically trudged away from the hospital's Main Stores loaded with supplies of free clothing. This uniform paraphernalia was a cultural variation on an established theme during the Victorian era which had spawned a militarist-type colonisation of most aspects of life to manage the various administrative threads running through the "real politic", as well as the perceived social crises erupting around the age. Institutional regulation, discipline and control was widespread and those invested with institutional responsibilities, more often than not, wore uniforms to distinguish them from their charges and to give further gravitas to their purpose. The principles equally applied to the organisation around ill health as much as any other field. For the control of physical illnesses, the staff of General Hospitals, Tuberculosis Sanatoria, and Fever Hospitals, possessed occupational keys and uniforms that divided them from their patients in organisations which ran with strict precision to effect an improvement in health and infection control. Equally, as part of the operation of institutionalised mental illness, the uniform regalia distinguished the staff from the patient fraternity but conferred a distinctly marshal connotation to the custodial function which they also pursued. In addition to all this, the Criminal Lunatic Asylum, with the authorisation of its dedicated Security Office, issued the security tackle of leather belt, key chain, key pouch, personal assistance whistle, name badge, identity card and hospital keys were variously affixed, pinned to, clipped on, and hung from, their persons. These prison affectations, incidentally or otherwise, undoubtedly had a compromising impact on the prospective therapeutic relations that were to be attempted, simultaneously, within an ostensibly mental health environment.

As demand for Broadmoor's specialised services expanded the secure hospital estate, nationally, expanded in turn. (Parkhurst Criminal Lunatic Asylum was a short-term stop-gap of about five years.) The severe overcrowding in Broadmoor was, eventually, considered so unacceptable that a second Criminal Lunatic Asylum,

Rampton, came into being in the County of Nottinghamshire in 1912. Like Broadmoor, it lay in the heart of the countryside, but surrounded by farmland, in this instance. Though the structure had a modicum of aesthetic attraction, owing to its relatively historical context, it did not in any way replicate the elegance of the older institution. These more prosaic buildings advertised themselves as an imposing, functional, State development, through and through, the grassed and arborial hinterland between the ward areas were interspersed with pruned, winding pathways. Moss Side Hospital was similarly commissioned and within the confines of its original buildings replicated the architecture and atmosphere of Rampton.

Their ongoing evolution came to involve their inclusion into the national services for mental health which was brought together in the enactment of the Mental Health Act (1959) at which juncture they had been relieved of their previous, awesome title as criminal lunatic asylums and acquired the less ominous, yet mystical, title of *Special Hospitals.* Their distinctive status as security hospitals prevailed on the criteria that, owing to the violent, dangerous, or criminal propensities of their patients, they would be *cared for in conditions* of *special security.* The *Special*, therefore, described conditions of restrictive detention without any mention of other management, treatment or therapeutic parameters! The absence of any treatment references implied not that custody, alone, would prevail but that the mental health care prescribed elsewhere in the National Health Service would be disseminated and implemented, but within the remit of secure conditions. Then, with the construction of the last of the "Special Hospitals", Park Lane, from 1974 onwards, with its inflationary security architecture of twenty foot, goose-necked perimeter walls the "Special Hospital" estate was completed. Park Lane – an ironic nomenclature if ever there was one – was erected directly adjacent to the Moss Side site. And, yet, there was some pertinence for the use of the iconic name in that, in terms of a security hospital, it presented the very best that money could buy. As a completely modern structure, it manifested the state of the art in security paraphernalia. The external perimeter was not only secure but escape-proof, its twenty foot walls being topped by a curved "goose-neck" which looped downwards, internally, thus preventing any potential escapee, or external assister, from gaining any sort of physical purchase. Internal entry to the hospital was through an electronically operated reception area with electronic doors operated from a Control Room from which personalised keys were issued in exchange for personalised identity cards. Beyond the bland block of administrative and professional offices, the residential areas took the form of separate, single-storey units which compromised any attempt at roof-top protesting by patients. In as striking a contrast as could be imagined the aesthetic achievements of Park Lane and Broadmoor lay at opposite poles. It must have been a deliberate architectural policy that Park Lane would represent a functional utilitarianism, laying down precedents for a contemporary, psychiatric stronghold, and that this would preclude any other consideration. With the complete absence of trees and shrubbery throughout the high-walled enclosure, little more than a furbished, lunar landscape could be appreciated. Initially, Park Lane absorbed what had, once again, become the burgeoning numbers of patients residing in Broadmoor.

The "Special Hospital" estate would leave an unforgettable image of imprisonment on any professional, relative or other visitor. But, was it entirely appropriate to develop a treatment regime in places with the aesthetic and operational ambiance of high security prison establishments? The positive prospect was that this incremental physical security would, hopefully, peel away shards of the security tasks from the nursing staff role and facilitate an improved focus on direct patient care.

There remained some residual issues which complicated this new-found incorporation within the mantle of the wider National Health Service. Firstly, unlike the rest of the health service, the "Special Hospitals" retained their long-standing political patronage. Instead of being incorporated under the umbrella of a Health Authority like all other mental hospitals and mental health services which, in turn, became responsible to the Department of Health and Social Security, they were directly administered by that Department as an exclusive entity. Secondly, due to the criminal contraventions which characterised the overwhelming majority of the "Special Hospital" patient group, the decision-making responsibilities around patient admissions and discharges were effected by the Home Office, who also controlled the Prison Service and Police Forces. This Home Office linkage also compelled the staff to sign the Official Secrets Act so that they were not at liberty to discuss professional issues in the open-handed manner that the rest of the health service was. This could only have perpetuated the relative separation and insularity that characterised these establishments. Thirdly, the "Special Hospital" staff maintained their unionised and cultural links with the Prison Officers Association which, within the negotiating arena of the

National Health Service, was not a recognised trade union. Fourthly, one of the major tenets of the 1959 Act was the promotion of an "open door" policy which democratised the use of mental health services. The asylum walls were demolished so that patients were no longer continuously confined; patients were encouraged to access the surrounding community and look to the prospect of rehabilitation; and the conditions for hospital admission were transformed by introducing a voluntary admission process for patients to supplement those still requiring "compulsory detention" (previously "certification"). Conversely, the high security hospitals retained and developed their perimeters, emphatically incarcerated their residents, severely limited their access to the community, and admitted but the merest trace of "informal" voluntary patients. These disparate guiding authorities, armed with their ranging principles, evolved into a complex constituency with many shades of purpose that was far more complex than the more straightforward purpose of the rest of the mental health services! Consequently, despite them coming within the auspices of the Mental Health Act, and the National Health Service, it was not wholly surprising that their entrenched affiliations predisposed these institutions to continue to assume a blatantly custodial operation nor that, in time, it became nothing short of a cause celebre that the "Special Hospitals" should eventually be disengaged from the constraining influences of direct Government control, and its erstwhile prison-orientated negotiating organisation, so that they could be freed up, managed, and represented under the broader mantle of localised Health Authorities. Conclusively, the more that the centre of gravity of mental health policy moved toward de-institutionalisation, democratisation, and de-stigmatisation – a veritable revolution over time – the more emphatically out-of-synch appeared the high security provision.

In turn, the emerging conflicting cultures between the Health Service and the "Specials" could only, at best, diffuse any therapeutic *insurgence,* at worst, relegate it to a subsidiary status. Most poignantly, during an evolving social climate, with changing political and professional pressures, all buffeting at the sides of tradition, the demand for custodial competence was preferred not to supersede, but to conflate with, therapeutic practice. Irrespective, for these favoured few there was only ever the *threat* of termination, only a fairly muted resolve that they should keep pace with the clinical advances in mental health care and, certainly, never any lack of need.

A remaining residual issue was the wearing of uniforms which matched the Prison Service. This had been taken for granted until the commissioning of Park Lane Hospital. From its inauguration the dress code was civilian "mufti" which represented a controversial break with "Special Hospital" tradition. The controversy was exacerbated by the construction of the Park Lane Hospital directly alongside that of Moss Side Hospital, on the same site, causing from time to time an eruption of hostilities between the two fraternities within the hospital social club since the traditional Moss Siders viewed this "mufti' ragbag as a provocation.

And, if it was the unpredictable, violent or criminal behaviour exhibited by a "Special Hospital" patient that determined the defensive management of the organisation so, in turn, this demanded that the resident staff be equipped to operate this part of their mission. Yet, these staff were not prison warders, guards, or private security personnel. Neither were the staff professionally trained in forensic detection, or custodial competencies, as appertained to the Police Service, or the Prison Service, respectively. On the contrary, the mandatory preparation of the professional staff was of medical, nursing, and paramedical care for physical and psychological ill-health. Any additional forensic or security skills, while practically incidental to their avowed professional preparation, were absolutely indispensable to the adequate fulfilment of their occupational roles within a high security organisation. Like it or not, everyone shared in the warden's task. Most poignantly, as each patient served out their time and accepted, or had imposed upon them, their range of treatments, every member of staff acquired a dutiful vigilance for inspecting and detecting any aspect of the patient's internal thinking, general predisposition, or outward conduct, which might hint at their prospective dangerousness. It was the indubitable case that, once having been found guilty, the "Special Hospital" patient had to prove him/herself innocent of any similar liability in the future.

At the most benign level, you could only be resigned to the requirement for a carceral glade that was necessarily ripped from nature's hosting forest in order to accommodate the perverse dwelling. That such a captive place needed to exist at all and that it was required for a unique minority of people too dangerous to be living among the general populace. That it should hold individuals whose offending behaviour was made all the more bemusing because it was directly or indirectly related to psychiatric morbidity – a truly defamatory master status if ever there was one. That it should fall to its remit as a psychiatric hospital to attend to the resulting business of what could be termed therapeutic custody – a place of almost total incarceration as a basic ingredient of care that would facilitate the medical and psychological treatment and rigorous assessment of future risk and dangerousness of its charges. That this would incorporate an advocacy of this patient class for their general rehabilitation, de-stigmatisation and de-criminalisation. In part accomplishment of that seemingly contradictory purpose a "Special Hospital" had to test its escape siren and remind the entire community within several miles' geographical radius of its presence and purpose. Anything outside of the advertised testing schedule, of course, denoted an actual escape and a pre-arranged public, police and institutional response sprung into operation. One such safety measure was for all surrounding schools to retain their pupils until their parents personally arrived to pick them up and ferry them home. All local motorists would discover that an encircling cordon of road blocks, at pre-determined spots, now barred their progress. Manned, jointly, by the police and hospital staff – the latter wearing bibs displaying the name of the hospital – the drivers and occupants would have pictures and descriptions of the escapee revealed to them. The whole scenario was nothing short of the black and white 1950s crime movies.

From a more malign point of view, the "Specials" were a holding centre facilitating an indeterminate detention for a significant social minority. This minority, if they were committed to an extended period of hospital stay, would have failed to secure the support of the major parties who could advocate a patient's release – the hospitals' Consultant Psychiatrists, the Mental Health Review Tribunals, the Parole Board, and the Home Secretary. For those whose release had failed, their official detention and their continued high security containment could be protracted over an indefinite period, much as applied to "lifers" sentenced to imprisonment. This had the consequence that a patient could repeatedly fail their release appeals in the same way a prison "lifer" could fail their parole hearings. This effective life imprisonment, then, sullied the beneficent philosophy of minimal hospitalisation and maximum rehabilitation and was facilitated by the Mental Health Acts.

000

"Special Hospitals." A vital role and function in the psychiatric drama. For all the connotations that attached themselves to their varied purpose these establishments played out their notorious role and lodged themselves in our professional mentality as strongly as it did in the public imagination. Their role had a distinctive difference from all the other players in the drama who were, otherwise, united in a liberation plot to free the mentally ill from their captivity, their illnesses, their stigma, and perverse associations, and to open up the possibility of social acceptance and integration. By contrast, the "Special Hospitals" moved about the mental health stage masking the emotions that would have revealed their countervailing beliefs, scepticism, and reservations toward the new zeitgeist. To any audience, they would remain professionally aloof with an entrenched and detached staff contingency; geographically isolated, total institutions with an overriding remit of social control; and a marginalised, chronic, mentally ill fraternity; and all garlanded around the glowering spectre of criminal insanity. So, hidden behind their inscrutable mask, they relaxed around the sure premise that there would never quite be a satisfactory public, professional and political consensus about their remit. As the evolving political mental health agenda gradually infiltrated and competed with the custodial regulations so was set in motion a progressive debate about the therapeutic and ethical limitations of the high security hospital and its professional operation. Additionally, the more an individual member of staff attempted to excavate their personal motivations about what they were trying to accomplish so they became even more exposed to these inevitable contradictions. An incorrigible and irreconcilable tension stretched between prevailing staff conservatism that perpetuated provincial institutionalism, traditional practice, stability and conformity, at one pole, and the aspiring professional innovation that seemed to promise only uncertainty and destabilisation, at the other. Regarding patients, the most dangerous among them performed the disfavour of casting a mantle of guilty association over the less severe majority. In respect of the media, the patients were nothing more than perpetrators of indecency, and purveyors of consummate evil, so that ideas of rectifying treatment, intensive therapy, restoration, indeed life, were often anathema blazed across their headlines.

This was the colourful, motley garb in which the "Special Hospitals" made their appearance and so distinguished them from the plainer purpose of all the other mental health cast. In addition, other colours were periodically stitched into the costume as it wore thin in places from glaring mistakes, shortcomings, and abuses and were forced to make repairs. For anyone fortunate enough to have experienced the high security mental health service, these issues, deliberations, historical contexts, contemporary dilemmas and contradictions, conflated into the patchwork Harlequin performance with which the nursing, medical and paramedical professionals had to acquaint themselves. I counted my own experience, there, to have been simultaneously fortuitous, stimulating and disturbing to an extent that I never viewed my professional role in the same light from then on. Naturally, the argument stood that my earlier experiences in other health settings necessarily challenged, predisposed and sensitised me toward given standards and boundaries that were appropriate enough for those environments but could only compromise the necessary paradigms of the high security estate. I would accept this to a point, but only to a point. I, and others – some nurses, but mostly those from other professions – had to hang on to a faith that the disturbing exposures which both quickened and distracted us were shared by a significant minority within the field. It was this common resonance which mutually sustained us for as long as we felt we could manage. As time and circumstance took their toll in these establishments a few of us came to experience a deliberate and targeted isolation which only enhanced our limited appreciation of the life of a "Special Hospital" patient as they, themselves, must have experienced it. Ultimately, it would be the admonishing investigations and publications of outside agencies that would come to vindicate our critique and sensitivities.

000

Not that there was any absence of dreadful imagery and awe in the general population when it came to the matter of the ordinary County asylums which were to be found outside all of the major towns and cities from the middle of the nineteenth century onwards. This could only have been perpetuated by the incarceration of the patients in these institutional colonies, outside of the regular boundaries of everyday society. The age of the lunatic asylum, the mental hospital, and the looney bin all but promulgated one of the most ingrained of prejudices – the perception that mental illness was a *madness*, essentially pitiable but more than a little tinged with dangerousness and uncontrollability. But, just after the mid-point of the twentieth century political pragmatism was to revise and rationalise the course of psychiatric history, psychiatric infrastructure, and mental health policy. The established provision of chronic hospitalisation was deconstructed and the appreciation of mental illness, its causes, its treatment, and its corollary, mental health, rendered anew. No longer was it deemed healthy, civilised, or financially viable, that the psychologically troubled should be held in psychiatric exile, in expensive institutions, segregated from a proper civilian integration. From then on, as localised relocation permitted, the County asylums were moribund and bound for obsolescence. So, with the effective dissolution of the mental hospitals in the 1990s, the predominant institutional stars of a hundred and fifty years imploded and their satellite fragments were dispersed into the universe of community care. As for the patients, they must have felt like time-travellers settling into alien culture-forms and unrecognisable landscapes. For many of the more difficult that could not resettle they were filtered into the replacement, medium security units that were regenerating some residual part of the old asylum sites. Within all this reconstitution, the age of the County lunatic asylum, the mental hospital, and the loony bin, entered the psychiatric paraphernalia of history, and the relics of an architectural past. However, the same scenario could not be said to apply to the handful of high security mental hospitals, formerly criminal lunatic asylums. For all the reasons outlined they not only persisted, but could be substantiated, as a fixed and luminous constellation in the psychiatric firmament.

Chapter 2

Acclimatisation

My employment at Moss Side Special Hospital commenced on 1st September which, in point of fact, was coterminous with the outbreak of Second World War hostilities when German forces embarked on the invasion of Poland! This trite association was, nevertheless, shortly to be accompanied by another extraordinary occurrence which could have indicated something portentous ahead. In these present days when meaningful interpretations accompanying natural events had been demythologised I could not be blamed for not taking more note of the event, at the time, but if I had been of a more superstitious persuasion it might well have augured the dubious future that was to befall the hospital, and better prepared me for my own travails. For barely two months after taking up my position, a meteorological scythe not only razed the countryside but was a portent of the coming wreckage that would trail through the "Special Hospitals", with the incidental felling of my own current ambitions. During October 1987, one of the BBC's weather forecasters – we all know the name of the poor soul – disputed a viewer's portent of a developing hurricane one autumnal night yet warned the nation to "batten down the hatches". What followed was Britain's "Great Storm" which strafed the land with its windy munitions, tearing the roots from fifteen million trees that crashed from life in an instant, and taking with them power supplies, transport systems, boats, buildings and workplace functions, and eighteen human lives. There was a sense of national emergency. The last storm of similar severity had subsided into history nearly three hundred years previously and, even more presciently from the point of view of the instability of the "Special Hospitals", a comparable event erupted within three years of this one. The storm, and its after-effects, changed the natural landscape while the inclement political and professional changes that followed behind saw the felling of a perennially outmoded institutional regime.

000

Acclimatising to the establishment was both exhilarating and perplexing from the very start and an experience which my one previous visit to the place – other then my attendance for my job interview – could never have provided more than an inkling of. Daily, I parked the car in the staff and visitor car park which adjoined the staff football pitch set against the low plain wooden perimeter fence. It could have been any fence demarcating a residential or commercial property and it was hard to take this seriously as the secure boundary of a "Special Hospital". Historically, Moss Side had admitted dangerous mentally defective patients, due to the impaired intellectual abilities of its residents, thereby demanding a perimeter that was the least imposing or defensive of any of the "Special Hospitals", and almost symbolic. It comprised metal fencing in some areas, and fairly low walls in others. I would take the short walk to the car barrier and the gate lodge, hand in my identity badge at the lodge window and await the uniformed nurse – in prison officer uniform – to search out my personal hospital keys which I attached to my leather belt; then accepted my personal roaming radio which I switched on, tested, and "joined the net" by connecting with the gate lodge communications centre; all after having briefly exchanged pleasantries with the keenly scrutinising gate lodge staff. As I sauntered along the short drive, in due awe of the manorial-looking administrative block, the camouflaging rambling ivy perfectly symbolised the mixed and uncertain purposes of the institution. The meandering, arboreal ivy cosmetically softened the sterner brick lines beneath so that no one would have defined either its medical or custodial possibilities. It could have fostered any enterprise on the face of it. Through the much abused entrance doors, and onto the worn staircase, I would register my arrival with the Admin Duty Nurse Manager. On this particular day, I was hailed by one of the two managers who occupied the line management tier immediately above my own. When you entered Harry's office he would always give an immediate indication as to whether the meeting was to launch a reprimand or accolade – the latter being a rare occurrence – but it was always business-like. On this occasion his constitution bore all the signs of very serious business. I was not invited to sit.

'Morning, Steve. Now, there's been a complaint made from a patient from one of your wards.' The tone was soft enough. So far, so good! 'Not to worry about that. I'm assuming you've heard nothing, yet?' was Harry's straightforward delivery. He was a uniquely tenacious man, chiselled into a short but robust physique, with a strident gait that belied his diminutive frame. The intense, sometimes bitter eyes, reflected the vehemence of an opinionated polemicist, who had a propensity to chew people off when he so wished. He could also be utterly charming when mellowed.

'No. What's that about, then, Harry?' I asked, any hint of intrigue deflated with apprehension. This was not the sort of news which was going to aid my inclusion into the unit fraternity.

'Patient Chivers claims he's been hit, not once, but twice, in the space of a few days, in the full view of other patients and staff, by one and the same person. Charge Nurse Sterns as a matter of fact. He's claiming that a few of the patients might be prepared to substantiate this. He *claims* he was punched the first time, slapped across the face the second, and then threatened if he should make a formal complaint. You know Sterns by now I imagine? Ex-Army man. Hard-nosed sort but decent enough, I think. Seems to like working with adolescents, anyway. Put up a pretty good show on that ward. We'll have to proceed with an investigation on this one. You won't be aware of the investigative procedure, will you?' I was not.

'Always hand it over to the police. That's the rule for investigating serious complaints. That way, we can be seen to be completely impartial, everything done above board. The greatest advantage is that no one can argue with the outcome, see.'

'To what extent will I be involved, Harry?'

'Not much because it's your unit. Can't be seen to be partial toward your staff's interests. We only ask the Charge Nurse for a written statement, then we leave all the rest to the police authorities to conduct their enquiries, speak to any relevant parties, and to collate whatever evidence they wish.'

'What about an internal investigation?'

'Doesn't happen,' he replied with a shrug of nonchalance. 'Simple as that.'

'But doesn't that give an impression that we're abregating our responsibility for what happens on our patch, and shunting the responsibility elsewhere?'

'Can you see any good reason for us doubling up and repeating the same investigation twice? I can't. The police will do a thorough job. We can't do better than that. I know what you're getting at – that there's a difference between conduct that falls short of professional standards, and behaviour which is illegal, and that they should be looked at separately. But take this case. If Sterns is proven to have done what he's accused of, his illegal behaviour will become a professional matter as well. On the other hand, if the matter wasn't considered serious enough to involve a police investigation we might then look at it from a professional standpoint, internally, and address it accordingly.' It all sounded plausible enough but as I sensed from Harry's increasingly brusque delivery that he would not appreciate a more protracted argument I desisted from voicing further reservations.

'Will Chivers handle that, all right?'

'Oh, if he's well enough to make a formal complaint to the hospital authorities, I have no doubt he can handle making a statement to the police. We'll have a member of the staff sitting with him during any interviews.'

'Suppose he'd rather not have a member of staff sit with him, after all, he'll be complaining about one of that staff's own colleagues? He'll be pretty inhibited don't you think?'

'We've always done it that way. Think of the opportunity a patient would have to say anything he wanted just to get his own back? Having the staff member present ensures that the patient can't blow things out of proportion. He might not, of course, but it's a safeguard and could save a lot of unnecessary aggravation.' It didn't seem quite the place to air the other reservations which seeped from this far from ideal process. In any case, I had no axe to grind and I certainly was not in the business of wanting to establish the culpability of Charge Nurse Sterns. Yet, if the complaint was true, and indulged in so publicly, then it could only raise concerns about what the staff believed they were entitled to do.

'What other steps have been taken, then? Presumably, I'll be down a Charge Nurse until the findings have been determined?' This presumption was based on my previous experience that, whilst an investigation into a staff conduct was in progress, the person against whom the allegation was being made would be temporarily suspended, possibly moved to another work area. This partly prevented any potential retaliation from the staff member but mostly protected that person from allegations of influencing the complainant, or of sustaining further pernicious complaints if the patient was so inclined to make them. This was the standard procedure within the wider Health Service.

'That's the point I was making. You'll lose Sterns from your unit but we won't lose him from our overall complement because he'll be assigned somewhere else, temporarily. This isn't a local Health Authority. We do things differently, here. You must remember that we're ruled somewhere between the Department of Health and the

P.O.A. The P.O.A. have negotiating rights with the Department and one of the most important principles that have been agreed is to have the police investigate complaints against the staff. A related bargaining chip is that the staff member will not be suspended from their duties during the investigative process.' I had determined during our short acquaintance that Harry was an intelligent man and that he must have packed away all reservations about this issue for pragmatic reasons. These hybrid ways of managing the organisation's problems were something to which he had accustomed himself, I imagined, and could see no good purpose in challenging them. He got on with his job within the prevailing parameters and that was an end to it. In any case, who was to say that such matters would be resolved with less satisfaction than appertained within a local Health Authority? 'It's a shame you have to face a difficulty like this having just started but it'll acquaint you with our internal affairs. How are you getting on in your unit, anyway?'

'Very mixed reaction from the staff but the patients are welcoming enough. As a matter of fact, they tend to swoop on me when I enter the units. They're yearning for personal contact – unavoidable when they're spending their youth in a tiny space away from family and peers. I wouldn't mind some privacy with them but both they and I are constrained by the presence of staff who seem very put out by my spending any time, alone, with patients. I'd like the opportunity to sit down with the lads on an informal basis but it just doesn't seem to be the done thing. My impression is that I've to listen to the staff reports and requests and then to bugger off! It's not quite how I'm used to doing things.'

'Well, you're a manager, why would you want to have some privacy with patients? If they have any queries they communicate them to the ward staff, then you don't have to involve yourself unless they can't resolve the issue. And that's rare. Besides, why would we need to employ managers if they're going to spend half their time doing the job of their subordinates? You're not paid for that, frankly.' His eyebrows were, by now, a raised arc of scepticism. And there was an end to it! His opinion was shared with good intent in his customary uncompromising way and provided yet further confirmation, if more was needed, of the desired expectations of the Nurse Manager in this hospital. I had not the least intention of accepting this state of affairs.

'They'll be watching you like a bunch of hawks. So, don't give them grounds for undermining you, and don't let them intimidate you. They're a bloody hard-nosed lot in this neck of the woods, you'll realise. But don't worry, if you're a survivor, as I'm sure you are, you'll find a way of handling it all, in time. Nothing flashy about it. It's common sense, really. You're in charge and no matter what they throw at you, you're the one carrying the can so they have to abide by your decisions. Bottom line is *be decisive*.' We were interrupted by the Duty Nurse Manager who had ambled through Harry's open door to share a query. John North, who always conveyed a slightly exasperated air, carried a staff duty sheet, in one hand, and his spectacles and a smoking fag, in the other. He was an inveterate chain-smoker who held extended conversations through the perpetual haze of exhaled smoke.

'Harry, Amber has cut-up again – a real good effort, this one – and the staff feel the wounds need a hospital visit for treatment. Now, I'm already sailing close to the wind on staffing and I don't think I can spare anyone from the wards for escort. I've trawled through the sheet and, frankly, I'm stuck. Now, I don't know whether you want me to call in people who are off-duty.'

'Why, what's so special that she can't be dealt with by Dr. Fish?' dubious that the injuries should warrant such a measure and showing immediate irritation.

'You'll like this one,' John said with a broad snigger. 'She's broken off her large toenail and cut all the way from her ankle up to the inside of her thigh,' he added, raising both eyebrows for humorous emphasis but giving way to a hearty chuckle that rattled his shoulders.

'Whatever next! Is she bleeding badly?'

'Enough to worry the staff, obviously.'

'Better call in a couple of staff, then.' Harry sat down and surveyed his desk of papers in a clear sign that John was dismissed, which indication I took as inviting my own departure, too. I followed John though the door and into the Duty Office.

'Usual charming self!' he said, with a sardonic smile. 'Right, I'd better get on with this, then. Everything all right with you, Steve?'

'Yes thank you, John.' I lowered my voice, checked over my shoulder, and turned back. 'Actually, I've just received a lecture on role boundaries,' rolling my eyes in Harry's direction. John retorted, equally quietly.

'Role boundaries! Oh, he'll have something to say on every imaginable subject. You'll soon learn the art of appreciative nodding while keeping your mouth shut, but staunchly disagreeing with him, whilst he's rattling on.' We smiled conspiratorially while I took up John's current task.

'She's a real challenge, that Amber, eh! Glad I don't have a female ward to cope with. I've seen the amount of paperwork they generate for Bill and it's astronomical!'

'I bet you are glad! She, alone, must account for a pile of accident reports every month. I understand she's cut every part of her body, do you know that?'

'Christ! I'll be seeing a lot more of her on my travels, if I see no one else. See you later, John. Must get back to the fray.' I departed the duty office and took to pondering how anyone could be content sifting the repetitive, routine problems and queries that would have to be fielded for hours, each and every shift, ensconced in this impersonal little hole. But, then, it often served as the very hub of all the immediate information that any of us needed to know. Perhaps it was this sense of centralised authority that he enjoyed? Or the enjoyment of scrupulous administration and being at the indispensable pinnacle of day to day decision making and the very proximate contact with the higher echelons? Or had he been merely bored, or stressed, even burnt out, from staff, patient, and ward contact over his years of service?

'Can't be much space left for her to get at!' was the trailing quip that pursued me along the corridor.

I strolled leisurely through the grounds on my way to the nurse managers' offices among which was my own, past the few wards that lay in this upper end of the hospital, reluctant to depart this aesthetically more pleasant environment. For these wards lay congealed into two equally expansive blocks one on either side of the Admin building. Even despite the barred metal windows and drab lines that indubitably proclaimed its utilitarian purpose as a state institution, and the fact that it lacked the crawling reaches of the Admin ivy, the whole assembly still managed to convey a small measure of historical appeal. To the back of the wards high metal fencing cordoned off the recreation areas which could be accessed by the residents when the staff so permitted. In one corner of this part of the estate a diminutive pond, sunk into an arboreal ring, and a clutch of contented, vocal mallard ducks within a trim of water foliage, posed as a secluded sanctuary. I passed on to the metal gate dividing this from the next quadrangle holding just a couple of single-storied female wards and the managers' portacabin, into a changing landscape that was completely bereft of trees and shrubbery. I entered the portacabin, briefly glanced at the internal mail, then left the suite to continue on into the furthest reaches of the site which were ever more barren and depleted. My key, taken from its pouch on its leather strap, remained in my hand while I negotiated the double set of high gates that would let me into the very furthest compound. Here was an unprepossessing landscape if ever there was one, confined and unsheltered, stagnating in the past, needing the sustenance of the vibrant world beyond. With the exception of the single-storey wards, the Education Centre, and the Industrial Unit, there were few visible artefacts other than a seemingly unused soccer pitch. In the fading distance, lay the tightly sealed line of a low-lying wall which was invitingly low to the distant eye but had had a trench gouged out along its entire, inner perimeter, effectively doubling the height of the barrier to the outside world. Cynically, this was called a "Ha Ha Wall" because, anybody believing that they could make an easy escape was, at the last, uncompromising moment, thwarted by an obstacle of unassailable dimensions and the derisive laughter of the hospital security system.

There was something more than a little seductive about the trappings of a custodial environment. The keys, alone, were more than mere accessories, more than constantly indispensable tools that gouged at doors, more then a symbol, even. They seemed a power in their own right which helped define the relationship, and differences, between their masters and their dependents. Each member of staff wore their individual bunch of keys on the long, leather straps that curled from the wide, black, leather belts around their uniform trousers. This differed from prison officers only in the small detail that, in their case, the keys hung on ostentatiously long, metal chains that clipped onto the back of their belts and, with every stride, swung with a menacing momentum. There was much else besides among the security paraphernalia. Those which adorned the person – keys, strap, key belts, key pouch, alarm whistle, portable two-way radios, staff uniforms, and the safety conscious detachable ties in the event of being attacked. The physical structure – car barriers, barred windows, iron gates and fencing, wooden fencing, brick walls, and "ha ha" walls. The security practices of escorting patients, radio contact with the communications centre, the warning siren, the scrupulous checks for patient numbers and whereabouts, incoming and outgoing mail content, patients' telephone calls and relatives' and friends' visits, personal and environmental searches, and patient access to personnel, instruments, utensils and space. Even the very idea of security. All evoked a sense of neatness, of control, of order and discipline, assurance and certainty. Was that an unconscious motivation for staff working in such environments that, compared with the vicissitudes of a society beyond its perimeter reaches, these were places which provoked a sense of psychological confidence, and stable reclusiveness?

000

Arriving outside my adolescent admission ward just as the afternoon hospital coach had arrived to pick up patients for the Education Centre and Industrial Unit, I had the opportunity to watch the business of what was termed "patient-movement". While the patients from the rest of the hospital stared from the windows of the waiting coach I unlocked the low gate to the nearest of my two wards, and unlocked and re-locked the double door entrance to the receiving corridor that constituted the security airlock. Along the corridor wall the waiting contingent – most of the ward patients – were being subjected to their regular "pat-down" search. They had not been out of the ward since the previous evening so any contraband found about their person would have derived from the ward environment. I wondered when the last successful find may have occurred and of the sheer tedium of such manoeuvres, day in, day out. The lads were spontaneously cheery as I watched them pass out through the airlock and scuttle onto the waiting coach, supervised by the staff who would radio in the movement-numbers. When they arrived at their respective work and education venues two or three minutes hence, they would receive another "pat-down" by an allocated staff member who would remain for the duration of the session in order to observe for safety. At the session's close, another search would accompany the patients' departure from the venues to ensure nothing was being removed from the area before yet another search hailed their return to their individual wards. This close scrutiny was an insurance that, at every stage of the patient-movement, the possibility of smuggling weapons and/or tools or other contraband in or out of the workshops, school, or any other area, were minimised. The procedure, which had sunk into the subconscious of the staff regime, was derived from the justifiable recommendations of the Carstairs Inquiry. Nevertheless, it would seem to be a template for everything else that happened. The previous evening, for example, I happened to be on the unit as the lads were preparing for bed. When so instructed they poured through the door separating the dayroom from the bedroom corridor, en masse, and stood outside the "boot room" whereupon each stripped his day

94

clothes down to the buff, handed them to a staff member who prodded them within the patient's allocated clothing space, in return for the night clothes which were passed out. None of this was accomplished within the privacy of bedrooms. Everything was public, everything routinised, everything group-orientated, even the baring of bodies.

And finally I unlocked the internal door which opened onto the unit dayroom. As always, I took note of the hasty grapevine as the staff registered my arrival and conveyed it to the nurse-in-charge who would be dutifully located in the office. As usual, this entry of mine felt like an intrusion and my presence unwelcome. This was not altogether unexpected, having experienced the sense of understandable intrusiveness in my previous hospital in which I had held a senior position. I had responded with similar emotions then but this was a qualitatively different level of response. There would be some grounds for believing that this was not only because I was a *new unit manager*, but an *outsider,* and *a member of the Royal College of Nursing*, and *not affiliated to the P.O.A.*! I had deliberately let slip this last information in order to register my intent or, at least, its early shoots having learned that there was not a single member of the entire hospital nursing contingent who was not affiliated to the Prison Officers' Association. Not until the arrival, that is, within weeks of my own appointment, of the new Chief Nursing Officer who also remained steadfastly aloof of the "officer" fold. As usual, as I looked toward the circulating staff, there seemed to be a palpable air of malign suspicion, and barely camouflaged hostility from some quarters, rather than plain inquisitiveness. It was the start of another afternoon shift.

'Afternoon, Mr. Burrows.' The greeting was offered by Charge Nurse Sterns who led the afternoon shift as I entered the ward office. Agitating on the window sill was the live ward two-way radio which sent out muted missives from around the hospital estate. Sterns' usually dour and somewhat abrasive persona did not appear to be in any way dented by the revelation about his alleged recent conduct. On the contrary, from his reception, he was rather enjoying his current celebrity and seemed to want to communicate to me 'go on, mate, catch me if you can!' This would fit in with the stance he'd taken toward me from the beginning which, I had fantasised, was that he viewed me as a young, witless Commissioned Officer compared with his own Sergeant Major's street-wise aptitude. 'Do you want tea?' This was the routine etiquette toward senior staff on all of the wards and very welcome when dealing with staff that you enjoyed meeting. I accepted, knowing that I'd be here a while. Charge Nurse Sterns leaned, unceremoniously, across me to the open door and yelled out, 'Masters!' Masters, one of the patients, who had been lingering in the proximity of the office, as if in anticipation of the request, jumped to the door. 'Cup of tea for Mr. Burrows!' Masters looked to me with a careless nonchalance. Presumably, there was some reason for this able youngster to have remained behind on the unit that day.

'Take sugar and milk, sir?'

'No sugar, and just a little milk, thanks.' I was reluctant to cooperate with the use of surnames which was the customary mode of addressing patients in "Special Hospitals" but, for now, I figured I would have to comply.

'A cup for you, Mr. Sterns?' This formality was the reciprocal custom allowed of patients who addressed the staff. All very distancing, all very demarcating, exactly the mode of the Prison Service.

'No, tah!' Masters disappeared to the ward kitchen and I watched a member of staff unlock the door for him for he was the hospital's equivalent of a trustee on a prison wing, given certain trusted responsibilities in return for limited privileges. Patients making drinks for staff was not entirely unheard of in the wider mental health services but to be routinely assigned to them, as a duty, most certainly was not. With all the perverse possibilities that came to mind in the preparation of the tea – poor hygiene practices, deliberately spitting into it, or contaminating it by some other means – I trusted that Masters had taken no great exception to me!

I was inclined to leave the broaching of the subject of the complaint to Sterns, if at all possible, not wanting to appear to be overly inquisitive or to be seen to give it too much of a priority. Play it cool, was the advice to myself. But before too much general ward business was covered, Sterns could not resist for long.

'You know, it doesn't seem right that patients, especially these patients, bearing in mind their backgrounds, have the right to take out complaints against the staff. What do *you* think?' If I had anticipated such a direct challenge as this, as perhaps I should have, I might have better prepared myself but the confrontation was characteristic of the man. The approach was quite in line with the essential agenda that mattered to the nursing staff, from what I had gathered. Was I on the side of the staff or the patients? I was so taken aback I jerked as if I'd been smartly pricked. Just how would I play this. What I wanted was to get on with setting out my principles of developing the staffs' clinical skills, promoting positive changes and abilities among the patients, and inculcating a therapeutic ward climate to make the best of things. I'd experienced all this authoritarianism in the old County asylum system during my earlier years. Been there, seen it, done it, too! But times had moved on as far as I was concerned! But, not truly knowing where to start, I fidgeted with unease, crossed and uncrossed both legs in a vain effort at delay. All to the faintly smirking delight of my inquisitor.

'Um... I can only say that if one of my relatives was in some institution I'd want them to be able to speak up if they were unhappy about something. And, I'd like to think someone or body would give them a fair hearing.' I had deliberately assumed a professional stance as it seemed pointless arguing the ethics if a colleague could really believe what he'd just proposed to me. It may not have been the smartest opening gambit but just as he opened his mouth to volley his chagrin in my direction I interpolated with, 'and, I would imagine you'd think likewise for one of your relatives.' The sails of his cheeks flapped with a momentary indeterminacy, before they filled out with a taught conviction as he tacked into the prevailing headwind of his personal philosophy.

'As it happens, if one of my own flesh and blood had committed what this lot have done I wouldn't be taking that attitude at all. I'd leave it to the people in the institution to decide what's best for a relative who had proven they weren't fit to live on the streets.' He keeled to one side as his confidence gathered momentum. 'So, you believe in protecting the likes of these? How do you make that out, exactly? What service do you think you're doing society?'

It was a fair point as far as it went. The adolescent unit I had inherited of two, thirty bedded wards with an occupancy of twenty five apiece had, in its time, held young males from the age of eleven or twelve, up to those in their mid-twenties. Many of these at the latter end of the range had been residents here for some years already and, at some point, consideration would have to be given to their internal transfer to wards for more chronic, older residents. Most antisocial and criminal acts were covered by the young fraternity, including serious assaults, arson, other property transgressions, and sexual offences. For many, their notoriety may have come not from one specific act but from a protracted profile of chronic delinquency, of multiple residential disposal, and chronic separation from family and friends. The two wards were differentiated along two main themes.

One served as an admission and assessment unit while the other's purpose was to offer so-called "continuing care", a bland and meaningless term for what you do with someone after an admission phase. On the face of it, it had to be said, based upon such an early forensic history, and without some very evident signs of improvement, you would not be overly confident of inviting many of the lads into your home for supper. Even when given trial leave, some had proven that they could persist with serious disorder as in the case of one current resident who was recently returned to our premises from a medium secure unit to which he had been transferred. He had inflicted a rape upon one of the female staff members.

'We all have a right to be outraged by the acts that some people commit, including our patients, but, that's a private confidence. We may even share it with fellow professionals. But, if that spills over to dictate our everyday management of patients it sure as hell will contaminate our professional way of doing our job, for which the country pays us, and our training should have prepared us. Now, I know the training for most of us was shit but that's what ongoing training is for, to keep us abreast of things.' This happened to suit my wider agenda, perfectly. 'We can never pretend to understand how young lads like ours could be capable of committing what they've done but, then, we haven't lived their lives. Who knows what we would have done if we'd grown up in their circumstances and, surely, it's those circumstances that separate us?' Masters appeared with the tea and Sterns nodded him in.

'You must be kidding. Even if they couldn't help what they did because of their circumstances, it doesn't mean they have the same rights as everybody else. Fair enough, I feel ruddy sorry for some of these blighters when I read about their backgrounds but I ain't going to go soft on them, that's for sure. They can be pretty damned canny, mark my words. It's just asking for trouble! If you're talking about professional responsibility then mine is to keep everyone safe by laying down firm rules and sticking to them so that these lads know exactly where they stand.'

'I have no problem with that, whatsoever. In the same way, though, we stick to the rules laid down for us otherwise anyone can do as they please and make up their own, don't you agree?' Sterns leaned toward me, his gesturing hands, and the frustration in his tone, a sufficient show of agitation to assure me that there had been a slight turn in the tide of the argument. Whether or not he believed me to be a complete prat he still needed to gauge where I was coming from, both for his own reassurance and in order to relay to the troops.

'Their families and schools have failed to bring them up properly and, if the likes of me fails, who else is going to show them how to behave? Put plain and simple, if I played up at home my dad would give me a bloody good clout round the ear, and serves me right. I respected him for that. Knew where I stood. Now, if *I* needed that to learn right from wrong, I don't see any harm in taking a firm hand with this lot. Just so long as it's meant in the right spirit.' I really didn't want to hear this and deflected the inference.

'I'll take it for granted you're talking metaphorically, not literally, of course,' I added, with some alacrity, not wishing to prompt an ill-considered answer which would lumber me with a crap dilemma. Sterns measured me with eyes that harboured a restrained disgust of my very presence in his office. Before any answer was forthcoming I elected not to pursue the point and Sterns let the subject go, also. Choosing a different tack to exculpate us both from this predicament, I said, appeasingly, 'I'm sure you have nothing to worry about regarding this complaint, Mr. Sterns. Good luck with it.' I rose and left the office, making a beeline for Masters who was to be found leaning on a cue by the billiard table, watching me, I noticed. I spoke up so that anyone in the vicinity could hear me.

'Thank you for the tea, Masters. What's your Christian name, by the way?' The extent of his surprise was evident in the delicious screw of his smile as he fully appreciated, as would others, the anarchy afoot.

'Trevor, sir.'

'OK, Trevor.' I then had to resist the temptation to dissuade him from this formal use of 'Mr' and 'Sir', but I was satisfied to have gone far enough and extended him a nod of acknowledgement. Then I was out of there.

000

Within a couple of days, the "Fates" descended upon the hospital to toy with the conflicting interests of the several parties before them and to spin a playful web of chaos. The current Chief Nursing Officer, newly appointed within a month or so of my own arrival, was called to make an executive decision from the start. With the backing of his Hospital Management Team he decided to prioritise the regulations governing the wider Health Service in favour of the localised agreement between the Department of Health and the P.O.A. and, by so doing, elected to *suspend* Charge Nurse Sterns from his post. This was an unprecedented move in the entire history of the hospital and created utter consternation among the dyed-in-the-wool staff and managers who were now playing on a field of distinctly different rules to which they were accustomed, and for which no single body, the Department of Health included, had prepared them. Those of us in managerial positions had tremendous sympathy for their position on just this principle. But for that minute sample of us who had hailed from the wider NHS a complaint into the conduct of a member of staff had the due consequence for that individual of a temporary suspension from their current duties, or an allocation to alternative duties, *and* an internal investigation. This expectation did not exist among the indigenous managers and the word was that some of them covertly supported the staff disquiet, not so surprising since all had come through the local ranks and still remained associated with the P.O.A., themselves. As things transpired, the hospital leadership of the P.O.A organised an emergency meeting for the nursing and occupations staff and a decisive outcome voted by a seventy-five percent majority to take industrial action. An increasing programme of industrial dislocation followed. The membership were instructed to desist from accepting any overtime availability and from any involvement in patient activities – recreational and rehabilitation trips, educational and occupational pursuits. However, an invidious escalation of reaction proposed that every one of the patients would remain locked into their individual rooms for a continuous period – in fact, this extended to ten days – and only let out for the barest minimum period. Among the nursing management, the Hospital Management Team, and other professional disciplines, all hoped that this unwarranted threat would come to naught because, in effect, the staff would be enforcing seclusion upon their charges for no good clinical reason. They effected to partly legitimise this dramatic action by maintaining the appropriate seclusion charts during the confinement which would ensure the legal requirement for a written record of each patient's progress, whilst so confined. The action, akin to that taken by the Prison Service, would be called a "lock-down".

The evening preceding the proposed acceleration in the dispute disturbed me intensely. Mixed with an anxious anticipation of the imminent debacle was my incomprehensibility that the staff were prepared to manipulate their patients' captive status as a tool in the dispute. The prospective outcome was not merely of a professional transgression, but of an allegation of "false imprisonment" which could be construed as an illegal, criminal, act. The position was indefensible, at any level, and had a number of other serious implications. Firstly, how much did it confirm the widely held view that industrial relations at the hospital were fundamentally adversarial and to what extent did basic human relations mirror this? Secondly, could there be any reasonable expectation of my gaining the confidence of the staff, personally, or in developing therapeutic programmes in the context of this show of callous disrespect for the patients' vulnerable mental states? And thirdly, I anguished about the longer term repercussions for individual staff, fellow managers, the hospital reputation, and, not least, my personal career. Would an association with the place come to form an immutable blemish on my own career prospects?

At 7.00 a.m. on the morning that the industrial action commenced, I was one of the nurse managers on duty and would have to admit to feeling variously dismayed and exhilarated to learn, as soon as I collected my keys from the gate lodge staff, that the proposed extension of the industrial action had been initiated by nursing staff and occupations officers. If I was being entirely honest, I was inclined toward prioritising the professional ramifications of the action. That is, that if the patients were to be found to be locked into their rooms, as if detained in cells without any clinical or safety reasons for doing so, then the senior nurse in charge of each ward should be held to account for issuing this instruction to the staff since this was a professional matter. I put these considerations to the other senior nursing staff who were present in the hospital at this early hour but I was prevailed upon not to follow this course. At this hastily convened managerial meeting it was determined that we should not pursue any form of disciplinary path against the vanguard of staff commencing this unprecedented event that morning. The grounds were that it would not be wise to confront the nursing staff at ward level since it was not only likely to further inflame the situation but would damage future relationships between them and the nurse managers. Further, this would likely lead to a deterioration in staff morale and, possibly, adversely affect the quality of nursing care to the patients. On reflection, this seemed valuable advice, which I adhered to, though it did not obviate my concern that in applying this light touch we might be perceived to be condoning the unprecedented stand by our colleagues. Our plan was to prioritise the monitoring of all patients, while avoiding agitating our colleagues, until we had sought professional and legal advice on a definitive way forward. For my part, I was allocated a number of wards whose patients it was now my duty to visit on an individual basis. I unlocked my way into the first of these, a female admission ward, and into an unusual and unnerving silence.

'Morning, Mr. Burrows,' was the insinuating greeting of the nurse approaching me, anxious, no doubt, to show me that this action was not of his choosing but an occupational, and communal, right.

'Morning, Mr. Cardew. How's it going?'

'Oh, what can I say, Mr. Burrows? The patients are taking it all pretty well and there've been no problems. It's all very regrettable. A terrible situation. I don't know what's to become of it? What happens if the patients cut up even more than usual, or something worse, and it's proven that our industrial action caused it?'

A peevish assertion of 'you mean *your* industrial action,' tripped out before I could help myself but he didn't wince or show too much concern and I surmised that he was just wanting to gauge a manager's perspective on their liability. 'Strikes me you've all got a good deal more to worry about even if not a single patient's mental health deteriorates during the action.'

'You really think so?'

'Damned right!'

'We're following the union's instructions, Mr. Burrows, that's all I can say,' he answered quite calmly, with more of a hint of conciliation than reproach. The ward Charge Nurse, a chap with whom I'd enjoyed very agreeable contact, came into view as we sauntered toward the office and I raised my voice as we came together.

'Morning, Steve.' The Charge Nurse, replete with his customary stressed countenance, unshaven, and blood-shot, acknowledged my appearance with his usual, amiable greeting and devoid of any hostility.

'Morning, Tony.' I said nothing more, wishing to infer my disappointment which he duly took note of I should imagine.

'Things are moving on apace, then, Steve?' As if I was delivering a missive to the entire nursing body I played the only card that seemed relevant, despite the advice I'd been given by my fellow managers.

'Let me speak plainly, Tony. You've got to be careful about this. However aggrieved the staff feel about higher management decisions in the hospital your industrial action is unlikely to uphold professional nursing standards. Not in anyone's books.' His next words were ambiguously apologetic and measured.

'It's regrettable but we've been forced into this by management intransigence.'

'But you don't get it do you? When it comes down to it, each of you will be held individually accountable for this! I don't think you'll be protected because it's a class action.' At least, this was the fundamental principle that had been inculcated by our professional nursing body. But then he surprised me by lowering his voice enough to be confiding yet not to the extent of being conspiratorial.

'I think the union have thought this through pretty thoroughly,' in an undisguised justification that would lend weight, so he hoped, to the gravitas with which the action was being undertaken. This could not have wholly dispelled his fears, or those of his colleagues, that their professional "tickets" could be on the line. He knew it, despite the sanctioning by the P.O.A. of the action, and all the staff knew it. The fact that all the registered nursing staff could be reported to their professional body, the United Kingdom Central Council, on the charge of unprofessional conduct had been a complete revelation to them, initially. Because, as already alluded to, despite having qualified as Registered Nurses, "Special Hospital" staff owed their occupational allegiance and guidance to the Prison Officers' Association which was not a self-regulating, professional body. And this was ever their "Achilles Heel". 'Will you come round with me, Tony, if I check on all the patients?'

'Sure thing, Steve. Lead the way there.' And we accompanied each other in a not so very disagreeable visit to every secluded patient on the ward before I took my leave. Truth to say, this initial staff reception was an agreeably appeasing overture in light of what could have been encountered and I dared hope that this was not to be something of a false dawn in relations with the strikers.

It was no easy business conducting yourself throughout an industrial action over a ten-day period. In principle, it sounded straightforward enough. While one side resorted to a premeditated work-to-rule routine that operated within the most basic working parameters with the intent to disrupt every facet of the organisation and force the other side into compromising negotiations and a conceding of ground, you attempted to act as a viable buffer and go-between. But there were essential differentiations to be made. This was no commercial, industrial or manufacturing enterprise where such reaction might be taken as the norm and where the target would be the industry's owners, products and profits. This was a public sector hospital where the target could only be its needy human beings and their proper care! And by "imprisoning" the patients, en masse – illegality aside – there had to be a justifiable speculation about whether proper care could be afforded them; how social, recreational, educational or occupational rights could be fulfilled; how there could be any compliance with the clinical team treatment programmes; and a serious possibility that there could be a direct deterioration in the mental state and general behaviour of the patients.

During the action, the management method was quickly established. For each and every one of us managers, each and every hour of the next ten days ushered us into the claustrophobic confinement of patients' individual rooms, checking on patients' welfare, and bearing the blithely admonishing presence of the nursing staff. Arrive at a ward. Proceed to each patient's room with the accompaniment of a staff member. Speak with the patient, ascertaining their mental state. Was the action – explicitly, the solitary confinement – having a detrimental effect on mental state? Encourage them to verbalise their concerns, while fully cognisant of the restraint they had to display in front of my staff escorts – their own staff who would, doubtless educate them of the error of their ways if they should criticise the staff action. But most unexpectedly, was the response of a handful of patients on Charge Nurse Sterns' ward who entered into a voluntary hunger strike in support of the man. This was completely beyond comprehension, at first sight, but there was the possibility that the hunger strikers might accrue for themselves some personal credibility and advantage which would sit favourably among those who lauded such singular power over their situation. After all, this action would have to end at some point and, perhaps, their would be a reckoning on everyone's account. Then there was also the equally viable prospect that they had resorted to this for purely altruistic reasons out of genuine respect for Charge Nurse Sterns and their sense of outrage at the accusation against him! As to the completion of the seclusion forms? It shortly became clear that they became a chore of form filling, an encumbrance symbolising the meaningless absurdity of managerial requirements as each member of staff, singularly appointed to the task, was found splayed among a melee of forms scribbling repetitive, fatuous entries, accounting for every fifteen minutes of their patients' progress in seclusion. At meal times, some of the wards would permit their patients to leave their seclusion in groups of four to six, and this would provide an abbreviated form of association. Yet, for us managers, with so many wards to cover, and the consecutive process of unlocking each room, there was little time for anything but the most cursory of contact with patients and, what little was accomplished, was hampered by the need to visit as many hospital patients as possible. In the main, it was not complicated by even a muted heckling, or show of open hostility, by the majority of the nursing staff.

On that inaugural day's visit to the first of my own adolescent wards, however, I was granted the pleasure of being accompanied by an unqualified nursing assistant who had pushed himself forward for the task at my arrival following hasty, and hushed, deliberations between the staff body at the farther end of the dormitory. This young, redheaded lad had proven himself to be a strongly opinionated, and audacious, combatant since my arrival as Unit Manager and he was not going to let up on showing me his mettle, now. For once, he was keeping shtoom but the object of the exercise was to inform me that he'd pore over every word, every glance, every nuance of bias I revealed in the patients' favour. He was so intensely present that it felt as if I had a lean fox, with a chisel faced curiosity, on hand to snap at any complicity to sustain his hungry animosity. I elected to keep my inquisitiveness to a minimum for, though I'd grown to like a good many of these lads, I didn't want to bring more undue pressure upon them than they already had to bear.

'Ok, then, Masters?' was my trite introduction on entering the trustee's room. Masters had adjusted himself from a supine position along his bed to casually turning, and leaning the side of his head on one arm, as if he was quite used to staff intruding into his personal space. I was mindful that this was the only intrusion he would have experienced because informal fraternising between the patients in one another's rooms was certainly not permitted.

'Oh fine, Mr. Burrows, no worries. Can't be helped.' The implication was that the "lock-up" must be a fairly relaxed affair, done with conciliation in mind, or to reduce the unnecessary complications for the staff, and that the patients were being given time, attention and company.

'Are you missing your ward duties?' I posed, trivially, searching for a different line than those I'd offered elsewhere.

'What do you think, Mr. Burrows?' he replied with a face that carried his consistently enigmatic expression that managed to impart scepticism, pleasure, and resignation, all at once, while probably masking any deep-seated resentment.

'I really don't know what to think. That's why I asked?' I replied, deservedly admonished. He maintained his curious expression, giving nothing away, as if expecting me to divine the truth of the matter. 'No, really, I'm trying to get a feel for how this situation is affecting different people. Perhaps you're grateful for the break from all those chores?'

'In some ways, yes, in some ways, no,' he said, confusingly, yet realistically.

'Well then, do you have anything you want to ask me?'

'Yeah! How long will management keep this up, do you think?' he asked, perfunctorily. Was this the patients' stance? Did they really blame the managers or had they been so successfully schooled by the nursing staff that the imprisoned patients had sided with the industrial action? This was all unexpected. And I suddenly realised I had no idea what I was to say, what to ask, or how to explain our position if the majority had taken this tack on the situation. I had made the assumption that my patients would set the agenda, complain about their imprisonment, provide me with some grounds for advising the managerial contingent on shortfalls in patient care. But none of this had been forthcoming. I felt impotent to accomplish anything remotely useful, in the immediate circumstances. Perhaps I could only await their cumulative frustration from the vantage of a detached and distant siege of the industrial action? On the other hand, was this a classic rendition of the "Stockholm Syndrome" where hostages eventually side, sympathise, and identify with their captors despite having nothing in common before their enforced encounter?

'What do you mean, exactly?'

'When is management going to let Mr. Sterns back?'

'He's been temporarily suspended while a certain matter is investigated.'

'There's nothing to investigate.'

'Well, it's not in my hands. There's nothing I can do about that for now.'

'Can't you put in a word for him?'

'That wouldn't make any difference, I'm afraid.'

'But you would if you could,' was the artless interruption from the Nursing Assistant's foxy presence as if he was regurgitating some bile.

'As I said, it would make no difference at this juncture.'

When I arrived at Caldicot's room the six foot three inch youth eyed me slyly – as was his wont – seeming to weigh the vigilant watchfulness of my attendant against an appreciation of my own delicate situation. This must have been a delectable conflict of interests to a confident, extroverted, young man, who generally informed me of his opinion in order to wind me up in a fairly convivial way. I was comfortable that he would commit himself to voicing not only his own but the general opinion on the situation.

'Is there anything you need that you're not getting, Caldicot?' was my pointed introduction.

'I've not had a woman for a while, Mr. Burrows, since you're asking, like'. And the slyest of self indulgent smirks sloshed around his eyes.

'That'll be enough of that, Caldicot,' interjected the redoubtable Nursing Assistant anxious to obstruct any conviviality, or to avoid any obfuscation of the proper issues as he saw it. It was a pity not least because of the audacious humour on show. We had to take it for granted that sex remained a complicated, but salient, preoccupation in captivity and we, the staff, deliberately underplayed it for the sake of convenience and safety. I peered at the walls of his room which were liberally splodged with magazine pictures of naked-breasted women and wondered how much this could satisfy the imagination, and frustrations, of a presumably sexually active youngster of about nineteen years of age.

'Well, you could say that because I'm straight I don't get the same sexual opportunities that some others do in here, Mr. Doyle!' The inference was clear, and perturbing, in all sorts of ways but it drew only a deep glare from the proprietorial Mr. Doyle who would, it could be supposed, have taken great exception to the suggestion. But I was determined to stick with this brazen lad.

'Is that so, now? Quite a spread you have, young Caldicot!' I continued, encouraging our conversation.

'Oh, you like, Mr. Burrows?' he said, insinuatingly. I smiled, appreciating his self-confidence in the face of the subdued harassment.

'Does everybody have these... what shall we say... adornments?'

'Not everyone, but most I'd say. Some have pictures of men!' he added. I looked directly into the provocative glint in his eye.

'Yes, thank you for that,' I replied, gently toning down the direction of the conversation. 'How are you managing, generally?'

'I'm managing fine. I think we all are. The staff are looking after us.' His tone then took on a demanding flourish. 'When is management going to settle all this? Mr. Sterns is a good Charge Nurse, you know.' I studied him, asking myself why on earth a confident lad like him should support the man if he did not believe this. He was bright and adaptable and never seemed to get himself into scrapes on the ward or, at least, was seldom discovered to be culpable. Surely, he didn't need to chalk up any future favours? I continued to stare at him, protracting the moment, asking the question, silently.

'That's pretty candid, Caldicot.'

'Pretty what?' he asked, amused.

'You're getting to the point, being straightforward without beating about the bush. So you think that management is to blame?'

'Sorry to say that, Mr. Burrows, you just having arrived and all that, but it does seem a lot of fuss over nothing.' I glanced at Nursing Assistant Doyle who was sniffing the air with a long-nosed relish.

'Depends what you mean by "nothing",' I concluded, as significantly as I dared, knowing that this would be fed back to the fraternity, then, turned to extricate myself from the scene with a parting, 'Thanks for your thoughts, I'll bear them in mind. Sorry, but I've got to try and get around to everyone.'

'Cheers, Mr. Burrows. Thanks for visiting.'

'My pleasure.'

000

Abundantly clear was this. The morale between the staff and patients had gathered momentum and it suggested that the staff had justified their actions to the patients in some detail and this had fostered good relations. Indeed, proving that the industrial action had directly caused a deterioration in the mental state and general behaviour of the patients would be problematic, if not impossible.

The newly appointed Chief Nursing Officer held regular managers' meetings. At one such I expressed my reservations that at no time had we directly challenged the authorisation for the massed patient seclusion and, furthermore, that nothing had been put in writing as to the actions which we had pursued. In his usual phlegmatic style he assured us that he had visited every ward and clearly stated management's position on the matter.

I will never forget the day, mid-way through the action, that the imperious grandees from the Department of Health arrived for a pre-arranged meeting with the nursing staff. The recreation hall accommodated the massed gathering of available nurses who faced the diminutive grandees, flanked by the unprepossessing guard of honour of nurse managers and the Chief Nursing Officer. The former had commenced their imprecations to the staff about the seriousness of their behaviour, iterating the accountability of every person for their individual actions, and the repercussions for their personal reputations and how it could jeopardise their careers. But after this opening salvo was delivered in an airy, upper-crust Queen's English to an indigenous community that hosted regional Scouser and Lancashire vernaculars, the P.O.A. leadership turned about and led the entire assembly from the hall in an orchestrated evacuation, leaving the Departmental dignitaries aghast and bereft of all dignity and potency. To have witnessed the pompous rendition tailing off to a gaping muteness was, it had to be admitted, something delicious to behold, but in all other respects, it caused consternation amongst us. And the repercussions would rail on for years as a minority of the patients, incensed by their confinement and with the encouragement of a local solicitor with previous connections to patient representation in the hospital, took out their own legal action against the P.O.A. What would come of this all, now? What would become of all this when, throughout the entire United Kingdom, there had been no known precedent for such a wilfully premeditated and unprecedented transgression against psychiatric patients – any patients, for that matter?

As events transpired, it was over in ten days. The police fulfilled their investigative duties and concluded that Charge Nurse Sterns had no case to answer. "MIND", the National Association for Mental Health, strongly rebuked all sides for the dispute arguing that a professional complaints procedure should be implemented at the hospital to replace the outdated, established one which, in the event that police did not prosecute a member of staff, left the hospital management with no possible course of action. Charge Nurse Sterns was reinstated.

How was the blame for this to be apportioned? Charge Nurse Sterns would have his share if he had assaulted the alleged victim, Chivers. The P.O.A. would have their corporate share for guiding the nurses into what, prospectively, was unprofessional conduct, even illegal conduct. To what degree did the hospital culture predispose the staff to conceive the social status of patients as fit to be used as industrial leverage? What influence had the individual personalities, their conciliation competencies, and career prospects, of the local P.O.A. leadership had on the way things had panned out? Every single member of staff in the action would bear their personal responsibility for committing themselves to the joint action. If Chivers' allegation was a false one then his responsibility was of a different order. He may have been mentally unwell, at the time, harbouring some paranoid ideas about his Charge Nurse and believing that he did, indeed, wish him harm in some way. An act, therefore, for which he could not be held responsible. Or, if mentally well, he may have chanced his arm in a pernicious act against someone to whom he had taken exception, or acted in desperation against someone who had previously done him an injustice. But it had to be said that Chivers, or any other patient, had a great deal to lose for daring to speak up against the staff, in any circumstances whether they were being truthful or otherwise. How much was the new Chief Nursing Officer blameworthy for instituting a disciplinary process which the hospital had not previously been acquainted with but which he knew to be valid? And, finally, to what extent was the Department of Health liable for decades of professional and organisational drift in the "Special Hospitals" which had permitted them to straggle behind the rest of the mental health system? In all respects, it was as if the "fates" had come to play.

All of the foregoing accountabilities had been played out against a background of accelerating concerns that the "Special Hospitals" were out of step with contemporary mental health care and organisational control. Several reports had pointed to their managerial failures, the continuing detrimental influence of the P.O.A. on matters relating to health management and institutional culture, and the need to educate the staff in the co-prioritisation of mental health and security principles. There was an additional element for this particular hospital emanating from its historical focus of generally admitting the mentally handicapped, as they were then called, hence, the somewhat low perimeter security. More recently, however, there had been an increasing admission rate of mentally ill and psychopathic patients for which the staff training and qualification had not adequately prepared them. Conflated with all this was the escalating tensions deriving from the perceived requirement to bring the "Special Hospitals" within the auspices of "general management" which had been in vogue for the rest of the National Health Service for a handful of years, already, from which they had remained immune and separate. It was no coincidence, consequently, that both my own appointment as a manager, and that of my newly appointed superior, the Chief Nursing Officer, had been conducted with officials from the Department of Health seated on the interview panels. Otherwise, I, for one, would probably not have succeeded in being appointed in favour of locally sponsored applicants. Before an interview panel of four, I remembered the opening salvo well.

'Tell me, Mr. Burrow – by the way, is it Burrow, or Burrows?'

'Burrow.'

'Tell me, Mr. Burrow,' suitably pausing for emphasis, 'just tell me what experience you have that equips you to manage the nursing staff in a "Special Hospital"?' The present incumbent of the post of Chief Nursing Officer speared this candid enquiry as much by way of sympathy than accusation, I felt.

'I can only believe that I can transfer any management ability I've acquired elsewhere in the Health Service to this hospital. I've worked with mentally disordered offenders in secure conditions and I'm aware of a good deal of the therapeutic innovations that are happening in the field. And what I've learned is to be a manager who can demonstrate to staff an enthusiasm about changes which improve the clinical activity on the wards that are expected to help patients.' His hint of dismay more than conveyed the impression of not believing what he was hearing as if I was way off course and, following my response, he proceeded to make what was more of a rhetorical statement in support of his original question.

'Let me put it this way,' and he thrust out a sceptical jaw, 'after all it makes no odds to me – I mean, I'm out of here pretty soon! I'm assuming that you've never dealt with the P.O.A. So do you have any idea what you're letting yourself in for? Let me go further. You are not a member of the P.O.A. You might wish to know that every single member of the nursing staff *are*!' he concluded, in parenthesis, 'You might bear that in mind.' These were unprecedented comments in the context of an interview, in my experience. It was as if I was to be a lamb to the slaughter and he was attempting to dissuade me from my well meaning blunder! He anticipated reaction, they all did, and I understood the intimation only too well. Naturally, he had a point. Yet, the two members of the Department of Health on the interview panel – luckily for me – favoured major change, and investing in staff who would merely perpetuate the established, inward looking system was not what they had come for. Somehow, I managed to persuade them that I was something approaching the man for the job – at least, from the available applicants. It would have implications for my whole career, way beyond my imaginings!

When the newly appointed Chief Nursing Officer, arriving shortly after my own appointment, replaced the previous incumbent who had interviewed me, he was to find himself in a similar position to myself with no previous experience of either the "Special Hospitals" or the P.O.A. Apparently, that did not deter the interview board either. But the Medical Director, who had also been recently appointed, a young vibrant individual, had had previous experience of both contingents. Together, they constituted two thirds of the Hospital Management Team, the remaining position taken by the head of Administration. Change was afoot and it was being imported, rather than nurtured indigenously.

The Chief Nursing Officer's interest in applying for this position intrigued me. He did not, in the first instance, make an immediate impression of leadership, nor had he any striking physical appearance, or any particular gravitas or charisma, yet he exuded an avuncular gregariousness, mixed with an understated imperiousness, which had its own drawing power. In his build, he was somewhat overweight concealed, to some extent, by the copious line of his dark, always dark, suits. This contrasted with the prematurely thinning grey hair and full beard and moustache which belied his years along with the youthful optimism of his brown eyes. His speech was regional – Norfolk, I believe – and ponderous, and laced with an amiable sarcasm. He obviously enjoyed human contact and positively relished the immense task of his office that lay ahead of him, with a smidgeon of grandiosity as I perceived it, along with a subdued, rather carefree, forthrightness. He was often to be found wandering the estate, introducing himself to the patients and staff, clad in an ancient Barber jacket that had seen better days. He had a far more conciliatory approach than I possessed, was magnanimous, and exuded warmth. He had done the rounds in his career, of course, part of which was a spell in a famous therapeutic community in Scotland. He had all the credentials for encouraging peoples' potential. It was impossible to anticipate whether he was capable of championing a floundering, rather backward, community of nursing staff through the turbulent waters of change but, to my mind, they could not have had a more affable leadership to attempt such transition. He was still single, had never been married, had no children, lived alone in a grand house a few miles from the hospital, and not a little time was used to speculate about his social interests, shall we say – which would have amused him no end. We discovered we were on mutually common ground when discussing the state of play in the hospital and, when I shared with him the difficulties I was to experience, would often commit himself unequivocally. I warmed to him heartily.

'Be assured, Steve, my dear chap, if I am able, I will support you in whatever changes you try to bring about,' I would hear him say with an avuncular display of loyalty. 'I know we have some bloody unbelievable retrogrades among the staff who want to block progress – God knows, I don't know how I refrain from bursting into laughter, sometimes, when they try to justify themselves to me – but we must show some understanding for these fellows. They're a long way off the pace and it's not entirely their fault. Besides that, I think the number of those with more forward looking attitudes gives me some room for optimism.' It was typical of the man to assume the best if he could. He and I had a couple of things in common quite distinct from our frequent discussions about the state of play in the hospital. We shared a general observation about the delight of now living in a flat, agricultural landmass which became home to visiting pink-footed geese and other huge flocks in winter, and swirling gatherings of lapwing during the summer months. More notably, that we two were the only members of nursing staff who were not to join the P.O.A. in the history of the hospital, and this would mark us out! Unfortunately, when, a couple of years later, the proverbial shit was mucked through the Inquiry fan, his generous, personable approach to the management of his nursing staff fouled his reputation and soiled his career inestimably.

000

One of the many surprises which confronted anyone who encountered "Special Hospital" patients was the relative absence of *acute* mental disorder when compared with other mental health units. In my experience, the most acute setting where consistent contact would be made with raw, untreated, psychological disturbance was the casualty department of a General Hospital. This was where the textbook descriptions came to life in the presentations of patients: the vividly psychotic with mumbling delusions of police conspiracies against their person; the hallucinating alcoholics who traced pink insects crawling over the clinic floors, ceiling and walls; the personality disordered who had swallowed a razor blade and other objects, or threatened the staff while still demanding attention; the drug users distracted and agitated, reeking from ulcerated injection sites; the very many depressed who had their stomachs pumped of poisons and the few who had thrown themselves into the Thames; and the successfully suicidal who had set light to the petrol they'd poured over their heads, or drowned in the Thames. This was not to say that

"Special Hospital" patients were not mentally unwell but that the vast majority had had their psychoses, and other manifestations of disorder, controlled over many years – the average stay being eight and a half years – plus the fact that a large proportion were deemed to have developed a "psychopathic disorder" which, though manifesting dysfunctional psychiatric symptoms, were rarely of the more debilitating nature of psychosis. Regarding the "psychopathic" group of disorders, it was partly this absence of acute symptoms about which so much controversy existed as to whether they were justifiably diagnosed with mental disorder and hospitalised, and acquitted of criminal intent, instead of being held responsible for there disturbance, criminalised, and imprisoned. In consequence, such a diagnosis could engender extreme reactions amongst health care staff in that they believed they were dealing with the notoriously "untreatable" because their antisocial and criminal perversions were not considered to be health related. Like most health care staff with whom I was acquainted I, too, had had my time of equivocation about any therapeutic optimism toward the most seriously disturbed of this group, bearing their histories in mind. The good news, however, was that those with a psychopathic disorder had a general potential for therapeutic work because they frequently had the capacity to have their behaviour challenged and, though not characteristically renowned for introspection, many were believed to possess the capacity for such. These, together with the increasing numbers of mentally ill patients, provided ample material for therapeutic work of some potential depth. I was extremely fortunate that the multi-disciplinary team, to which I was attached in the adolescent unit, thought likewise. The clinical team of psychologist, social worker, consultant psychiatrist, and a member of the occupations workshops – the school education department could rarely spare a member of staff – were all in place when I was appointed, and attendance at the weekly clinical team meetings was effected with our patients' mental health at the forefront.

Another significant surprise for anyone not intimately acquainted with the "Special Hospital" mentality was not only the relative lack of commentary on the residents' mental disorder but the pre-eminence afforded to their criminal offences. If an inquiry was made about a particular patient about whom you had little knowledge the retort was, almost invariably, a rendition of the criminal history, especially the index offence for which they had been hospitalised. Little wonder that the working ideation was of disciplinary and security routines, rather than clinical intervention.

All this was responsible for another surprising shortfall in the service provision – the total absence of "parole" opportunities to the patients. Briefly, this was a policy used in secure mental health services which afforded individual patients who were progressing well to be granted specified periods of time off their units as a first important step in their rehabilitation to outside hospitals. Emanating from the historical use of parole as a show of trust toward captured war prisoners, the patient was being entrusted with the responsibility to use this free time appropriately and to return to his/her unit at the appointed time without undue occurrence. Nowhere in this hospital was this facility afforded to the patients which curtailed their rehabilitative potential.

The format of the weekly, clinical team meeting on the adolescent unit was that the five of us would cramp ourselves into the meanest of meeting rooms, along with a senior member of the nursing fraternity, for a couple of hours or so. This ward representative would generally include one of the Charge Nurses, provided they were on duty, or the next senior member of staff in their absence. The pecking order was extremely important to the staff and each day's ward allocation from the duty nursing office was a calculated listing of the staff in descending order of seniority. Within a very short exposure to these meetings, it became apparent that essential splits persisted in the team, with the rest of the team branching away from the prescripts of the nursing staff, and a fairly neutral occupations officer. I was sensitive to an adversarial model which lined up a prosecuting nursing team against a patient's defending counsel comprising the remainder of the professionals. How much I had accelerated this division I could not judge but I was a willing party to it and it took me no time at all to determine my side of choice. The format of the team meeting was pursued in the following manner: The nursing representative would present an account of each patient's progress during the preceding week, giving particular emphasis to any misdemeanours, and then produce some predetermined recommendations arising out of the nursing team's admonishing deliberations. Even when there was evidence of a patient having achieved something positive it was virtually voided by evidence of any negative infringement. Behaviour which did not conform with nursing expectations would have remunerative repercussions – it would hit the patients where it hurt most – in the pocket! Not that hard cash was the prize. The "Special

Hospitals" had long ago instituted a no-cash policy within their jurisdiction because of past experiences when cash had facilitated the escape of patients. The "rewards system", such as existed, required, it would seem, a scrupulously clean sheet in order to gain any "stage" advance. Any blemish, on the other hand, could demand a "stage" drop. As was the case with any staff presentation, the nature of the patient material presented by the nurses said as much about their prevailing attitudes – prosecuting attitudes, in many instances – as it gave an objective account of the patients' overall conduct, psychological symptoms, and interpersonal progress. This had significant consequences.

The hospital's "rewards system" was designed to motivate the patients by offering financial inducement as a way of improving behaviour – a modified form of behaviour modification. This would have been even more of an attraction among these young people who would not have had much of an opportunity to experience an economic wage before coming into hospital. This para-financial system enabled them to receive fortnightly credit, not money, which they used to purchase personal items. The exact amount ranged over what are called "stages". Each lad began at the lowest stage and rose through the superior levels according to his improved conduct. Although this sounded a feasible arrangement it had a particularly pernicious edge in the way in which behaviour was interpreted. Anything positive that the lads achieved was immediately cancelled out by the slightest infraction. Plainly, the staff seemed to have specially honed antennae for patients' shortcomings and none was tolerated. It was quite obvious that staff would brook no opposition, no challenges to their complete control and this was transmitted through a reduction of the patients' reward stage. It was, in short, a powerful tool for demanding conforming and unresisting behaviour. Among young men this was not an appropriate model to help their development especially when having to live in such unusually constrained circumstances. I could only view the system as a thoroughly inappropriate and misguided way of ensuring institutional stability and dependency, and dampening any real, dynamic development among them as a group striving towards independence. The ultimate concern would be their adaptation to the outside world when they were finally released. They would not have acquired the self-motivation which they would need to adapt outside of the establishment. So, patients had two essential choices. Unless they managed to avoid any adversity, whatsoever, they were essentially pushing the Sisyphus Stone. This could de-motivate them so that they not only gave up trying to improve their staged rewards but it could contribute to a state of decompensation whereby their psychiatric condition and social motivation actually worsened. Perversely, if they should manage to hold onto a sense of themselves by kicking against the traces this might actually prove to be a better outcome for their future prospects because they remained somewhat emotionally independent, if economically impoverished.

'Baird has been his usual manipulative self. Monday, he was, I suppose you could say, just plain cheeky, continually demanding to see you, Dr. Cook. By all accounts, he wants to appeal against his return to the hospital after the rape he committed. Says he shouldn't be the only one to blame and why should he carry the can, alone. Says he's been victimised would you believe!' Mr. Spiller, the Staff Nurse in question, had intoned this through his characteristic, high pitched, local accent, heavy with sarcasm, and accompanied with suitably rolling eyes and a quizzical smirk. I had discovered him to be a major opinion leader among the staff who saw it as his avowed duty to convey the detrimental behaviour of his charges with uncompromising tenacity and he expected nothing short of a rubber stamp for his efforts. And a rubber stamp was what he had generally achieved, I had realised very early on. 'Well, he carried on insisting that he see you, Dr. Cook, so the staff counselled him about taking responsibility for his actions. Honestly, some people don't know when they're well off. He could be languishing in jail! Anyway, the school report said that his performance has deteriorated this week and he's moaning to them, too. So, seeing as he's not been very compliant we suggest that his stage be dropped. A brief silence frosted among the rest of us before the Consultant Psychiatrist commenced the uphill attempt to view all this in more therapeutic terms.

'Aren't we being a little too hasty? I'm perfectly happy to see Baird and discuss the matter with him, actually. We can organise that directly the meeting is finished, if you like. He's clearly adopted a rather distorted stance which deserves to be reviewed with him if he's to gain any insight into the rape and the reasons for his recall to the hospital,' he proposed, in his characteristically apologetic, shy fashion, not wishing to stir Mr. Spiller, but anticipating that he'd have had the backing of the rest of his nursing colleagues. He was, perhaps, the least assertive Consultant I'd ever met but this was more than compensated for by his undisputed conciliation and championing of the patients' cause. The horrified muteness that accompanied Mr. Spiller's stare suggested his thoughts were of the order of 'You must be off your bloody rocker, mate!'

'Sounds to me as if he's providing us with an excellent opportunity to examine his account of what happened at that unit. Whether he'd felt out of his depth, what sparked off his rape of the staff member, his modus operandi in relation to the rape, whether he believed he could get away with it, his perception of the possible consequences – so much that we could glean about his ideations,' interjected Heinrich, the Clinical Psychologist, clearly wishing to give support to this reappraisal. More horrified muteness!

'Do you really think it's worth digging up the blindingly obvious, with respect? We know he's a young psychopath who's prepared to risk doing antisocial things. He's impulsive, don't consider the consequences, and don't learn from his mistakes. He's a classic example, don't you think? The ward "sex awareness" programme made a big difference, then, didn't it!' Reluctant grins of cold acknowledgement rippled around the assembly.

'Well, the ward "sex awareness" programme, excellent initiative though it is, only does what it says. It's a basic education. The point is, that we have all the confirmation we need that Baird has learned very little from his stay with us. On the contrary, he's graduating in the wrong direction! And probably because we've failed him.'

'Failed him! I don't know about that! He's failed himself, if anybody has,' was Mr. Spiller's exasperated retort.

'I would say we all failed, personally,' replied Heinrich, with narrowing eyes that more than hinted of his contempt. I think the issue is how we follow up on this: to give Baird a real chance to explain the circumstances of the rape; to re-evaluate his attitudes and behaviour toward the whole placement; for us to learn the lessons of what we failed to put in place for him; and what the receiving adolescent unit failed to put in place that enabled him to commit that act, also,' harried Heinrich, casting an assured look around the rest of our group.

'Would you be happy to do the following up, Heinrich?' suggested Dr. Cook. 'Perhaps, I could suggest that to him during my interview?'

'I'm not sure I have the available time just at the moment. It's a busy period for me. I've already got a couple of "penile plethysmographs" to get done, and there could be a place for this in his treatment, without a doubt, but, along with so many of the patients he needs some really skilled interventions to get him on course. I'm busy enough putting together my "arson programme", I'm afraid.' A "penile plethysmograph" was a proven technique for measuring a person's sexual arousal when a coil, attached around the male penis, was transferred to a monitor and calibrated. The aim was not to assess sexual arousal, per se, that is to say, normal sexual arousal, but to give an indication of an individual's inappropriate sexual stimulation and how he misinterpreted others' non-sexual behaviour as sexual cues.

'I wouldn't mind taking up the sexual angle, actually,' interjected Julian, the Social Worker, who had a real commitment to turning round these lads' lives. 'Ideally, there should be a sex offending group programme but, in the absence of that, I'll tackle the issues with Baird.' From the stunned, momentary inhibition of Mr. Spiller, this was far more than he bargained for. Julian's softly spoken voice deceptively masked an intense and intelligent disposition and one who weighed his words carefully. 'As it happens, it fits in very nicely with a related concern I have of the patients' access to pornographic material.' This had been a major contention of his which he had wanted to air for a while.

'How do you mean?' queried Mr. Spiller, snapping at the morsel of criticism. 'I wouldn't say they had any access to pornographic material!'

'I beg to differ,' Julian pronounced with a deceptive calm. 'Some patients have told me they're allowed to view videos with explicit sexual content and that the staff sit alongside to watch.'

'I admit we do allow the occasional racy video but I don't think we'd allow anything too explicit. After all, it's not in our interests to stir up their sexual frustrations. There's enough sexual activity as it is. We believe in being realistic, though. These are young lads with sex drives and I think we set limits as to what is appropriate material.'

'Thin end of the wedge!' was Julian's slow and deliberate reply. 'Some would say that no explicit sexual material was appropriate,' he added, insinuatingly. 'For example, that even sex magazines are totally inappropriate.' I was going to find this challenging, too!

'You saying there shouldn't be any sexual material in their possession, or on the ward, whatsoever?' uttered Mr. Spiller, ratchetting with exasperation.

'I'm saying more consideration should be given to the issue than is currently done because distorted sexual thinking is a huge issue among a good many of these youngsters and it's not appropriate to pretend that chauvinistic, sexual attitudes, however well-intended, does anything other than feed their distortions. Plus, we have sex offenders, here. What message are we sending out to them?'

'Which is what we attempt through the "sex awareness" programme, partly,' asserted Mr. Spiller, barely able to contain himself. 'You'll be saying sex is wrong, altogether!' I pondered how much seething contempt was festering beneath Julian's outward, unabashed calm as he left the comment, unanswered, spinning like a limp leaf between the lot of us. For we all realised the hypocrisy of this in that there would be serious repercussions for any of the lads caught indulging in sexual acts with one another, mutually or otherwise.

'The sex awareness work is vital, nobody's disputing that, but more in-depth work wouldn't go amiss and, maybe, Julian has a point,' added Dr. Cook, in a concerted effort to display some vestige of assertiveness and to conclude the interchange in order to move the meeting along. 'It seems to me this deserves further consideration than we can do it justice, right now. Anyway, in the first instance, I'd be obliged if you tell Baird that I'll arrange to see him and that will, no doubt, lift his spirits.' Dr. Cook adjusted himself over Baird's file, prepared his fountain pen, and moved to add a written commentary on the proceedings.

'And what about the "rewards", meantime? Are we agreed to drop his to the lower stage?' continued the redoubtable Mr. Spiller. It was time for me to take my own stand.

'Has he done anything positive during the last week, something to be weighed against his preoccupied behaviour?' I posed. Mr. spiller was not prepared for this having only come prepared with Baird's shortfalls. He simply returned my stare and raised his shoulders. 'Has he taken part in all the other activities that he's supposed to?'

'I don't think he's opted out of anything, exactly, but that's not the point.'

'I think it is. He's not quite upset the applecart, has he?' I was on dangerous ground for this would not sit credibly with the nursing staff but it was a signal of unequivocal intent that I meant to send out.

'He failed to respond to staff counselling!'

'Perhaps, if he had been granted the interview with Dr. Cook it would have settled him down for the rest of the week?'

'You're saying *we're* in the wrong, now?' This epitomised Mr. Spiller, tenacious to the bitter end! My stance was complimented by Heinrich.

'The whole point of the rewards system is to encourage appropriate behaviour and that's the clear message that every patient should be consistently receiving,' he added, helpfully.

'And will you ask Baird's "Primary Nurse" to make sure that a nursing care plan has been drawn up around this issue?' I added, with some vehemence. 'This has become a new priority in Baird's care. If he has any difficulties in putting it together, tell him I'd be glad to help. OK?'

'OK! I really didn't know there was a nursing care plan for sex offending? That will be interesting.' Mr. Spiller could never be described as being crestfallen but he was certainly baffled and would make a meal out of this, later, for sure. And now was not the time for me to admit to having no clear idea what a nursing care plan for sex offending should look like, either!

With the clinical meeting terminated and the Education Officer and nursing member departing, the four of us habitually tarried for informal chatter prior to lunch. Dr. Cook would be gasping to fag it, but he welcomed the conviviality and the commitment of his team.

'Do you know, I think we may be making some headway with all these issues on the table, I really do!' he enthused, smiling through blackened teeth which suggested his lifelong antipathy toward dentists, or a reluctance at self-management. 'And I must say, Steve, it's very encouraging to have a clinically interested Nurse Manager who's not focused on the habitual housekeeping issues. A very welcome change, I must say. Welcome aboard!'

'Agreed,' Heinrich joined in, much to my gratification.

'That's good of you. It's not much appreciated with the ward staff, though. They think ward activity is their domain and it's not my job to interfere. But that's not how I see it. I'm only too thankful for this venue, and the mutual support, I can tell you! The rest of my week can be a pretty isolated existence.'

'I'd also go along with what the others have said, Steve,' the lugubrious Julian joined in, nodding his appreciation. 'It's gratifying to feel able to speak frankly in front of you about nursing matters.'

'Thank you. Perhaps, this is a good time to ask you all about what you feel about the competence of the nursing staff? Frankly, are you satisfied with their input? It would help me to know.'

'I admire your candour, Steve, as if it's quite important to you,' remarked Julian, with more than a hint of conspiracy.

'Well it is, of course. I'm supposed to represent the nursing staff and I feel I've a long haul ahead of me. If I'm compromised in that, then, bang goes my personal reputation and I'm just not prepared to sacrifice that!'

'That's fighting talk!' shrieked Dr. Cook with a cackle of glee. 'Well, I'm no judge but if I have any view it has to be that the nurses' professionalism can't possibly be helped by their P.O.A. association, surely! Be that as it may, the pragmatic thing is that one really has no choice but to get along with the staff,' he added noncommittally.

'That doesn't tell me whether you're satisfied with their service, or not,' I queried, looking directly at the Consultant. Before he dredged up enough energy for a further non-commitment, Julian had intervened.

'Which,' drawing in his breath in something of a depressive resignation, 'brings me to a point I'd like to make. I honestly don't know what antagonises me more about nurses working with adolescent patients: the illusion that they offer some sort of moral benchmark, or the apparent insistence on their patients' irretrievable culpability which justifies any or all of the security, *and* the lack of therapy! For starters what, precisely, did Mr. Spiller mean by "counselling"? Nothing that equates with my notion, that's for sure! They've managed to adulterate "counselling" to give a kind of professional camouflage to "putting someone straight". It's a glorified "ticking off"! They've not the slightest idea about counselling from a facilitative point of view. I mean do these chaps get any in-service training or any professional development because, for the majority, the informed man in the street would have a better grasp of counselling, quite frankly. Surely, either professional training is required for our present staff group, or we need to recruit staff with more appropriate attitudes, even if they don't have an especial skills base? Now, as the Nurse Manager, Steve, is there anything you can do about that because I don't see any end to this impasse?'

While the ideas were not entirely unwelcome since I had, myself, come to the same reluctant conclusions, it did very much feel as if I was being provoked into taking out the pin from a managerial grenade. The latter suggestion of staff changes would be of a more immediate possibility and would suit my own purposes in potentially improving what I wanted in terms of a more enterprising team, but I anticipated a backlash as a result of the social disruption it would engender.

'I agree, there is a need for better staff. I'll have a word with my boss and negotiate some personnel changes. As to the training, well, these guys are supposed to have qualified in "Mental Handicap Nursing", so they should know all about "behaviour modification" and adapting patients' behaviour! In fact, I'm not convinced that's the issue any longer. What they really need is to be re-trained in "mental health" principles, and to better prepare them for the mentally ill clients who are being admitted these days. So, there's a mixed bag of professional issues floundering about and they're not entirely to blame for that.'

'Nevertheless,' said Heinrich, expansively, 'One would have expected staff with "Mental Handicap training" to have, at least, a working knowledge of behavioural therapy but I see so very little evidence of this. It's discouraging because you feel you have to set out all the basic parameters, when they should be "au fait" with them.'

'Well let me make *myself* clear. The state of the regime in this hospital takes me back to when I first started out in the old County asylum system, about fifteen years ago. In fact, it has to go beyond even that! There's so much that can be done and it's been done elsewhere. We can catch up, I'm sure, no reason why we shouldn't. I'm really excited about the prospects.'

'I hope you can sustain that enthusiasm, Steve,' was the lugubrious Julian's pensive conclusion. But his considered stare might have been saying the proverbial 'famous last words, sir!'

'Things can only get better,' I rounded off, though this certainly said more about my personal enthusiasm for, and the presumption of, change rather than that it represented a calculated appreciation of the process by which it could be fulfilled. The pause that followed might have applauded the sentiment, there again, it could have disdained the misplaced sense of righteous endeavour. It was hard to interpret.

'It all rather feeds one's scepticism about what on earth anybody means when they talk of these places as "*Special Hospitals*",' Julian derided, as if the notion left a distinct distaste for him. 'If anyone can tell me what's "special" I'd be grateful.' We all shared in a round of quizzical grunts and acknowledging nods which was broken by the affable Dr. Cook in high spirits.

'And on that note, methinks it's time for lunch!' he concluded. 'Can I offer anyone a lift?' And we rose, in unison. As Julian and I slowly passed along the empty corridor, together, I jokingly probed his contribution to the sex debate.

'It will be a job abolishing the sex material from an environment like this. We might have to be quite pragmatic and give way in the end. Do you have strong personal views about sexual material, Julian?'

'Strong "feminist" views, *actually*,' he replied, through a not so approving smile.

This, then, was the nature of the therapeutic environment into which Baird, and all the other adolescents, had been directed. Baird had come to the "Special Hospital" as a twelve-year-old – not quite the youngest candidate in its history, but certainly to be counted among a small band of minors aged around eleven or twelve years of age. After a troubled childhood, when he was considered to be uncontrollable at home and at school, he had acquired a wide history of antisocial conduct. It had not involved rape or any other sexual offence, though. His parents had visited him at intermittent intervals but he could lay claim to few family ties or friends. After a few years of "treatment" in the "Special Hospital" adolescent unit, the relevant authorities felt that he deserved a chance to undergo the slow rehabilitation into the community. He was transferred to a dedicated adolescent, medium secure unit, on a trial basis, one with a highly focused therapeutic regime. During this sojourn, he had found himself in group sessions with a female Occupational Therapist who, perhaps, had underestimated the pent-up potential of a teenager with a cumulatively deprived history. For on one such occasion, when a group had decanted from the activities room, he had lagged behind, closed the door, and swiftly overpowered her. He wasted no time in raping her. Thus, rape had been added to his catalogue of deviant transgressions. He was unceremoniously and, on the face of things, deservedly, recalled to the "Special Hospital" where his rehabilitative prospects would now take many years having succumbed to such a transgression so early on. He knew it, and he was fighting his corner! What people might find difficult to cope with was that he was an extremely affable young man who had, perforce, been required to spend the majority of his teenage years living on wit and resilience in secure conditions without any opportunity to fulfill a normal teenager's development, or to learn any of the more sophisticated social conventions outside of a confined, institutional context. The question needed to be asked, what chance had he ever had of succeeding when he had been so woefully unprepared for the transition? More to the point, what were the expectations of the Department of Health, his psychiatrists, and other authorities, of his realistic rehabilitation having spent his formative years in unmitigated, restrictive captivity? Had it been taken for granted that this therapeutic captivity would hone him into an obliging temperate youth devoid of a recidivistic potential? This was not to condone his rape, it had to be said, but there was a case to be answered that with so little exposure to normal social intercourse, with so little supportive rehabilitative structure, what motivation or capacity did he have for not taking any chances that presented themselves? In any event, hopefully, everybody would have learned the lessons. One such was the necessity for "sex awareness" educational programme which was set in motion on the unit. But for this client group such a standardised programme, though relevant, would have skipped across the deeply rutted disturbance of the seriously sexually deviant. For many of these kids an abnormal psycho-sexual development, including inappropriate sexual arousal and sadistic fantasies, and actual sexual violence, perhaps arising out of their own childhood sexual abuse, would have been the order of the day. Relative to these sexual offences, as well as the broad range of other serious disorders, the rehabilitative shortfalls of sending youngsters with these types of background back into the community, without being properly prepared, were unconscionable.

000

Over the period that I remained on the unit, Julian proved his commitment to our lads and raised my appreciation of the Social Worker's contribution to a clinical team by doing more than producing comprehensive "social circumstances" reports of each client's history, family and school background, and sorting out the client's financial benefits, etc – the standard contribution of Social Workers. He used these tools, and the associated personal interviews, and his general attitude of acceptance, to build his rapport and gain the confidence of the unit's clients. Unable to fulfill his aims during the normal day because of the patients' attendance at the Education Centre or Industrial Workshops, he would make time outside of his normal hours to pursue relevant therapeutic issues. He seemed to pilot a non-threatening course that caused little disturbance among the nursing staff while he hardened himself toward a regime which he likened to a correctional Borstal. And with each subsequent Clinical Team Meeting he would feed in information gathered from his intimate sessions which none of us had got anywhere near. I envied his commitment facilitated, in part, by his status as an individual practitioner in a professional discipline which permitted him a measure of independence. I, on the other hand, without such independence, with a rather narrower remit, and always answerable to

125

a wider body of colleagues, was far more restricted in my range of activity.

Julian took upon himself another more focused, problem-solving, therapeutic initiative – what was called an "empathy group". In principle, this would have been appropriate for any of our lads, provided they had the cognitive capacity, to aid their appreciation of the effect that their general behaviour may have had on others. Selected patients from the adolescent unit joined this closed group of only Julian and its participants and pursued the complex disclosure of feelings, motivations, and self-awareness. Its longer-term purpose was to generate some insight into other peoples' sensitivities, especially actual or potential victims, past or future, of the participants' own offending propensities. This empathy-building must have been an arduous project for both Julian and the group members, the latter probably never having been expected, or encouraged, to expose personal feelings during their prior period of stay!

Julian and I had become particularly sensitised to the emotional needs of the lads on the "continuing care" ward of our adolescent unit which catered, in an overwhelming preponderance, for young men with mild mental handicaps. These debilities had often resulted from earlier brain injuries, either at birth, or from accidents or infections, and although the damage was never extreme, could be manifested in a number of ways, including speech deficits. As with the lads from the "admission and assessment" unit, these lads exhibited evasive, immature and impulsive characteristics made even worse by their intellectual deficits which rendered them more *uncontrolling* and *uncontrollable*. Only now, they knew nothing other than restrictive control: perimeter fences, locks, keys and radios; locked doors to their rooms; personal and room searches; continuous surveillance and escorted movement to any location; checks on incoming and outgoing mail and packages; sanctions for inappropriate behaviour; a rigidly circumscribed daily programme and regime; the need for permission to engage in any activity; and the inability to access any normal adolescent lifestyle. Other structural factors contributed to this social and emotional isolation. Relationally and economically, residents' families tended to live at some considerable distance from the hospital limiting their access to just occasional visits. Architecturally, the layout of this part of the hospital was separately constructed and each single-storey unit was completely separated from their neighbours. The office accommodation for all the personnel of the clinical team, myself included, was straddled across the estate in distant offices so that only the nursing staff resided on the wards – a structural deficit which more modern units endeavoured to diffuse by incorporating all the team in the same suite. The nurses had been abandoned to their singular devices and the patients had, in turn, been abandoned to the unmitigated company of the nursing staff. And it was my impression that for the longer serving medical staff, who wanted as little disturbance as possible, this was as comfortable an arrangement as the nurses' desire to limit any outside interference. This mutually cosy scenario meant, in effect, that the units were detached, satellite locations which, perforce, perpetuated a nurse-dominated culture. So dominant was it that even when we members of the clinical team came to the wards, for whatever reason, we were marked onto the daily ward reports as "visitors", as if we hailed from some outside agency. Incredibly, this also included myself as the unit nursing manager! Then there was the exclusion of female staff from the unit which mitigated any genuine effort at a normalising relational environment.

We also posited that these youngsters' personal problems were accentuated within the hospital boundaries by the "dualist" mode of management to which they were subjected. This was manifested by the social separation of staff from patients; the separation of the client's offending behaviours from their mental incapacities; the separation of ward-based staff from other professionals in the team; and the separation of security procedures from therapeutic endeavours. The end result was that patients would have to prove themselves to the staff via an individual competitiveness which would reveal which of the individual patients were positively responsive to the controls set by the staff. Then there was an assumption that these external controls would, somehow, recalibrate the lads' internal controls through sheer repetition and example. Contrary to this control model, Julian and I noted the yearning for attention and, if we to dared to admit it, *affection,* as was evidenced by their corralling of any visitors to the ward whose presence was more intermittent than that of the regular nursing staff. We favoured a more "integrated" model which also acknowledged that the derivation of problems were often contextual to both the wider social context of their lives, and within the hospital, and that a collective pooling of patient resources had the potential to find a group resolution to many everyday matters.

Part of our solution was for Julian and me to set up a modified, ward "community meeting" for these needy residents with mild mental impairments. In any case, activity on this unit was far less organised than the admission unit and could do with more structured input. It was an unnatural venture in a therapeutically sparse, correctional atmosphere but we hoped it would serve the patients and engage, at least, some of the staff in a new enterprise. For one of the guiding principles of a "community meeting" was that it should be an inclusive affair, democratically accepting all grades of staff and patients on an equal basis, and affording each individual an equal status. Well, the rest of the clinical team did not attend because of the late timing, and – surprise, surprise – neither did the nursing staff who remained steadfastly detached from the venture. As the Nurse Manager I could have insisted, I suppose, but preferred to wait for their interested spontaneity to be excited. Hence our need to modify the forum. In order to involve as many of the residents as possible it was scheduled as a once-weekly, late afternoon, meeting, following tea, and we were delighted that, on every occasion, virtually every resident turned out.

At that first session, we invited everyone to draw the dayroom chairs into a large central circle and the throng of eager anticipation, at such an anarchic act, was palpable. It really seemed as if a circle had never been created in the ward and, for a few minutes, Julian and I basked in the sheer pleasure of listening to the clamouring enthusiasm displayed while cognisant of the nursing staff surveying the anarchy from the adjoining office. For our part, we wanted to be facilitators, demonstrate the task of facilitation, and to contribute just enough input to keep the scene manageable without being intrusive. We intervened with a few rallying calls to settle and congratulated everyone for turning out, then suggested that we establish some "ground rules" that would provide a common understanding for future meetings. Among the most vital were that no one should deliberately interrupt another while they were speaking to the group, thereby directly countering the clamour to compete with one another, but to interrupt with some thought for the other. And discussions about the self-absenting nursing staff should be entirely off limits for if the staff thought the group was a vehicle to criticise them then they would sabotage it, for sure. This was not the most favourable of circumstances because, ideally, this was exactly the kind of forum where the patients should have had the legitimate opportunity to tackle the staff about their routines and decisions and for them, in turn, to justify those practices and to reciprocally bring up their concerns for the patients' consideration. So, the situation was markedly skewed against the most optimum potential for a community group, but legitimate enough for all that. Naturally, as an innovation which provided a relatively open-ended forum for allowing the residents to express, and which they would not risk jeopardising, we could not have failed. Remarkably, bearing in mind their relative incapacities, the group functioned even better than we could have imagined but, then, if the participants were only permitted to deal with a limited area of their communal lives then it had little reason to fall into much conflict. It should have experienced conflicts because the staff and residents should, inevitably, have had to deal with demonstrations of differences of opinion, and challenges to the system. But the group was never provided the opportunity to advance to that level of maturity. Within these limits – increasingly disappointing, with time, because so many issues and grievances needed to be reigned in – it was good enough that we continued to hold the forum in the knowledge that it served the patients, enabled an additional therapeutic input from ourselves, and subverted the one-dimensional "nursing apartheid" that so distinctly separated the body of nurses from that of the patients. Not least, it ever so slightly confounded the disciplinary management by the staff which was inextricably bound to a criminalisation of the patients which predisposed them to apportion any "care" to entrapping any deviant behaviour which was identified, while relegating any "therapeutic" intervention to a secondary status. This imposed a perception of the patients in terms of criminal justice and criminal transgression, rather than of psychiatric intervention and psychological shortfall.

Strategically, in respect of my own role, I also applied the more integrated model in favour of the dualist schism between nursing staff and their managers. By opposing the tribal herding of the nursing staff I endeavoured to engage them in working more independently with individual patients, rather than camouflaging themselves in a team identity; encouraging the clinical activity to be taken as seriously as the custodial routines; elaborating the more subtle psychological needs of patients as well as concentrating on obvious deviant behaviours; and working alongside them as a clinical resource to help plan the care with them, rather than allow them to confine my own role to managerial supervision. I also began to move one or two staff off the unit whom I thought were obstructing this shift toward a therapeutic orientation and, initially, this had the appearance of a normalised staff development programme. This was a project ripe for younger, adaptive staff, especially outsiders from other hospitals, but you were hampered by yet another localised agreement which expected that a person promoted to the rank of Ward Sister or Charge Nurse to have acquired at least four years' previous experience of the "Special Hospital" Service. By then, of course, the dye would be cast. But within eighteen months, and the replacement of three or four of my unit Charge Nurses and one or two junior staff, in the process, it became clear that I was partial toward some staff and was prepared to dispose of those who would not adapt their approach. Despite these moves and changes I still could not find the right therapeutic blend. I was, finally, to give up seeking an optimum therapeutic compromise. I was to renege on all compromise, in time.

000

'Steve! Is that you Steve? You'd better come in here, lad!' was the call I heard as I conversed on the Admin corridor. Recognising the voice of John North, the Duty Nurse Manager, I presented myself to the duty office. 'Don't suppose you're up to speed on the latest,' he said in a grave tone which managed to elevate my apprehension immediately. I had just returned from my rotared two days' leave and would have had no inkling of the "latest". 'How long have you been with us – not six months is it? Well, you're probably going to start believing that you've been handed a poisoned chalice, old son. Sit yourself down there. Better still, would you like a coffee or something because what I'm going to tell you is going to be something of a shock, I imagine.'

'Oh my God, what the hell's happened now? I'll forgo the coffee for now. Just let me have it,' I replied, mightily apprehensive now.

'Please yourself, then. Sean Walton? One of yours on the adolescent admission ward?' I nodded in affirmation. 'Dead! Sorry to break the news.'

'What! He's only about twenty!'

'*Was*. Found dead in seclusion while you were off. We didn't ring you at home. Nothing you could do and it would only have ruined your days off. The circumstances…' and he trailed off to review the notes on his desk replacing his spectacles that were always hung from a neck chain. 'Let me see, yes, here we are. Apparently, the day before – that would be on your first day off – he was discovered making sexual advances toward one of the other lads in the toilet area.' He raised his eyes in my direction. 'You'll know that Walton's history was sex offending,' and returned to his notes. 'Then he was given the task of mopping the toilet area as punishment, if you like. He didn't take too kindly to that and gave a V-sign to one of the Nursing Assistants. A bit of a commotion followed and he is said to have attacked the Nursing Assistant with the mop in an unprovoked attack. He had to be restrained by staff, and was placed in seclusion. Quite disturbed by all accounts, anyway, seen in seclusion by a new Duty Doctor who supported continuing seclusion until the nursing staff saw fit to let him out. Next morning – that would be your second leave day – he was found lying on his back on the seclusion bed with his trousers round his ankles,' long, in-drawn breath, 'not moving, unresponsive, could not be resuscitated, and was later pronounced dead. There are some dodgy details emerging from some of the patients about what took place around that scenario but there you have it, I'm afraid.' He drew heavily on his fag and exhaled, demonstratively, anticipating my response. I pushed myself back into the seat, flabbergasted.

'What are these "dodgy details" you mentioned, John?'

'The Nursing Assistant in question, Grimes, good lad by reputation, is alleged to have hit young Walton over the head with a billiard cue,' he added in a hushed, confiding voice while pausing and scrutinising me.

'What!'

'That's the info I'm getting. The police have begun investigations.'

'Has Grimes been suspended?'

'No! What, after the last debacle? Our masters have thought better of it this time. They've gone for a straight police investigation according to the *old* agreement with the P.O.A.'

'So, back-tracking on suspension, then?'

'Seems so.'

'Christ. I wasn't here. Oh, thank the Lord I wasn't on duty! Who's conducting the internal inquiry? Not me I trust?'

'No. No internal. It's with the police.'

'Well, they won't be able to prove anything. You mentioned the use of a cue. Who says?'

'Patients naturally.'

'Patients?'

'More than one patient, by all accounts.'

'No doubt they're willing to speak up over a death of one of their own,' I mused. 'Well we've all done something we've regretted in our careers but...was this done in full view of the patients?'

'Whatever occurred took place in the dayroom, in full view, yes.'

'Bloody hell! Do people think they're untouchable, or something?'

'Well, there we are. I can't help you any more.'

'Look, thanks, John, you've been a great help. What do I do, now?'

'Carry on!' I rose, tentatively toward the door.

'I'm bloody cursed. When I arrived here I was told I'd been handed the best unit in the hospital? That's what everyone said, as if I'd been given a special favour! Life sucks, don't it!'

The police presented their report of the incident and subsequent death to the Crown Prosecution Service who determined that there were no grounds for taking any further action due to uncorroborated evidence, and the case was dropped. This despite the replicated statements of a number of the patients that Sean Walton had been hit over the head by Nursing Assistant Grimes. Furthermore, the local pathologist had found nothing unusual to report on his investigations of the body and the Coroner, in turn, accepted that the body could proceed to cremation.

000

More industrial action followed one year on from my first encounter with the process. This time it was due to the "Clinical Grading" exercise which had been rolled out across the nation for every member of the nursing fraternity in whatever field they functioned. The aim was laudable enough. To prescribe a compendium of new nursing roles, in terms of identified managerial and clinical competencies, and to evaluate current roles against these criteria rather than assuming, as had been done in the past, that these competencies were automatically acquired by the simple process of advancing seniority. In short, the profession required a much more stringent definition of what nursing roles constituted rather than the generically unhelpful "Staff Nurse", or "Ward Sister/Charge Nurse", etc. This was a window of real opportunity for me to show how I would support any nurse who wished to improve his individual grading potential. Via the individual interviews which all managers were committed to I encouraged the staff to consider their future professional development, and the advanced training which would promote their appeal chances. This was also advantageous to me since

I needed better qualified staff for the therapeutic projects I had in mind for the adolescent unit. For during my early orientation to the hospital, the absence of a single nurse or manager with higher academic qualifications, or advanced professional training, was evidence enough of a somewhat retarded professional culture. No organisation could keep pace with changing demands unless the illuminating benefit of continuing education enabled them to expand their horizons. Truth to say, despite the presence of an on-site educational department, not even a continuing "in-service" programme of basic development was in place.

As always in such a process, the Clinical Grading exercise did not exactly excite people's expectations but each person had an appeal process that they could access if they felt they had been incorrectly evaluated. For the staff of this hospital, the process itself was a sufficient cause for appeal and so, without accessing the formal appeal procedure to justify their individual claims for a higher grading, the staff resorted to a group action and appealed to the P.O.A. again. Further industrial action ensued. The P.O.A. implemented a ban on all overtime working, and any escorting of patients from the wards to any other area of the hospital, for whatever purpose. This time the nursing management was better organised and had prepared a definitive list of all the "patient movements" that took place during a normal week. Many, such as patients' social events, evening adult education, activities clubs had to be temporarily suspended. Referrals to a range of treatment and investigative clinics such as G.P., ophthalmic, chiropody, x-rays and EEGs, were limited to just urgent cases. The weekend church services, and patient visits, were re-located to the wards instead of centrally organised. And the whole Christmas entertainment programme for the residents remained under threat at that time. Again, it was a difficult time for everyone and, presumably, it was understood that secluding the patients again was far too problematic. One of the eventual outcomes of this action was that a significant number of nursing staff were named and reported to their professional bodies on charges of professional misconduct. The charges were not upheld by those bodies and though this, rightly, sent the message that health staff had the right to take industrial action, in this particular institutional context, it fuelled the potential for further aggravated disputes as an automatic entitlement. And yet a further dispute was exactly what transpired!

000

The limited calls from *within* the hospital for change came from individuals who had a desire to be on a par with other mental health services, had a fear of becoming becalmed in a therapeutic doldrums, and also a concern with their own professional viability and personal anonymity. These calls were mooted by a loosely confederated minority who counted among their numbers social workers, psychologists, a couple of psychiatrists, and a handful of nursing staff. They vehemently opposed the therapeutic vacuity, the toxicity of industrial relations, and the reactionary tenacity that so disadvantaged the patients' progress and development. An analogy that had come to form in my mind was of an amateur theatre company which had generated two opposing cliques under its single roof as its membership had evolved. Each clique vying to promote its own players, each vying for control of the theatre's direction and its repertoire. The "Treadmill Troupe", the established set and predominant in overwhelming number, walked the boards with recitations and incantations that heralded their old gods, revived their indigenous mythologies, preserved their ancient catalogue, while protecting them from the heresies of the modern era. For they were the guardians of an established venue and programme tradition which hailed the classical themes of warfare, conflicts, revenge, and rites of passage, which were unashamedly portrayed during their vociferous, protectionist productions. While the stage remained dominated by the "Troupe" the minority players of the "Therapy Thespians" sat in a hushed and whispered cluster in the auditorium fidgeting for the day that a wider audience would come to take their seats, and when informed critics would adjudicate the relative merits of the competing players and their dramatic pieces. And when, by turn, the residual company of "Thespians" pushed themselves forward to act out their alternative, lyrical, empathising scenes the majority "Troupe" jeered from the stalls and hung garrulously from the gallery in a rite of whimsical objection. It was clear that there was little prospect that such a slow and deliberate attrition would have so radical an effect as to convert the whole company but the palliative performances continued, often to empty houses.

000

In 1989, the "Special Hospitals" came under the orbit of the "Special Hospital Services Authority" which was created for the purpose. Indefatigably, it amounted to a "regime change". As a distinct health authority, in its own right, it was now to give account for the four high security mental hospitals. This, effectively, meant the end of the historical patronage of the Department of Health and Social Security, and the adoption of the managerial and operational mantle of the rest of the National Health Service and its driving force, "general management". Following its inception, an early plenary executive forum at a centralised plush hotel incorporated the managerial roots of all the hospitals' professional disciplines. Top of the bill was the performance of the new Chief Executive, a dapper-dressed and coiffered, suave, man, who coquettishly strutted his slight build about the dais upon which he was raised, and set out his strategic vision in a mellifluous, protracted delivery. The dramatic incongruence of this erudite, entrepreneurial image, set against the staid, prosaic traditionalism of the majority of the assembly, could not have been missed by anyone. It was all but a cavalier proclamation by King Charles I before the puritan sobriety of a Roundhead assembly and his expectation of their necessary genuflection.

'We are a virgin authority. We have an unequivocal, operational remit to provide continuity to hospital security, and public protection.' Pause after protracted pause, and bated silence. 'Nevertheless, there is an additional component which will be pursued with the utmost vigour. Our 1700 patients will have the right to expect an improved investment – an investment both material and professional - in their care and rehabilitation. How we implement this is our responsibility as an organisation. The most important message I have to impart to all of you is contained in a single word. That word is "*subsidiarity*".' Every sentence was delivered in an unusually measured, calculated pace which dramatised the whole performance and this last operative word was pronounced with all the sensual undertone of a sex act while he waited for the word, and its weighty intonation, to seduce us into an anticipatory receptiveness since none of us had the slightest inkling of its meaning. An advantage which he exploited fully. 'By subsidiarity I mean that, though the Special Hospital Services Authority will be the central organ, as much decision-making, managerial responsibility and accountability, will be devolved down through the four limbs of each of your own hospitals. Each hospital now has its dedicated General Manager, in situ, and in the future every ward throughout the four hospitals will have its dedicated Ward Manager. The measure by which I shall adjudge the success of this subsidiarity will be the extent to which my desk will be clear of all impediments to my day.' The audience allowed themselves a relieved hum of laughter. 'The less I have to do the better because it will indicate to me that the organisation will obviously be functioning as it should. And I do aim to achieve a cleared desk!' Hum, hum!

For all this inspirational and illuminative reorientation it did not take much to appreciate the irony of the exercise in one respect, at least. For the creation of the Special Hospital Services Authority, to the "Special Hospital" staff, must have had the semblance of being abandoned by the Department of Health as in the manner of unruly kids who were no longer controllable by parents or society at large. In health professional terms, the "Special Hospitals" and their staff were now seen to be a deviant class who were to be specifically legislated for, as had been the case with their patients. The appointment had become precipitous as the evidence stacked up that the "Special Hospitals" were out of sync with the pace of change taking place in the rest of the Health Service. In the previous year, alone, there had been additional disturbance to the public relations image of the "Special Hospital" system following Broadmoor Hospital's inspection by the Health Advisory Service, an independent watchdog which had concluded, at every level, that the hospital was not up to the mark. It highlighted the lack of collaboration that could have included the patients' involvement in their treatment and care, a consideration which would have been expected elsewhere. This single aspect epitomised a system of care which was un-therapeutic, put too great a stress on the use of seclusion and excessive custody, was outdated, depersonalising, and resistant to change. Nursing staff with experience of more enlightened approaches to care, it posited, were unlikely to remain within a system in which virtually all grades performed the same, customary routines with little differentiation of skills. The S.H.S.A. was officially sanctioned to sweep into power on the back of this critique of fundamental deficiencies. The S.H.S.A. would comprise a predominant institution with the authority to institute uncompromising managerial efficiency in order to exert greater control over its professional charges, and no one could but appreciate how, in principle, this paralleled the present staff domination and management of patients. This virgin authority, with its unprecedented remit, would be perceived by the hospital group and staff as a discriminating, oppressive, victimising perpetrator who would victimise its subordinates. The victimisers would be punishing, un-protective and neglecting of the staff's past status whilst they, for their

136

part, would reciprocate with as much defiance, resistance, and sabotage as they could muster.

It was particularly ironic in light of Nursing's governing, professional bodies who now had high hopes that the "Special Hospital" nurses would now move away from mere custody, and strengthen its care base.

000

If there were specific clinical phenomena which would alert anybody to the distressed condition of the hospital, and lead them to question its viability as a therapeutic establishment, it was its record, and management, of self-harming behaviour by its resident patients, and the prolific use of seclusion. The act of locking a person in a room, on their own, against their will, could only be legalised if the patient showed a significant level of dangerousness toward others. Of the range of independent causes for which an individual was secluded in this hospital, there were two major causes. The more general cause was for some act of aggression or violence for which it was considered necessary to separate them from their peers or staff. The other major cause was self-harming behaviour which applied, in most instances, to the female patients though this was not to say that violence did not come into the frame on occasion. But, the actual numbers involved, particularly regarding the female patients, were utterly astounding. With the sole exception of the integrated, pre-discharge ward, this involved every single female ward. In point of fact, a veritable contagion seemed to have caught hold of the female patient fraternity. It was inconceivable that a visit could be made to a female ward without encountering someone, sometimes several, who bore the tell-tale marks of current self-harm. The most immediately obvious were those who sustained the marks of "head-butting". Indeed, the severely indented contusions to the middle of the forehead, present among so many, could have represented a pathological, religious symbol. To have reached this level of damage an individual would have subjected themselves to a repetitive collision of their forehead against a wall, or floor, or other firm object, with a considerable and continuous force. Rarely would it have been accomplished with single assaults.

Despite my earlier career in a diversity of health care settings, including a year and a half spent in an Accident and Emergency Department, none had prepared me for the extent, severity and elaboration of the self-harming behaviour which I came to encounter within these precincts of "Special Hospitals". Within the hospital wards, virtually not an episode occurred on the adolescent unit, nor the gender-integrated, pre-discharge unit, and the male population exhibited it to a significantly lesser degree than the female population even though the numbers of the former outnumbered those of the latter by a ratio of 7:3. The one male exception was one by the name of Hennessey who, perforce, needed to reside on what functioned as an intensive care unit. His exceptional case illustrated the most extreme of examples engaging, as he did, in near daily exhibitions of the phenomena. But the issue was so widespread among the females that it reflected the well-documented scenario that persisted among the female populations in the country's prisons. There was such an embarrassment of self-harming incidents, in fact, that the running hospital register – kept by one of the three most senior nurse managers – referred only to the incidents of "self-mutilation" as if he could not dare accept the complete reality. The nursing staff, on the other hand, all too keenly conscious of the plethora of related incidents, would make entries in their notes of most of the remainder. By no means exclusive, a veritable potpourri of such behaviour could be identified: lacerating with an implement, facial punching, eye gouging, biting, scratching, inserting foreign bodies into wounds, swallowing articles, tying a ligature around the neck, picking at wounds or stitches, head banging, friction burns, fire burns, electrocution burns, cigarette burns water immersion, and throwing oneself in front of a vehicle. It should be pointed out that the tying of a ligature around the neck was not always accompanied by an immediate attempt to draw it taught but it gave some signal of intent and did not go unnoticed. The most predominant behaviours were head banging and self-laceration which accounted for about half of all incidents. The latter was particularly significant in that to obtain some sharp implement took a measure of versatility in ward environments which were so vigorously scoured, via frequent ward and personal searches, for the presence of such potential weapons.

So intrigued was I by this riot of self-harm occurring on a daily basis that I gained permission to conduct a survey of the phenomena over a six month period. The findings more than verified the clinical impression. The in-patient population during this six-month period was 300 or so and over a fifth were identified as self-harming patients during that time, alone. Young Hennessey, regrettably, was reported in no less than a fifth of all the incidents, while less than a fifth of all the remainder were ascribed to the male population as a whole. This left the remaining females – only 30 percent of the total hospital population – responsible for the majority two thirds of the total, accumulating just shy of 300 incidents between them! And these were only the observed and recorded ones! Not every female appeared in these figures, naturally, but over half of them did! By dissecting this group by psychiatric diagnosis, the most significant picture was that these self-harming females assigned the diagnosis of "personality disorder" constituted over half the total self-harmers in the hospital. Just under half of this personality disordered group had engaged in "poly-injurious" self-harm which meant that they had incurred between three and seven different forms of self-harm during this six-month period alone.

As striking, was the nursing management of these self-destructive patients, incidents and their concomitant injuries. Predominantly, the patients were administered extra doses of medication in a medically prescribed attempt to quell the disturbance. On 50 occasions patients were placed within individualised restraint garments, after the act of self-harm, and some with an additional personalised helmet for good measure. Following approximately a third of all incidents the patients were placed into "seclusion". While on 11 occasions patients received extra medication, then secluded, and then placed into restraint garments and/or helmets, as a package, in attempts to prevent further acts of self-harm. In other words, the patients were as incapacitated as they could possibly have been without being manacled or physically held down. Such was the concern that this form of behaviour created for the staff!

Looking at someone's body after it had been subjected to their personal scarification prompted conflicting emotions – revulsion, I'm afraid to say, was very prominent, initially. Always perhaps! If there was one self-harming method which caused the greatest impact I would have adjudged it to be self-laceration whereby an individual generally used a sharp instrument to cut anywhere on their own body surface. Clearly, each self-lacerating patient had their unique modus operandi and this might vary over time. These might constitute single or multiple lines of superficial cuts, some traced in neat parallel lines, approximate in length and space, suggesting a methodical, orderly, precision of thinking and action, in the manner of someone crafting a creative work much like a tattoo. There might be a spontaneous rash of chaotic-looking slashes, long and short, deep and delicate. In more extreme instances, when the cuts graduated to grosser carvings or gouges, the gaping blobs of fatty tissue bubbled up, and the rising claret spurted out. These could be freshly laid across old patterns, often at different angles, so that the whole was much like a healed mesh with broad bands of scarred anger and frustration, over time. There was fascination when listening to explanations by patients who might often talk, positively, of emotional relief from their cutting when the red pipes of warm blood must have spurted to the surface and burst with life over the cold white of their skin and suicidal thoughts. It was disconcerting to reflect on how much private planning and rumination must have gone into the whole process: the procurement of instruments – the razors, nails, stones, glass, staples, batteries, hairpins, drawing pins and chords, etc; the selection of a location – dayroom, toilet, bathroom, bedroom or dormitory, or exercise area; the timing of the act relative to the daily schedule and the presence of others; the method by which the act would be effected; the choice of the body part on which to inflict the injury; and the introspection concerning the visual injuries, the scarring after-effects, and whether any benefit had been accrued. As disconcerting was the tenacity to carry through a desire to self-harm despite the defensive reactions of staff about them. Often, verbalised intentions or actual attempts would cause the perpetrators to be isolated in spartan rooms, cleared of all artefacts and personal clothing, placed in canvas clothing, searched, and then locked in. Despite these measures patients exhibited what had been called a "morbid resourcefulness" in scheming their way to self-harm in opposition to all efforts to deter them. For example, by "posting" a weapon or instrument in their vagina, where they could not be legally searched without special permission, they were able to extract the implement at the time of their choosing and to fulfil their intentions relatively free of disturbance. Implementing the seclusion, in fact, often appeared to have facilitated the mutilatory activity rather than prevented it.

To counter the possibility that the patients' motivation was "attention-seeking", and that this was being reinforced by the elaborate arrangements needed to transfer the injured to general hospitals to receive necessary treatment, a revised policy invited the services of a local General Practitioner, Dr. Fish. His remit was to provide an "on-call" service and to attend the hospital to suture the wounds "in-house". An experimental period assessed the value of applying the sutures without the use of local anaesthetic in order to further minimise the treatment-provoking response. This did not seem so barbaric as the patients did not incur any physical discomfort from the procedure, and this concurred with their admission that little pain was sustained during the actual inflicting of the wounds. On the contrary, many spoke of the sheer relief that was liberated during the act of cutting. But it was soon discovered that this was not in the least aversive, gained no advantage, and the practice ended. I was to overhear the commentary of Dr. Fish who attended these suffering and perplexing women and I could not have faulted his attempts at convivial rapport and understanding as he sutured the gross tears on someone's arm, or removed an instrument that had been inserted into a previous wound, or re-dressed a laceration from which the sutures had been steadily unpicked by the injured party. He knew that he would need to return: to treat the same patients; to treat them time and again; whatever, and however, he tried. Neither could fault be found in the sympathetic stance adopted by some of the nursing staff who, to their credit in view of the lack of comprehension, gradually began to tolerate the patient's need to inflict harm on themselves, and to offer as much reassurance and personal contact as they believed appropriate for each case.

There was no dearth of speculation about the derivations of this apparently perverse expression of disorder. The causes were mostly ascribed to *intrapersonal issues*, that is, derived from *within* the individual predisposition. From this stance, the large-scale of the phenomenon had to be located in the extensive damage to individual personalities: that is, from personal isolation, low self-esteem, boredom and hopelessness, receiving bad news, a disturbing event; depression, or psychotic delusion; purging of guilt, impulsiveness, masochism or narcissism; sexual frustration and stimulation; regressive self-stimulation, where he/she returned to an earlier stage of their life; depersonalisation, where he/she lost touch with their sense of their own self and external reality and attempted to establish an ego boundary via contact with their body. Of the most touted was that the female patients simply comprised a smaller contingent of more severely disturbed people than their male counterparts and this was reflected in their magnified self-harming.

The causes could also be *interpersonal*, that is, between individuals: conflict with others, taking revenge, and gaining some situational advantage such as wishing to avoid other peoples' company or having to attend work; social contagion, whereby behaviours learned and imitated from one another were experimented with, or even used to compete with one another; as an adaptive way of communicating anxiety and need which could not be managed verbally; or reinforced (rewarded) by the guaranteed urgent, anxious and attentive responses by the staff to their actions. Another line of inquiry which was gathering momentum was the causal link between self-harm and earlier sexual abuse which seemed to feature in the emerging social histories of the female patients. Though not to be underestimated, arguably though, this did not take sufficient account of the possible sexual abuse of male patients, which might not be so readily admitted to by male patients.

The figures, the description of injuries, the lamentably limited treatment methods for managing the self-harmers, most especially the gender bias, deserved some viable sociological, and social explanations, and their solutions, also. Much informed debate centred on the relevance of gender stereotypes which, in the first place, was said to discriminate in favour of a judicial and professional prescription for the medical treatment of female criminality, rather than the customary imprisonment and punishment which appertained to the male population. This would somewhat account for the concentration of this minority within the high security mental hospitals. The gender stereotyping, it was further proposed, magnified the defaulting position of female self-harmers because of their failure to comply with society's expectations of femininity, domesticity and motherhood. In turn, this caused them to accumulate an assortment of adverse "master statuses" including those of offenders, failed women, self-abusers and, in some instances, personality disordered which provoked a more extreme staff reaction toward them. The adoption of a lesbian lifestyle only precipitated further adverse discrimination. Other proposals included the idea that women did not have the same coping strategies as men to manage stressful, particularly custodial, environments; that female socialisation promoted an expressive, caring, home-centredness as opposed to the instrumental, assertive and competitive qualities of male socialisation which would not cause such a painful dislocation from a familial and social network.

Intuitively, these sophisticated explanations, though wholly applicable to some degree or other, required a more prosaic topping-up in order to serve as a sufficient model for explaining the epidemic of female self-harmers and the associated treatment strategies. This prosaic precept was that the localised, micro-social, toxic mixture of an uncompromising grip of custodial power exercised by the marooned, ward-based nursing staff; the virtual absence of any purposeful activity, or lifestyle, or ambition, to which the patients could aspire during their protracted "Special Hospital" stay; the prospect of their indefinite detention in a "Special Hospital" with no clear release date in sight; and a proportionate dereliction of professional, therapeutic training and education by all professional parties in respect of the patient dysfunction steered the cause toward an institution-generated phenomena.

Professional training, education and supervision was entirely redundant and staff had to negotiate a psychological survival path that was necessarily intuitive. We were also all prisoners of what one therapeutic model, Cognitive Behavioural Therapy, called a "cognitive dissonance", whereby we simultaneously held competing, inconsistent thoughts about the issue. The more automatic staff response was a tendency to adopt a pragmatic shorthand for the persistent self-mutilatory/harming repertoires by interpreting them as perverse, incredible, maladaptive, and attention-seeking acts which deserved little serious emotional investment on their part. It was, after all, no easy business trying to empathise with patients who often presented no clear reason for inflicting such permanent destruction upon themselves and this very fact, more than any other consideration, persuaded us that the patients' behaviour was irrational. The advantage of this was that it could then be dismissed, discounted, invalidated, packed away from serious reflection! As too, could our clinical incapacity to deal effectively with both the physical wounds and the psychological trauma that must have precipitated each incident, and certainly persisted afterward. The more the patient mutilation and its motivation could be explained away as illogical, the less need was there for us to reproach ourselves for not being able to fathom the business. In turn, this rationalisation relieved us all of any responsibility. Nevertheless, responsibility was precisely what was demanded of us in the form of a professional duty of care towards clients, whatever they may be. We had no professional right to object to a patient's condition. And so, these dissonant notions of perverse self-centredness battled with a sometimes reluctant, seeping appreciation of the patients' psychological suffering.

We of the nursing staff, had long since reified the act of self-laceration as "cutting up". In itself, the phrase conveyed the staff's generally derogatory posture toward an enigmatic range of behaviours for which they could not account and toward which any sympathetic understanding of the dynamics that motivated it had long since been severed. Speculating on its symbolism and the underlying dynamics was a seductive exercise: 'if you patients cut your bodies, you will sever any sympathy we staff have for you'. The plain fact was that we, the staff, had to unconsciously expel our ignorance, our lack of empathy, and our inability to prevent the self-lacerating, and to project all the blame for this cumulatively uncomfortable situation onto the patient-perpetrators. The patients became not only self-harmers, in the instrumental sense, but the psychological cause of the staff guilt, anxiety and incompetence and this explained the force of staff reaction toward the phenomena and the patients, and their need to distance themselves from it in the phrase "cutting up".

Speculation on the possible causes of the self harming phenomenon could not distinguish the respective strengths of psychological illness, from non-disordered despair, from plain resistance. For the patients, an awareness of the staff's competing attitudes only added to their own dissonant thoughts. The long hours of ruminating preparation prior to acting out the self-harm, as well as more impulsive responses, had to encompass the short and long term consequences for themselves. What would be the physical damage to the body? Would this self-harm persist in the future as a life-long habit and could it, eventually, be fatal? Would the visual and emotional impact deter both themselves and others from having intimate social and sexual relationships? Would there be a lifetime need to cover up the body, secreting the issue from public view and curtailing participation in public activities? And, if drawn to public attention would not the most expected reciprocation bound to be revulsion and antipathy? All these distractions could be set against the several advantages of indulging their self-harming inclinations, not least, that the patients accrued some genuine benefit, even if only a part solution, to an ongoing difficulty to which they could conceive of no other, given their circumstances. Perhaps it even gave back a measure of control to patients knowing that their behaviour represented a psychological frontier beyond which the staff, all staff, were incapable of understanding or controlling?

Radical proposals were imperative to puncture the swelling epidemic, take the pressure off the hospital and staff, and discover other ways forward. One such was that the more prolific self-harming female contingent would be congregated on one newly created facility where the habitual self-damaging dynamics could be intensively investigated, and where the females might find some mutual benefit in identifying with, and supporting, each other. I rather envied the Nurse

144

Manager who was promoted to lead the nursing staff in this genuinely therapeutic initiative. A gregarious, affable, and humorous man, Ben Lamb was notable for his natty state of dress and an unmitigated enthusiasm for life which was often mirrored by a frequent boyish expression of "okey-dokey". I was also struck by the energetic gate which propelled him in long, buoyant bounds which made him readily identifiable from any distance. He was the natural selection for the task in view of his current responsibility for the female admission ward but you suspected that these convivial personal qualities, to which might be added an irrepressible resilience, were also considered in order to sustain the staff morale in the face of the travails to come. The team leader with the necessary gravitas for the exercise was the Consultant Psychiatrist, Dr. Graveney. Contrasted with the vigorous Ben Lamb, at his side, he cut a more unprepossessing image – physically gaunt, pallid, unremarkably attired, less boisterous, and a bustling gait, but this would belie the avowed determination with which he approached the project. He being the most vociferous of the complete establishment's "Therapy Thespians", if I was any judge. Willing to accept the input of any interested party they welcomed my intention to visit the unit, along with several others. I remembered the first occasion with some clarity.

'Oh, what have we got here, then! It's Mr. Burrows!" was the opening salvo which issued from among the knot of about half a dozen youthful females huddled against a corridor radiator that lay off of the dayroom. The brightly painted walls and inner ward railings, and the floor space which had been covered throughout with a newly laid carpet for a more homely comfort, was an agreeable start. It was significant that the ladies had congregated in the corridor – free range, so to speak – while the rest of the hospital units generally battery farmed their charges, confining them to rigorously prescribed areas where their limited mobility could be supervised with the minimum of staff inconvenience. So, this was a policy innovation, a policy risk indeed, since this entrusted the patients not to take adverse advantage of it! 'What you doing here, then? There ain't no one in seclusion and this ain't your unit, anyway!' The verbal challenge, delivered in a course London vernacular, was neither a polite introduction nor a frank admonishment but a calculated piece of mickey taking. It came from one of the more notorious of the personality disordered, self-mutilating females who had become a leader amongst her sisters. Abi had acquired her reputation for the aggressively forthright challenges to the staff, and system, coupled with her propensity to scarify her face with roughly-hewn lacerations. Approaching this small band, I discerned their air of palpable suspicion and exclusivity which, at that moment, was being engineered to cause me maximum discomfort. But Abi could manage this all by her lonesome! Slightly abashed, I scampered for the nearest explanation I could muster. After all, it was not easy to rationalise what was, in large measure, an idle curiosity.

'Actually, I've popped in to see how things are shaping up for you all, Abi.' The use of patients' Christian names had also been a policy innovation and I tried to milk it.

'A bit free with the Christian names, aren't we?' Appreciative giggles from the rest of her number. 'And why would you be interested in what happens to us?' Good point. I was on the back foot in seconds! 'Come to see how the real nutters are doing, have we?'

'I wouldn't put it that way, at all,' now not knowing how I should address her.

'How *would* you put it, then,?' she said with a mocking relish. A satisfied wave of derisive appreciation flickered through the now very attentive group.

'Um,' I stammered, with no choice but to accept my embarrassment, 'no, actually, I'm really excited by what's happening down here and... I wanted to offer my encouragement,' I stumbled, pathetically.

'*So* glad you're *excited*. We're *ecstatic* ourselves, *actually*!' I was stymied. At one level, this could be interpreted as an example of the ability of a personality disordered individual to complicate interpersonal relations to gain some perverse advantage over another. The rest of her entourage, though savouring my struggling efforts, might have preferred that I would move on allowing them to conspire further, perhaps.

'We're still locked up. No difference there,' added one of the group.

'Well it is different though, surely. You wouldn't be nattering on a corridor back on the admissions ward or the other female areas without being supervised,' I replied, vainly trying to break some ice here and to assert myself.

'*So*,' was the exaggerated reply, 'we supposed to be grateful, or something?' continued Chrissie, another leader of the pack. 'Ain't we got nothing better to do, then?' again, in a similar tone to Abi.

'He's come to cure us, haven't you, Mr. Burrows?' was Abi's defiant jibe. I was mightily stymied, now. I was lost for a ready answer and wished I'd come better prepared. And that said it all, really. I was, in truth, wholly unprepared for making any contribution other than a vague support.

'You used the word "cure". What are you looking for a cure of?' I countered, coming directly alongside Abi.

'Ooh! There's a question! What are we looking for a cure of girls?' she retaliated, rolling her eyes in derision. The rest languished over the radiator and against both walls.

'My sex drive!' sang another of them to peals of laughter from all.

'Don't make me laugh! You ain't got no idea how to cure nothing, you lot. All you're good for is locking us up. You do a pretty good job of that. So why you've put us in 'ere for God only knows,' was the sarcastic prod of Chrissie. 'Admit it. Go on bleeding admit it!' There were one or two gasps of surprise.

''Ere, watch yerself, girl, he'll report you. You going to report her for swearing, Mr. Burrows?' prods Abi.

'Now I'm worried! Can you see me quivering?' says Chrissie, enjoined by others' laughter and I wondered if there was any mileage in trying to prolong this. Abi came alongside the pace again.

'What's the game, anyway? They've gone and stuck us in here for "cutting up" but we're in the hospital for being nutters. Why ain't they getting our mental illness better, that's the real problem, not "cutting up". Barking up the wrong tree if you ask me, mate. Now we've got something else to convince the ''Ome Office about. That's on top of our mental illness and index offences. You don't have an answer do yer?' I had, by then, determined that the best approach was simply to hear them out.

'Course he don't. Oh, come on girls,' interrupted Chrissie, disgustedly.

'While we're at it,' continued the redoubtable Abi, intent on fielding the several issues at stake, 'can you tell us why we still have to put up with male staff when this is supposed to be a special unit for us girls?'

'Isn't that an effort to provide you with as much normality as possible?' I ventured.

'I don't mind the men, meself, so long as we get the right ones – good lookers would be a big help, not these ugly muppets!' interjected Chrissie, to the shrills of the whole group.

'Speak for yerself. I don't think it's right that they're here having a good oggle at us, especially when they lay their fucking hands on you, strip you, and throw you into seclusion. Downright bloody liberty! Bloody perverts!' added the aggrieved Abi.

The group, other than Abi, peeled away in a show of boredom cum disdain but I was relieved when she responded to my next query and stayed put. I wanted just a small chance to redeem myself. Glaring toward me, her light brown eyes fermented with emotional distance and concerted lack of respect. Yet she stood her ground, a little less confidently perhaps. She blinked with contempt and waited on my discomfort. How naïve was I! What was I doing here projecting my own optimism onto these people who, now I realised, had little cause for celebration.

'I take your point. I only…'

'Oh, what point was that? I didn't know there was one.'

'Well, why should you be excited, I suppose? You're still in hospital wherever you're placed. And do you really believe the presence of male staff makes for more difficulties?' She examined me quizzically and waited some more. I surveyed the coarse scar tissue that had obliterated most of the skin to her cheeks, chin and forehead. There were fresh scratches, severe lines of anger. What anger there must have been to rub out your face! Otherwise, the face was singularly pale, the cheeks fallen in, as if the severed muscles could not sustain them. The light brown eyes, tired and slightly irresolute now as if she could only maintain an antipathetic energy for so long, looked away. 'You do realise, I hope, that this unit could be your ticket out of here, in time.' I didn't really know that I believed this but felt an urge to offer up something hopeful. 'Your chance of a transfer out of here has got to be improved, don't you think?'

'Oh, and when's that going to happen then? Coming to this unit's just made things a hell of a lot worse. What have I gained, what have any of us gained, from being stuck in here and concentrating on "cutting"? That ain't done any of us any favours. Just added another burden to getting out. Any case, I ain't got nothing to look forward to even if I did get out.' From the degree of facial disfigurement I did wonder how much it would affect her prospects "on the out", let alone the years spent in institutions that she was alleged to have endured most of her life. And that was the salutary measure of it! It wasn't just mental disorder we were facing, but an existential loss of meaning in life itself, perhaps! And in the face of all the staff who came and went with fervent goals, and ambition, who smiled when they came on duty and offered up supercilious words of encouragement when there was no comfort to be gained. She, on the other hand, could not face the world, so she cut off her face, bit by bit.

I would wish to believe as we drifted apart that I would have learned much of value if I could engineer more contact with the unit.

It would have compensated for the frail impotence I was forced to accept at that moment. Yet I was grateful for what I'd learned in those few minutes, too. Not that it was to do too much for Abi, I presumed. She was to fair well on the unit, though. So well, she was eventually discharged to a medium secure unit. Some of the staff believed a real victory had been achieved, and so there had. Only one day, within the relatively relaxed regime of a new institution where no more was known about repairing psychological disfigurement, or existential crises, than any other custodial establishment, she could face life no longer, baracaded her room, strapped up her neck behind its door, and turned her face from the world once and for all.

I never had the chance to determine the impact her death had had on Dr. Graveney. He had opposed the outdated regime of the hospital, fought the P.O.A., gently revived the staff on his unit, and believed in a sound future for his patients. By that time I had deserted my managerial position.

Chapter 3

Disillusionment

The use of "seclusion" was one more of the remarkable facets of this hospital. When I had started out as a "mental nurse" in the 1970s, the excuse we could have had for an incomplete understanding of the proper use of seclusion was that it was not specified within the earlier Mental Health Act (1959). Emanating, as I had, from one of the standard County hospitals within the wider mental health service I had been well acquainted with the use of seclusion as a "correctional isolation" – indeed, had used it for that very purpose on a number of occasions myself – not that we called it by half so grand a notion. "Bang him up" was the conventional phrase for the enforced confinement of refractory patients who had contravened some unwritten rule and this was common practice. The "banging" was never made absolutely explicit but there was a presumption that it was derived from the practice of slamming, and locking, the door on a reticent patient who had no desire to be placed in a separate room and who, generally speaking, would have been forced into it against their will. The slamming was required because the staff were beating a hasty exit and did not wish to be clobbered by the patient! Nor was I a stranger to how the justification for that enforcement could be as malleable as suited the predilections of the staff. In fact, when its use was not confined to frank dangerousness for the safety of other patients and staff, but for our own ends of reprimanding patients for what we considered to be generally unacceptable behaviour, then, it represented an abuse of the procedure, plain and simple. In the County mental hospitals, patients were known to be secluded for swearing, for uttering threatening intentions, for causing damage, for confrontations with other patients, for drunkenness, or for any other non-compliance with the rules. Our rules. The ones that were partial to one member of staff or another.

This was not the position by 1983 when a revamped Mental Health Act deliberately elaborated the use of seclusion in an accompanying *Code of Practice.* Any patient who was deemed to be severely disturbed and likely to cause serious harm to others, require protection for their own sake, or to avoid causing serious harm to others, could be locked alone in a room which would then be supervised. No one could now be in doubt as to the strictly limited and authenticated purposes for which it was now to be used.

What the Mental Health Acts had not formally accommodated was the utilisation of patients' individual rooms as spaces in which their inhabitants could be locked for the entire duration of the night. In plain point of fact, when "Special Hospital" patients went to bed they were delivered, en masse, and locked into their bedrooms until the following morning and were required to use a chamber pot for their nocturnal elimination if the room did not contain separate toilet facilities, which they generally did not. Come the morning, patients would "slop out". Mirroring the very same conditions that persisted in the Prison Service this conveyed the indisputable notion that each room was, in essence, a cell. To my astonishment, this was the state of play when I entered the "Special Hospital" service and it disturbed me from the outset that this could ever have become an acceptable practice. Intuitively, it just seemed wrong. However, it had a historical and economic justification in the sense that it required only one member of staff to be allocated to each ward.

Another justification for secluding patients had also eluded the Mental Health Act it would seem. There had never been any intention to justify the seclusion of a new patient on their arrival as a hospital admission!

000

My own impressionistic sketch of the arrival of a newly admitted patient to the hospital was configured with an extrapolated account imparted to me by a long-standing member of staff. Rising earnestly from the institution with a heavy sigh of relief, the withering, greying light strayed into the firmament, abandoning the stern lines of the brick dwellings, the speared metal tips of the railings, and the grass-chamfered verges of the pathways. During the hours of sun, and in the absence of any spreading trees in the vicinity, any passing flight of crows would hang, momentarily, like black portraits against the brilliant hues, but never tarry. At its close, the heavy dank breath of the winter air retired over the chilling embers of another "Special Hospital" day.

Tearing a jagged slash across this evening screen the visiting vehicle droned its uncertain course from the main gate to the rear entrance of the establishment. The van contained the cooped-up, searing senses of the institution's most recent recruit who anxiously reached out for signs and portents of what was to befall him in the coming few years and who wished for something more certain than the bland reassurance which his two staff escorts were offering him. The first of the huge, metal-barred, entrance gates swung open on their leering, metal limbs with a grating, mocking bow of greeting and, as the van and its occupants drew to a halt before the second of them, the first gates returned to their accustomed fortifying position, closing out the world beyond with a resounding, iron slap of finality. The uniformed soul on gate duty, swinging a key on its leather strap, sauntered pass to unlock and push aside the next grilled obstacle, and ushered through the van into the sombre, inner compound. Already alerted to the prospective arrival, the gateman pointed toward a low building among the several similar ones that were dispersed like a diminutive, barren township in a large clearing, devoid of foliage, human activity, and colour.

Accompanied by the gate-duty staff member, the van was escorted to the unassuming front door of the unprepossessing dwelling to which it were to deliver the charge. It disgorged the passenger, along with several large polythene bags of possessions, as if to pass on a parcelled delivery. Another uniform, another face, appeared turning another key from the other side of the door, and all moved into the receiving airlock. The so-called "airlock" gave the staff an opportunity to better control the human comings and goings. Now the inner door of the airlock slammed and locked shut and the newcomer smelled the airless stuffiness of the dayroom and spied the cruel glares of some of the other patients, and the curiosity of others. That moment's attention was also fixed on the carefully choreographed presence of the crossed arms, feet astride, five staff members of a reception committee. The escorts would have admitted to having a quiet admiration for the staff of a high security mental hospital whose raison d'etre was to control the more intransigent and dangerous of all psychiatric inmates – a uniformed band of gentlemen all who appeared eminently confident of their remit and completely un-phased by the prospect of yet another unknown quantity in their midst. The new arrival was ordered to stand before one of the junior staff, hold out his arms, spread his legs, and turn about, while his body was prodded in a routine search for contraband which might have been carelessly overlooked by the escorts.

The senior member of ward staff would have proceeded from the dayroom office, and with a deliberation born of studied repetition, postponed introductions beyond a brief exchange of names, and charged his latest entrant to follow him through the nervous atmosphere of the disturbed ward, which also doubled as a hospital admission ward. While the ricocheting clap of a metal gate, dividing the ward from a dormitory corridor, was locked behind them he would have strode, in the company of perhaps a couple of the staff, to the far end of the bleak, furniture-less, narrow corridor where the party briefly halted while locks were screwed open to reveal the stark tile and enamel of the washing and bathing facilities. One of the three members of staff would have reached down into the chipped, white, enamelled bath, inserted the bath-plug, swivelled the ageing, green-stained, copper taps and stood back as the forceful rush of water filled the bottom of the bath to a few inches before the tap was closed off. It seemed hardly enough to bathe in, but there were sound reasons for such apparent frugality, and the newcomer offered no complaint.

'Right, lad, we need you to take a bath so get undressed, dunk yourself in there, and give yourself a good scrub,' directed the bath filler. The newcomer would have shed his outer clothing down to his underpants and peered questioningly back at the bath filler. 'Yes, everything, come on, hurry up about it, we haven't got all bleeding day!' Underpants were duly drawn down. None of them made any effort to remove themselves, or look away in a concession of politeness, as he drew up his naked, pale body to the enamel side and swung his legs and privates over the cold lip and lowered himself into the shallow pool. 'Make sure you give that hair of yours a good clean, while you're at it.' A bar of soap was flung into the water and he made the best of the short time available to bathe and scrub his hair under the scrutinising beam of this company while verbal notes were made of his person.

'Two inch scar to upper left arm. How'd you get that scar?' one of them would have questioned.

'Got them in a fight last year. Some bloke nicked me with a blade.'

'Got them in a fight, *Mr. Williams*!' Williams, the enquiring nurse, would have insisted.

'Got them in a fight, Mr. Williams,' he replied, keen to oblige.

'Christ, you started early! Got any more distinguishing marks on your body?'

'No, I don't think so, Mr. Williams.'

'Well, let's have a look.' And that was partly the purpose of the shallow bath – to peruse the body for signs of infection, or bruising from previous physical abuse, or other singular marks of identification. The newcomer meekly rose to his feet, withstood the inspection, peered up for an acknowledgement, and lowered himself into the restricted waters. 'Nothing! Right, hurry up and finish.' The bather lathered himself as best he could with the material at his disposal, doused himself, scampered over the bath side, and dried with the worn towelling put aside for him.

'Now, put this on. Pyjamas aren't appropriate at the moment.' The lad dared not ask why this was the case and why his apportioned attire should have to be a sleeveless, canvas tunic, or what was to become of his clothes, so he yanked on the faded garment, the like of which he'd never clapped eyes on before. Mr. Williams, pointing to the dishevelled clothes strewn on the floor proclaimed 'Right, pick that lot up and follow me.' The arrival swept up his gear in a flurry, pinched his damp feet into his shoes and followed on until he was delivered to a side room where the ritual unlocking was repeated. 'Fold that lot up and put them down there,' said Mr. Williams, indicating a spot outside the door. Not needing to be invited, the newcomer stepped into the room containing but a floor mattress, pillow, sheet, reinforced canvas bedcover, and urinal. Pointing to the latter, Mr. Williams indicated 'There's your piss-pot. Now, get your head down. We don't want to hear a peep out of you, my lad. We'll keep an eye on you so you'll not be forgotten. Got that?'

'Yes. Mr. Williams. Can I have some supper, please, I haven't eaten since midday.'

'Hum. Didn't you eat before you left your unit? Supper's finished, here. I'll see if something can be rustled up but I'm not promising anything.' The lad was tempted to engage them further, to enquire whether he would be able to retain his belongings, why he didn't have room furniture, not even a chair or bed, what was the routine, and when could he meet the other residents? But he confined himself to one comment.

"Why am I sleeping on just a mattress, Mr. Williams?'

'Because you're here for observation. It's for safety purposes and you're an unknown quantity to us. We want to observe you and we also want to find out if you've got any contagious diseases. Can't have anything circulating around the place. You might have T.B. or some other nasty little disease. Might have "crabs"!' he declared, brashly, while enjoying the accompanying chuckles of his colleagues.

'But I was checked out in the secure unit and I haven't got no T.B or nothing, so far as I know. And I didn't have to do no "solitary"!' said the newcomer, optimistically.

'Solitary! Whatever gave you that idea? Look upon it as "isolation" until we're sure you're infection free! That make you feel any better? You'll get your meals brought to you and the staff will check you on a regular basis so if you need anything you can ask on their visit. Then, provided you behave yourself, you can join in normal association.' The recruit gathered enough resolve for one more enquiry.

'How long will I be in here, Mr. Williams?'

'Until we tell you otherwise!' interjected the previously silent one, the one in charge, who was now reaching for his key.

'Well, I mean, will it be a day, a couple of days, what?'

'As long as necessary, lad! All in good time. We'll get you out as soon as possible. Now, you just make yourself at home and get your head down.'

As I have said, the foregoing scene was an extrapolated account of a typical, patient admission to the hospital as reminisced by a colleague who had seen out his entire nursing career there as man and boy. His reminiscence was, I could presume, an informed one which I had absolutely no reason to doubt after having shared a sound acquaintance with him. It was an unrepentant account of a regularised adherence to what was, ostensibly, a protective isolation to combat any incubating contagious illness might have eluded an initial medical health examination. The "protective" became a euphemism for "protracted" isolation, by implication. For when I enquired of the length of this unquestioned, routinised "protective" isolation/seclusion the revelation was that it lasted "weeks". 'Weeks', I exclaimed! He returned my astonishment with a look of stoic insistence. 'Weeks,' he reiterated.

The information was imparted in the context of a more general exchange about the widespread use of seclusion in the hospital. After the time of which my colleague had spoken, and probably because of it, seclusion had become a legally sanctioned strategy within the field of mental disorder so that the confinement of a patient in a room, against his or her will, was predicated on the grounds that other people in the vicinity may need to be protected from them because of their manifest dangerousness. It functioned as an intervention of last resort when all other strategies had failed and, decidedly, did not come within the remit of medical treatment. It was supposed to be a short-term containment of a patient who might, otherwise, be causing some harm to others because of their deteriorating mental state, and should be terminated at the earliest opportunity following the patient's improvement. Although confined, alone, such a procedure was intended to be regularly and punctiliously supervised by an observer. Of course, what my informant was confiding by implication, but did not openly admit to, was an earlier rendition of the confinement process where the prevention of physical contagion – though laudable, in principle – was also a means of rationalising a disciplinary warning. So obvious was this, that I merely looked askance at my colleague without bothering to confirm my deduction that the procedure was a deliberate induction of the patient into their subordinate status. That it was meant to send out the message that this was the end of the road for them and that, for any seditious behaviour, there was the prospect of a separation from their immediate peers and loss of further privileges.

000

As a Nurse Manager I was charged with the dedicated remit of only two wards but it was expanded to cover the whole hospital during certain hours. During *shop-time*, a "Special Hospital" phrase denoting the nine-to-five working hours when the occupational workshops opened to equip selected patients with some artisan skills and productive occupation, my responsibility lay within my unit, alone. Outside of these hours I shared, on an intermittent basis, along with other managers, a responsibility for managing the entire hospital site and this would include the occasional night duty. It was during these unsocial hours that I came into contact with the majority of the hospital's secluded patients whom I was committed to visit as one of my explicit managerial tasks. In effect, on any particular shift, this would require that I commence a veritable round of ward visits for the purpose! Managerial overview was a requisite of the official seclusion procedure. It amounted to ensuring that, at a minimum, four-hourly interval, a manager would check on the situation: that the reason for the seclusion was appropriate; that the patient was being properly cared for, that any concerns about their condition or mental state, by either staff or patient, were aired; for listening to, and advising on, the rationale for any ongoing confinement; and that the staff rationale for continuing the isolation was valid. In many respects, this could have been viewed as a mere formality. After all, the staff in charge were trained in their occupation, qualified to an acceptable standard of nursing, entered onto a national register of expertise, and expected to exercise their professional judgement on matters clinical and organisational at ward level. In short, there would need to be some extraordinary grounds before a manager might question the actions of the ward staff. Furthermore, managers were only in the vicinity for a matter of minutes, much of the time, and simply had to trust that their staff were fulfilling their responsibilities to the patient. Nevertheless, most of the managers, as far as I understood, took the opportunity to look in upon the secluded patients and converse with them. This was acceptable to all, in principle, but you had better be careful about how you proceeded!

The bottom line, obviously, was to militate against any abuse of the procedure. As with any hospital, a manager would be accompanied to the room allocated for the purpose of seclusion by, at least, one of the permanent ward nurses. The seclusion room door would be unlocked by them while a visitor such as myself entered to speak with the patient, face to face. It was always my policy to walk into the room and approach the patient unless I had been given a warning brief by the staff that this would be inadvisable. The experience of having the staff standing behind you, in the doorway, listening while you made your enquires of the patient and heard their own explanation of events could be very discomforting indeed, especially if the accounts contradicted each other. There was always a concern about the repercussions for a patient who vehemently denied the nurses' story. If you found yourself suspecting that the staff had been "gilding the lily", somewhat, too much scrutiny might have the adverse effect of protracting the patient's seclusion. A forthright objection to the seclusion, on the manager's part, and the ordering of an immediate cessation of the procedure, might lead to the staff finding further grounds for re-secluding once the manager's back was turned! In so doing, it would then be claimed that the original seclusion was well-founded and that the manager's own intervention to terminate proved to be fallacious, thus undermining their credibility. This was a matter which all the managers were agreed on – challenging the decision was mightily awkward and potentially detrimental for all but the secluding staff especially if you actually released the patient. Then, there might also be the consequence of the incident being reported to the P.O.A. for further guaranteed admonishment.

One bleak weekend afternoon, in my capacity as a Duty Nurse Manager, I called on the male intensive care ward to monitor one of its patients who had been secluded earlier. It had become an expectation for me that the ward frequently secluded patients. This defied my past personal experience when, as a Charge Nurse of an intensive care ward, we rarely secluded patients and, then, only for overtly violent behaviour. The whole rationale about "intensive care" was that patients were designated to that area for brief periods of focused treatment of their particular disturbance and then returned to the area from which they had originated. Needless to say, the current operational objectives were to contain what were perceived as the chronically refractory class of patient. This was not the modern purpose of such a unit.

The patient, MacDonald, a young colloquial Glaswegian lad, had a disturbed history on the unit and was known to me for the reports of his episodic aggression. That said, I had always found him to be an articulate and humorous individual, with a guarded, distant feel about him, one who was consummately institutionalised, but I had warmed to him nonetheless. On the other hand, I had never taken to one of the permanent Charge Nurses, who happened to be on duty that afternoon, owing to his unabated, supercilious hostility toward me. There was no pleasure in dealing with this gentleman. On my arrival, without ceremony, Charge Nurse Walters immediately led me to MacDonald with two of his staff following behind as we cut across the dayroom.

'Afternoon, Mr. Burrows,' was the greeting from a consummately self-injurious Hennessey, a patient who generally made a point of approaching or calling out to me on most occasions that I visited. He reclined in an armchair against one of the walls, with his personal helmet at his side, without a hint of self-consciousness. He did not rise. He was often to be found wearing his helmet because of his regular propensity for episodes of fearsome head-banging. Looking at him, now, I noted his chronically deteriorating forehead and the gross indentation that years of smashing his head against objects had produced. The lips that he once had were now mere scar tissue, also the product of years of self-biting. He had gross visible wounds to his arms and hands which had also been sustained during his self-biting phases. In fact, he appeared on the ward report on nearly every day for one act of self-harm of another and was one of the most prolific self-harmers in the history of the hospital. I did not stop at this juncture and called across to him.

'Afternoon to you, Hennessey, I'll come and have a word, later.'

'Thank you, Mr. Burrows'. I turned to keep astride of Walters' pretentious ambling.

'Macdonald's on a "dirty protest",' was Walters' finite introduction to my reason for being called here. He unlocked the seclusion door, stood back, and revealed a totally naked MacDonald standing in a concerned posture against the far wall. The sole article in the room, other then himself, was the polythene covered mattress, bereft of sheet or canvas cover. As I roundly glared toward Walters, to the side of me, he narrowed his eyes as if to say 'and what are you going to do about that, then?' I knew I was now on the spot and would flounder to find a ready solution to this predicament.

'Well, Macdonald, what's up then?' I proffered, as cheerily as I could, while subduing the anxiety about my own, and the patient's, humiliation. For a young man, Macdonald was noticeably thin and ashen, with a tightly drawn face and prominent cheekbones. From such a frail skeleton issued a resonating voice.

'I don't feel very well, Mr. Burrows.'

'I see. Can you say any more about that to help me understand what's going on?' It was not so easy treading between concern for him and the palpable mantle of scepticism about me.

'Just don't feel well.' The dark frown around his round brown eyes was creased with anxiety. I looked at the walls about us to verify the staff claims. There were clear signs of hand-smeared faeces on the paintwork.

'Can you explain your reason for smearing the walls, then? I asked, hoping vainly for some explanation that might help get us somewhere.

'Don't know. I can't help myself when I'm angry.' Walters was silent but I fancied I could feel his presence sneering at my inquiries and implicit protestation.

'Why is he naked? Why is he not wearing something, if only a canvas?' I demanded.

'Because he's shitting himself, and his clothes, and the bed clothes. As soon as we bathe him and dress him, he dirties again. So, there's no point in giving him more clothes to mess up until he's more settled,' was the peremptory reply.

'Well he can't remain without clothes or a blanket and sheet, indefinitely. How long do you figure on keeping him like this?'

'When he's more settled, and he's not messing up, we'll give him back his stuff,' replied the unflappable Walters. I was in a spot. Did I dare countermand his decision in the face of this spectacle, this humiliation, this travesty, or did I let things run their course in the manner which the staff intended?

159

'Has anyone spent time with MacDonald trying to discover what's going on?' I posed, searching for a minimally therapeutic angle in this philistine atmosphere.

'Yes, we've tried all that, naturally. But he's threatened to smear us with shit, too.' Walters' voice was a symphony of sarcasm. I appealed to MacDonald and made my intentions as plain as I dared.

'Well, will you try and settle down and speak with the staff about what's bothering you. Will you do that for me?' as I took the risk of being paternal.

"Yes, Mr. Burrows."

'Be sure you do now. Is there anything else you want to say to me?' I leaned against one of the side walls, my hands deliberately, casually, lounging in my trousers, attempting to appear un-phased, looked as directly as I could at him and awaited whatever he wished to share.

'No,' was his truncated response. It was not feasible to tarry long, but I lingered to be as supportive as I could, and reluctantly I pushed away from the wall.

'Okay MacDonald, let's see you getting back into the dayroom, eh? I'm going to ring the ward later this afternoon to see if you're making any progress. It would be great to hear that you've just stopped smearing. How about that? Stop this smearing and I'm sure Mr. Walters, here, will let you out.' He nodded, unconvincingly, while I feared that I'd done little to help him. I could, of course, have asked to speak with him alone but that would be seditious. And what if he had decided to smear or assault me during the process? That would have been my just deserts in everyone's eyes. I retraced my steps into the corridor, almost belligerent as I swept past the staff in the doorway. 'OK, good luck then,' as the door was relocked.

'You haven't actually said he's remained violent since you placed him in seclusion.'

'That's because he's probably got what he wanted. He threatened that he wasn't able to control himself and didn't want to hurt anyone, particularly the staff, so could we put him in the box. He's done it before. He'll calm down in time.'

'Giving him what he wants, in this fashion, isn't solving anything. We're reinforcing all this disturbance without getting to the root of it all.'

'Better than the staff getting hurt or shat on,' he replied, quite un-phased as I returned a long chagrined look.

"Well, I hope it won't be long before he's back in some clothing, in the first place, then I would hope he'll come out soon after,' I stated vehemently. I wrestled with whether I should lay it on the line: 'Remember he shouldn't be in here if he's not a danger to others,' but who knew what that might have provoked?

'Of course,' was the apathetic agreement. I returned, briskly, to the dayroom intent that my body language communicated my disapproval of this scenario. On re-entering the dayroom, I approach Hennessey but my escort was in ambling attendance, hanging about the office doorway.

Hennessey had an unnerving persona (or should I admit to being somewhat unnerved!). Though a young man, in his early twenties, who exuded the most haunting and pathetic unhappiness, this did not capture the extent of the emotions he stimulated. His countenance was prematurely aged and drawn across a tight swollen face of a freckled pale hue. The narrow reddened eyes hinted at a lack of sleep as if wearied by a constant inner vigilance. He had death in his eyes: toward himself, toward others, perhaps everything; a self-rejection muddled with suspicion and hatred, perhaps an underlying suggestion that you should not encroach to close if you feared the consequences; eyes that were mean and inscrutable and defied empathy. There was no sense of being able to get in touch with this blighted life which sustained a daily ritual of self-hurting, seemingly, in a physical and mental attrition of his own body and mind, his very person, and mirroring the moribund relationship he had with a world to which he could not relate, and which failed to communicate with him. Words were expelled between his scarred and cadaverous lips as if they had never belonged to him and had no purpose, no destiny. And you felt consummately defeatist in that, despite anyone's attempts to modify his destructive lifestyle – which had been very considerable in one form or another – not much had changed. So why should any fleeting verbal exchange with myself make the slightest difference? Naturally, all this was as much my own projection of how I viewed him, as much as it accurately represented his own experience. Still, I was always mystified by his clamours for contact that intervened in a monotonous preoccupation with his own relentless oblivion. It could only be a travesty that when I came to look back on the content of those several brief exchanges I could only glean a semblance of them as if they had left but a memorial scar. How hopeless must the staff have felt!

'Do you live locally, Mr. Burrows?'

'I live not so very far but not locally, exactly, Hennessey.'

'You don't want to live too near the hospital,' he posed,

insightfully, and with a grin that tightened his already narrow eyes.

'You're dead right!'

'You need to get far away when you're off duty. Are you married?'

'I am.'

'How long have you been married?'

'Oooh! Now you have me, um, a year and a half, thereabouts.'

'Do you have any children?'

'Not yet.'

'Do you want to have children?'

'I do, very much.'

'You like children, then?'

'Umm, I wouldn't say I liked all children just because they're kids. No. Any more questions?' I added, appreciating his efforts but restlessly aware of the staff scrutiny.

'How many?'

'Pardon?'

'How many kids do you want?'

'Got me there,' I answered, truthfully. 'Two or three?'

'They'll be happy, Mr. Burrows.' Though the sentiment was amicable enough this had the flavour of a rote enquiry that he would proceed through with any newcomer. And the peculiarly forthright nature would have been just a little uncomfortable, perhaps, had I not realised that he was not only gaining some purchase on who I was, and the context of my life outside the hospital, this ward, but of an outside world that he could only experience vicariously.

'Why, thank you, Hennessey.'

'That's all right, Mr. Burrows. Thanks for stopping by.' Then he looked away and his voice wound down like a receding spring, seemingly deprived of further volition beyond a brief encounter, and he laid his head into the headrest of his chair either to muse upon what small scenes he'd just gleaned of the outside world, or just to shut down for a while on his long journey to nowhere.

000

Broadmoor had not gone unscathed during the time I had been away since my orientation visit. The year 1988 proved a difficult one for the old criminal lunatic repository. One of its patients, a black African-Caribbean by the name of Joseph Watts, died in the hospital in similar circumstances to another African-Caribbean named Michael

Martin, four years earlier. Both patients had died in seclusion. Both patients had been restrained by numbers of nursing staff and administered high doses of medication which were given via enforced injections. Joseph Watts had been involved in a violent altercation with another ward patient and was escorted by the nursing staff to a seclusion room. During the ensuing period of seclusion he had further contacts with nursing staff where, on at least two separate occasions, up to ten staff members restrained him. He was stripped of his clothes and administered a substantial quantity of medication – 200mgs chlorpromazine which was four times the recommended dosage. At Joseph Watts' inquest a verdict of "accidental death" was recorded as a result of cardiac failure associated with the administration of phenothiazine drugs.

In 1991, yet another African Caribbean male patient died after being secluded at Broadmoor Hospital. The patient, Orville Blackwood, had attempted to strike a male psychiatrist who had commenced interviewing him after he had been displaying signs of being unsettled, restlessness and non-compliance with his treatment programme . After having been restrained and secluded he had been administered a different chemical cocktail of anti-psychotics, this time Sparine and Modecate, which was considered in some circles to be an uncommon practice. Again, the inquest returned a verdict of "accidental death". This inquiry, which linked all three deaths, was deliberately subtitled "Big, Black and Dangerous?" because of the authors' belief that there existed a widely held misconception that this was how health staff characterised African-Caribbean offender patients.

So contentious had the seclusion issue become in the "Special Hospitals" that it became the subject of a research study by a nurse researcher at Ashworth Hospital. Tom Mason, the researcher, actually used the study as a basis for a Doctorate. His findings confirmed that the use of seclusion by "Special Hospitals" was a "cultural practice", that it was generally over-prescribed, and was sanctioned to maintain control over the patients, rather than being positively utilised for their care. The disproportionate usage in the management of female patients was especially problematic he posited.

000

'Steve, how do you feel about being a co-therapist in an arson group?' This surprising, but welcome request, was launched by

163

Heinrich who had become a bit of an authority on the management of patients with a history of setting fires as part of their psychological problems. He had published papers on the issue and put together a therapeutic package which he intended to implement at the hospital. Unsurprisingly, we had a number of clients whose histories included a fire-setting criminality. Truth was that I was as keen to continue setting the therapeutic agenda to my nursing staff, as actively participating in the venture. 'I've drawn up a provisional list of likely candidates and allocated some space at the social rehabilitation department. All I need is someone to convene with me. How about it?' I was delighted at the prospect of further clinical work and for being valued for having something to offer – neither of which I had had much cause to celebrate during my high security experience, to date. I accepted without reservation even though I had no explicit experience in work with people of a fire-setting propensity. But therapeutic skills, and motivation, are readily built upon and infinitely transferable commodities and my inclinations were toward clinical work which, as far as I was concerned, did not in any way compromise my managerial role.

'It's a done deal, Heinrich. When do we start?'

'Good man. We start in a couple of weeks. As you know, there is some more industrial action in the offing so I'll probably require your cooperation to help escort the patients to the rehab unit as well. OK with you?'

'I'm your man!' I replied with some exhilaration. For some months now, I had spent a fairly unproductive time attempting to engage the staff in devising bespoke nursing diagnoses, and treatments, for individual patients without notable change. And as time had passed, my attitude toward what I conceived as their entrenched traditionalism had become hardened and was fast approaching an uncompromising intransigence of my own making.

In preparation of our inaugural meeting a couple of weeks later I presented myself to the admission adolescent ward in time to collect the arson group members. One or two of the very brightest lads immediately asked if I had come for that very group, which I confirmed. Was I taking them, myself, because the staff were on industrial action? I confirmed this, too. Without delay they turned away and their voices rose above the general cacophony in an amused and sarcastic cry.

'Arsonists! Arsonists! Line up! Mr. Burrows is here to take you to your arson group!'

I didn't even need to present myself to the staff on duty since they were now pursuing a third spate of industrial action – within two years of the start of my high security service – and, as anticipated, were refusing to provide an escort for the patient group. Around the ward the derisive rallying cries continued like a chain reaction echoing around a county courtroom: 'Arsonists! Arsonists!' Accordingly, I waited for the "arsonists" with the intention of linking up with Heinrich who was duly collecting the other arson members from the adjoining continuing care ward. If he and I had declined the task then the start of the group would not be happening. I noted the staff talking with one another in the dayroom and office but not approaching me. Sheepishly, the arsonists duly presented themselves at the dayroom gate and I accompanied them along the corridor and out of the unit. Heinrich and I joined forces, informing security at the gate lodge, via my two-way personal radio, of the prospective journey of our group movement of patients and two members of staff to the rehab centre, on foot. And we proceeded. Now we had to rely on the cooperation of the lads, themselves, for if anyone attempted an escape, the pair of us would be hauled over for our presumptuousness at taking on this task without the usual nursing escort. This was no minor achievement as the usual mode of transporting patients was via the use of a hospital coach. Our rebellious act was to walk them out of one compound, across a middle one, and through to a third, where lay the venue within the Rehabilitation Centre. And back again. The two journeys – repeated on subsequent dates – were not accomplished without a modicum of reasonable apprehension of the deleterious consequences if we should have read this wrongly. But confident that we had a great deal to prove while in this predicament we were not disappointed by our patients, who did not deviate from the objective, and we negotiated the several thousand metres, uneventfully.

Heinrich's programme sprung from his conviction that no treatment was being provided for the socially unskilled patients whose history – and index offences – included arson, and that they required to be confronted about their resorting to such dangerous solutions to the problems that life threw up for them. His programme, as it unravelled, revealed an important therapeutic principle which I was to incorporate into all of my own future therapeutic practice. This was to communicate to the members of a therapy group an appreciation that their deviant behaviour, at one level, was an extreme variant of conventional interests and that the therapeutic goal was, in some respect, to enable them to attain that level of appropriate participation in that activity without resorting to a level of risk and dangerousness. Most people were excited by fires and incendiary events, and practices, constituted a sizable part of everyone's interests. So we opened with the diverse ways in which normal society invoked and utilised "fire": firework displays and annual bonfire nights; garden bonfires, refuse fires, camp fires; how people marvelled at forest and brushwood fires sparked by heatwaves; how the Armed Forces utilised bombs, flamethrowers and incendiary devices for military advantage; self-immolation as a political gesture; and how fire was used in a religious Christian context to reflect God's punishment, and to threaten the prospect of Hellfire for unrepentant sinners; etc. The message was that we were all surrounded by fire related phenomena, that interest in these was rational and normal, and that our participants' involvement had some understandable derivations for deviating from this which could be explored and improved upon. However, it was then essential to convey to the group that their own use of fire-setting was not just a pathological exaggeration of normal fire-setting interest. Therapeutic optimism was based on the principle that, as in the case of the "empathy group", this was a problem-solving venture. In tracing the personal histories of these people their fire-setting was motivated by their personal and social ineffectiveness which precluded their ability to bring satisfactory changes to their lives so that, once a particularly triggering event stimulated them, they resorted to setting light to buildings and the like to register their anger and attempt to bring some advantage to bear on their circumstances. The problem-solving extended to the prospect that each of them could gain some insight into their peculiar aberrations, that their predilections were redeemable, and that they would be afforded the chance to adopt less problematic strategies to manage their life problems without resorting to fire-setting solutions. On the principle that the fire-setting was a way of solving everyday difficulties because our lads lacked the general social skills enjoyed by the majority of other people to solve them in more conventional ways, the aim was to enlarge their general social skills repertoire, and inter-personal assertiveness. To effect this, one of the major therapeutic techniques was to confront their behaviour in a supportive manner which encouraged their self exploration. There had to be a therapeutic optimism for change!

000

Of course, this therapeutic emphasis had muddied the traditionally crystal clarity of the hospital waters. There was an understandable disjunction for nursing staff who had relied, heavily until now, on a distorted brand of behaviour modification which only rewarded an institutionally stereotyped conformity, rather than encouraging behaviour considered to be positively adaptive *in relation to their individual psychological problems.* As described earlier, the institutionally established method for encouraging patient change was somewhat one-dimensional – the twelve-stage "rewards" system. This attempted to motivate favourable behaviour, un-blighted by any deviance, by moving the client onto a higher level of purchasing power and their selection of goods and items of their choosing. Money never changed hands during a process which merely translated monetary values into "virtual" purchasing power. Conversely, behaviour deemed to be undesirable and maladaptive was reflected in a demotion to a lower purchasing stage. Perversely, the reward system had failed to link individually desirable criteria to advance each patient's personal development but had been converted to a pragmatic tool for promoting universally unproblematic conduct. In plain terms, the rewards system was a euphemism for potential punishment. You did not have to be a therapeutic purist to comprehend a practice which aimed at a socially conforming baseline appropriate to an institutional climate rather than one that was instrumental in tutoring each patient toward an individually adaptive development. Having said that, there could be no avoiding the need for some generally approved behavioural standards in order to maintain safety and order within an institutional context to avoid the associated repercussions from neglecting to monitor the deviant propensities of each individual resident, plus the more remote possibility of their concerted uprisings as a body. The trouble was that the two competing sets of dynamics were fudged by an incorporation into the one corrective, essentially non-therapeutic, system.

It had also to be borne in mind that the nursing staff had been traditionally trained in the field of what was called "mental handicap", or what became "learning disability". However, the more contemporary intake of hospital patients had been increasingly comprised of patients with diagnoses of "mental illness" and "psychopathy" for which, arguably, they were not professionally prepared. With a view to assisting them to make this adjustment I had produced an assessment schedule which was to help them to take account of a range of relevant indicators, highlighting individuals' mental state, which would apply to these new patient categories. For some of the staff this appeared to be very welcome and I had the schedule produced in the form of an assessment document for use on the adolescent unit.

A subsequent initiative was to approach the Director of Nurse Education about this shortfall in training for the nursing staff who now had to manage new classes of patients. Between the two of us, we agreed to develop an introductory course which would equip our staff with incremental knowledge to manage patients with mental illness and psychopathy. I had not the slightest doubt that effecting this continuing education package to enhance the competencies of my staff was a necessary part of my managerial remit but it should have been an explicit requirement for staff across the hospital and instituted long before I had proposed it.

000

'I'll tell you what,' said Hal, reintroducing the subject of why a huge tranche of nurses, including himself, had been reported to nursing's professional bodies for a second instance of industrial action and accusations of "unprofessional conduct". 'There's nothing those bodies can do to us – we're too important.' As one of the Charge Nurses I'd acquired via my staff movements, who had proven to be very responsive to my aims on the unit, I was more than prepared to hear his soundings on the matter.

'The false imprisonment of patients has added a new dimension to industrial action, don't you think, Hal?' I countered, refraining from an outright condemnation. 'That's unprecedented as far as I'm aware. Maybe I'm wrong.'

'No, no, you're right I'm sure. It may be the first time that's happened but it don't mean we're going to be blown out of the water. Look at the numbers involved – not a handful, not dozens, but hundreds, and I'll tell you what – they couldn't afford to get rid of us. If they dared to strike us all from the Register who's going to run this place without the nursing staff? They'll not get the police in, they couldn't transfer the patients, they can't close the place, they're stuck with us, pure and simple.' A garrulous, gregarious individual whose lower teeth protruded a little further than the upper set, creating a slight whistling accompaniment to his conversation, Hal had a view on most subjects. And he was no fool, either. He fingered his slipping, smudged spectacles, yet again, prodding them further up his nose as was his characteristic wont. 'You see, we're different from the rest of the Health Service. Nobody else wants these patients once they've been disposed of here. Their own Health Authorities won't have them back if they can help it. They'd sooner pay up and have 'em stay here. The Home Office would be forced to disperse the patients among all the bloody prisons in the country and, I'll tell you what, they sure as hell aren't about to do that! "Special Hospitals" are here to stay, for all their faults. What's more, "Special Hospitals" represent the end of the road for these patients. They can't get any lower, see!'

'Still doesn't mean you have carte blanche to do as, and when, you like with them,' I replied, contradictorily.

'No, true, but I'll tell you another thing. They won't get rid of Special Hospital staff, unprofessional conduct, or otherwise, because, at the end of the day my friend, the "Special Hospitals" – God bless all who sail in her – are *political*! Ultimately, this has nothing whatsoever to do with humanitarianism, therapy or mental health care; this is all about politics!'

For me, meanwhile, the perplexing sense of working in an industrial relations climate of the order of a heavy industry, or heavy manufacturing, or the docklands, and which was completely at odds with the public purposes and professional ideals with which it was charged to carry out, was now engrained into my psyche.

000

It was abysmally easy to break the customary code operating within the hospital and I managed to do so on a fairly regular basis. A number of indicative events soon served to illustrate how out of sync were my own proclivities with that of the local climate, none of which I regretted. I had become increasingly frustrated by the formality of patient contact and the apparent incursion that you were made to feel by talking with them on a free and informal basis. On arrival at a ward, and within the confinement of the staff office, the visitor – even a Nurse Manager such as myself – was allowed a sieved, verbal update on the residents from the nurse in charge before a mutual indulging of one another's latest contemplations on the state of the hospital and other gossip-strewn distractions. You were not expected to truncate these in preference for making a personal acquaintance, relationship, or assessment of patients, so I conjured every opportunity to protract my stay and invite a personal contact with them. This did not conform to custom and was never a comfortable exercise. The patients felt scrutinised by the staff while I did so, and I most certainly was distrusted by the staff for taking leave of protocol.

A graduated defiance of etiquette predisposed me to lapses on other units so that, on one occasion, it precipitated a rounded admonishment. Appearing on one of the ward dayrooms outside of my own unit, in my capacity as a Duty Manager, I had tarried to converse with a patient who had engaged me in a snap conversation. On then proceeding to the ward office, the office door was closed behind me and I was treated to the Charge Nurse's vociferous disapproval for not, in the first instance, having reported to him immediately I had arrived, as was the customary expectation. I was further admonished for speaking with a patient without seeking the permission of the staff, first! This convention was rationalised on the grounds that the patient may have been unstable, psychotic, and conceivably dangerous and he, personally, would have had to pick up the pieces if I had sustained an assault. There was merit in this, to a point, but, as I argued at the time, I would have wanted to know why such a patient exhibiting such a potential risk was not being closely monitored by an accompanying staff member rather than be left unsupervised? Otherwise, he or she could not have been causing that much concern to have been left to wander freely. I interpreted the whole scenario more as an indicator of the nursing staff's mantle of absolute control of ward proceedings, of the possibility that the patient might confide a complaint to me, and their perception that I represented an unwelcome external interference.

Similarly, I baulked at the formalised address system which so distanced the staff from the patients in the manner of the prison service. The nomenclature was limited to surnames, only, with the staff distinguished by adding the prefix of Mr., Mrs., or Miss according to marital status. Never did I hear patients, even our youngsters, being referred to by first names. With time I indulged myself in breaking this taboo and, by the by, refused to reprimand any patient who chose to call me by my own. In this respect, breaking the code was a risky business for the patients but once the bolder opinion leaders, such as Baird and Caldicott, had tested the water the way was cleared for others to venture forward. I was excited by their show of resilience since it must have brought some pressure upon them. However, as more patients adopted the informality there was not much the nursing staff could do if the manager was promoting the matter.

Then there was the situation when I had learned that a patient of my acquaintance, whom I had encountered at the previous medium secure unit at which I had been employed, had been transferred back into high security. He resided on a ward outside of my own managerial jurisdiction but, thinking nothing of this, I determined to visit him to discover the reasons for his return. I duly presented myself to the ward, explained my purpose, and was permitted a closed session with him, alone. He and I had enjoyed a good rapport at the medium secure unit and we took up, again, with some ease. His could offer no sound explanation for being returned to the high security establishment but was aware of the detrimental impact this would have on his future prospects of rehabilitation. To have sustained a failed transfer to a lower level of security was, effectively, worse than if he had not had that opportunity offered him at all. I had to agree that his return was a surprise to me despite having been party to discussions with the female staff of that unit who had voiced concerns about the guarded and enigmatic manner in which he conducted himself when in their presence. It was true to say that he perturbed them. These concerns, which were not replicated by male staff members, may have been largely intuitive but we had all taken them seriously. I promised, nevertheless, to keep in touch and departed only to be hauled before one of my senior managers, a day or so later, following a complaint about having stepped beyond my area of jurisdiction without due cause. I had contravened another manager's jurisdiction without his permission. Protestations of ignorance, on my part, about the necessity to do so were accompanied by an enquiry about the source of this complaint. It turned out to be the Unit Manager of that unit, an individual with whom I shared the same suite of offices and with whom I had a very reasonable relationship, but who had not had the assertiveness to broach the subject with me personally. It was the way things were done, I supposed.

A further situation was perhaps the most illuminative in terms of where I was determinedly now heading. It was probably during the third episode of industrial dispute, in the two years of my managerial stay, that the refusal to collect the hospital waste started to have effect. One minor repercussion was that a considerable proportion of rubbish, undoubtedly ejected from the patients' windows, had accumulated within the confined exercise areas of my adolescent admissions unit. Approaching my ward staff about what was to be done I learned that they would not concede any ground taken by ancillary staff who were exercising their "work-to-rule" rights. In short, they would not be clearing up the rubbish. For my part, not being a member of any striking body and having no justification, therefore, for supporting the deterioration about me, I insisted that I would clear up the rubbish myself and would engage the services of a couple of the young residents who were prepared to assist me. The staff didn't have time to contact the P.O.A. before I had called out, in the dayroom, for two helpers for the task. Volunteers abounded and I selected one or two with whom I enjoyed a particularly good rapport, including the audacious Caldicott. And by now, I was aware that Caldicott was an opinion leader to the lads on the unit – a valuable ally. But they would also need to be trustworthy of me since I was prepared to proceed into the exercise yard without the customary two-way radio which normally accompanied any patient-movement! Since I was not operating as a hospital-wide Duty Manager that day I, too, did not have a radio on my person. The ward radio was expected to reside on the ward itself and would not be offered to me. This was sacrosanct to the safety of the staff at all times. But I did not want it. I unlocked a side door and, with both lads in tow, ventured outside of the building to the muttering strains of the staff who warned about the inherent risks. I would have to admit that that was a nervous time. I was not only breaking one of the unbroken hospital conventions, but the P.O.A. would be informed, and it would be brought to the attention of higher managers, and to the security department, for certain. And there were potential risks. But no one realised this more than my assistants who had probably never been anywhere without an accompanying radio, who anticipated the flack that I would receive, and anticipated the flack for their own defiance. They confounded the staff predictions by acting impeccably. It was an act that I was determined to fulfil whatever the consequences, hopefully, even to provoke discussion about the need for the reasonable flexing of rules. The most favourable outcome of the deed was that it perpetuated my good relations with the unit adolescents from both wards and, by this time, I valued this as much as anything. The act also triggered a telephone call from the Chairman of the hospital P.O.A. who, in a surprisingly conciliatory fashion, warned me of the dangers of compromising the hospital's security arrangements and breaking the terms of a legitimate industrial dispute. Other dangers were not spelt out.

I would venture to say that such examples of petty grievance and scrupulous observance of rules should not have been expected in a contemporary mental health environment, but that there had to be rational grounds for their expression. In a closed environment which was so dictated by policy and instruction – from the Department of Health remit for the hospital, via the hospital management policies, and the guidance from the Prison Officers Association – allied to the relative absence of therapeutic endeavour, there was very little room for more personal initiative, democratic decision-making, or tolerance of change, which might facilitate staff initiative and self-validation. What amounted to an "aggravated territorialism" had to have its roots in the tenacious need to control what slim opportunities for initiative of which they could avail themselves. Indeed, anybody with knowledge of the past history of the County mental hospitals would have been familiar with the predicament. But that was the past and this current situation had to say more about the collective insecurity and paranoia that was ingrained into the psychological fabric of the hospital staff and which was undoubtedly contributed to by the regular reports of assaults on staff by patients. There were also the abiding mythologies that haunted the establishment. If the Carstairs incident served as the most prolific of these, then this establishment could certainly lay claim to its own. In the not so distant past, one of the current Ward Sisters had sustained a life-threatening assault by a female patient in her charge and despite the Sister being able to return to work, it caused irreparable injury to all staff-patient associations. Yet another, universally publicised catastrophe, had lived on in the collective annals though.

Of its singularly infamous clients no one was more renowned than one who went by the name of Patrick Mackay. As with the youthful Graham Young from Broadmoor he had acquired a seriously disturbed teenage history. Having set fires to a pet tortoise and a Catholic church, robbing local residents, attempting to strangle his mother and aunt, and attempting to kill a younger boy, he was admitted to this hospital at the age of fifteen and diagnosed as a psychopath (the admission criteria could include this category). Discharged in 1972, Mackay was befriended by a Catholic priest who paid a high price for doing so. In 1975, Father Crean was so severely battered by Mackay that his brain was exposed and he died as a consequence. Mackay was aged twenty-two years. As yet another serial killer, he was convicted of three murders, but confessed to the murder of eleven, mostly elderly victims. Again, like Young, his behaviour had fatal consequences for the general public. His trial yielded a life sentence and the remainder of his years have been spent in prison.

000

In my efforts to conjure a therapeutic nursing team appropriate to visiting the rehabilitation requirements of a younger client group I reluctantly accepted the advice of my line manager to have the obtuse Charge Nurse Walters transferred to my unit. My line manager had previously revealed his thoughtful insights into the man and believed that I had underestimated his potential. I had not rated my superior as a particularly insightful fellow, not least, because at some point during most conversations he managed to distract himself with fatuous references to Liverpool Football Club of which he was a perennial season ticket holder. I thought it propitious, in light of his seniority and past help in transferring other staff, to accept the recommendation while reserving the aspiration that Walters would not wish to take up the offer. This idea was misplaced and he commenced what I, nevertheless, presumed would be a fairly short sojourn. He came onto the unit, played a very reserved game indeed, in my company, and offered no obvious clues as to how he felt about his move. However, the pugnacious glint of his eyes provided sufficient evidence that he was not here for my benefit.

Thereabouts, I started to observe some not so subtle changes in my relations with the nursing staff. When I had commenced my position at the hospital I had volunteered to represent the hospital football team which would also help me to integrate into the fraternity. Accordingly, most weekends, I played alongside other staff and it was my firm belief that this lowered the barriers to being considered an outsider. As the most current game approached, I was advised to turn up at an appointed venue, at a prescribed time, to meet prior to travelling for an away game. Which I duly did, only to find that everyone else had departed. Having no idea of the precise location of the match, only the general area, I determined to rush to the appropriate village in order to show my commitment and, in the hope that a genuine mistake had been made concerning the arrangements. It was a wet morning and the road surface unforgiving for a hasty, lost driver and, en route, I ploughed my car into the back of two which had preceded me over the brow of a bridge, damaging all three. Having later arrived at the hospital for duty I was sent home to recuperate.

On my return to work, I recall recounting the tale to many a member of staff, that day, as I moved about the hospital and did so, once again, before Charge Nurse Walters and one of the staff closely aligned to him, on my appearance at the adolescent unit. When I reached the point of careering into two other drivers and disengaging my car from the one into which I had directly smashed, the two of them burst into spontaneous, raucous and sarcastic laughter which would have been difficult to fathom but for its audaciousness. Subsequent events put it into perspective! To begin with, no explanation was forthcoming from other team members as to the incongruent pre-match arrangements. Then the realisation dawned that the staff were far more hesitant in their responses to me and that I had to put direct questions to them before I received any verbal contact. Neither was I invited to partake of the customary cup of tea when I arrived to fulfill my managerial duties. A few days of this repeated scenario disconcerted me no end.

000

My position was deteriorating, and my motivation was lapsing in all but my dealings with the unit patients and the colleagues from the non-nursing professions with whom I enjoyed sound relations. A few of the patients now openly addressed me by my first name and confided various snippets of information. The kindly affirmations of the residents of the continuing care unit were particularly affecting because of what might be expected as their more limited capacity for emotional expression. Young Billy Baird made a special effort to express himself. On one momentous day, he came alongside me, inclined his head close, hushed and confiding. The proximity quite took me by surprise, briefly.

'Steve, watch yer back! The staff are out to get you!'

'What!'

'Yeah, watch your back, I'm telling you. Be careful of the staff. I can't stop, but I wanted to warn you.' And with that he scuttled off to blend in around the snooker table.

000

I began to share my misgivings with the other members of my clinical team and the detrimental impact it was having on my spirits and motivation. Something, I declared, was definitely amiss! Julian was the first to proffer an opinion.

'I didn't want to mention anything to you, Steve, but it would seem that the staff are adopting a discreetly hostile response to you. I didn't want to worry you but since it's become clear…'

'Some form of discreetly hostile response! Whatever do you

mean?' I interrupted, anxiously.

'Well, the background, I suppose, is that there has been a long-running personality clash between you and them and, with all the staff movements you've effected, they're all feeling that they could be next to be moved off the unit. There's considerable insecurity among them.' His ambivalent smile suggested that a dark lining of rebuke lay around what was, ostensibly, a sympathetic disposition. Heinrich leaped in emphatically.

'I don't think that's a bad thing, personally. It's good for them to have to earn their place on the unit. You're keeping them on their toes, Steve, and I support you in filtering out the dead wood. I think that will attract the better staff from the remainder of the hospital. Besides, I think you've tried to bring in some really important innovations and you've been a good role model for patient care, I do really. And, in my estimation, it's been a difficult ride for you.'

'All very well but, when you're replacing staff, better the Devil you know and all that,' replied Julian, less ambivalent, now.

'But you've agreed to all my staff movements, to date, surely, Julian?'

'To a point, Steve, to a point. I would probably argue, if anything, that you've been a little too enthusiastic. A little heavy-handed, maybe? In one instance, I'd dare suggest that you moved off the most intelligent member of staff amongst the two wards.'

'But I have to say, in my defence, Julian, and I know to whom you refer, that he was a damned difficult bloke to work with.'

'But at least he had a brain, some potential that we could work with!' Julian replied with unconcealed exasperation. A protracted pause followed. 'Now I'm concerned that the staff could become very obstructive to all our work.'

'Well, won't that make a change?' I retorted, disdainfully, gradually suspecting that I was not to receive the support I currently required from the team. 'In any case, that cannot apply to those who I'm very satisfied with. And they'll know who they are. Do you get a sense that anything's going down, then?'

'Well, yes, don't you?' Julian replied, more enigmatically.

'Don't you worry, Steve. You have our support,' said the indefatigable Heinrich.

'Appreciated, Heinrich. What, exactly is going down do you think?' I enquired, but looking to all of them, in turn.

'Haven't you noticed anything yourself, Steve?' interposed Dr. Cook.

'I have certainly noticed a change in the staff attitudes toward me, yes. A lot more reticent, I'd say.'

'Maybe you need to consider the impact this might have on your personal mental health,' Dr. Cook continued in the most conciliatory manner.

'On my mental health? What *do* you mean?'

'Didn't you know, Steve? The nursing staff have "sent you to Coventry".'

000

This was not an unprecedented event, nor was the element of reprisal a stranger to the place. We were all similarly aware of a handful of professional staff who were entrenched in their own personality clashes with staff. And as I was to learn from Hal, one of my Charge Nurses who had had proven himself to be rather a good mate toward me – a commodity in fairly short supply at ward level, at least – there had been a past precedent of a senior member of staff being ritually ostracised. He had been a psychologist. It would appear that the psychologists, above all others, were the one professional group which was more prepared to object to the prevailing hospital culture.

'Hal, could you spare me a minute or two in private? I'd appreciate it.'

'Be my guest, Steve.' He invited me into the ward office and appreciated the sensitivity of closing the door.

'Now I hope I'm not compromising your position but am I right in assuming that the staff have sent me to Coventry?'

'You're not compromising me in the least, me old mate, but there's no use in denying it. And I'm sorry, I really am, but you have been.' With the sensitivity with which this was offered, I could feel the sentimentality rising to choke off my efforts to speak and I dared not try to do so for a few struggling seconds. 'It's a crying shame because I think you've been bloody good for this unit and I support what you've tried to do, but you've definitely rubbed some peoples' backs up.'

'What's the score then?'

'Well, they're going to give you the cold-shoulder. It's not how I feel and I'm not going to support it, neither, but you'd better consider your options. Such a shame 'cos, I'll tell you what, you never had much of a chance from the beginning in my opinion. And you couldn't have made a better start when you arrived. Playing for the football team – that was a smart move. Nothing better for getting yourself accepted. What happened to that, by the way, 'cos you dropped out by all accounts?'

'Oh, one or two of the team decided to play "silly buggers" by misinforming me about a pre-match arrangement so that I missed a match. Then the replacement manager, you know, that State Enrolled Nurse, came into the job and decided to drop me to reserve for half a match. Well, we were losing at half-time so he brought me on and we won. Anyway, I decided they could stick it, frankly. I think, since I was a manager and an outsider, people were putting me in my place. That's how I read it, anyway.'

'I know what you mean and I reckon you've got that about right. They can be funny buggers, this lot. Anyway, joining the soccer team showed you were prepared to get stuck in and get yourself accepted. It was always going to be hard going in your position. Listen, don't feel too bad about it. It's our loss.'

'That's kind of you. So, what do I do about it in your opinion? Have things gone too far do you think?'

'I honestly can't tell you! Not that all of us agree with it, by any means, if that means anything to you like. And perhaps you don't know but this is not the first time this has happened. Not that I'm equating you with this other guy. But not so very long ago, we had a psychologist here – very elevated position within the hospital – who took it upon himself to slag off nearly everything the nursing staff did. But he did it in a published article in a highly influential organisation which came to the attention of the staff, needless to say. I mean, I ask you? Well, the reaction wasn't surprising – the nursing staff refused to have any working contact with him, or any personal relationship. He was a leper as far as we were concerned.'

'Did you agree with that?'

'Afraid I did, 'cos he wasn't one of us, was he? All very well slagging off his own kind but what right did he have to drag us through the mud. He didn't have the right to do that. That's why I don't feel the same way about you. At least you've got your hands dirty and tried to show the staff where we should be headed – and you're right. I know that. Things are going to have to change around here whether we like it or not.'

'So, going back to the psychologist, what was the outcome?'

'Well, I'll tell you what, he certainly got his comeuppance. The situation deteriorated so badly, he had his car damaged, he got loads of abusive mail, threatening phone calls, and the like, and needed a personal escort at times. Needless to say, he had to leave pretty sharpish like!' Hal really didn't know whether to break into a smile or preserve his sensitivity toward my own predicament. God bless him!

000

On a subsequent day Billy Baird approached again, presumably a little more emboldened since he took no very great care to conceal his intentions this time.

'Steve, is it true – you're leaving? The staff have told us, you know. They're bloody pleased, but we're not.'

'It's a shame they're pleased but, yes, I'm leaving shortly.'

'It's true, then!'

'Afraid so, young man.'

'They've been giving you a hard time, haven't they? I warned you they would, didn't I? We've seen it when you speak up for us. *And* they talk openly all the time about you going. They don't mind if we hear, like!'

'Hum! Well, I'll be out of here in a couple of weeks so you'll not hear much more.'

'You know, Steve, I'm really going to miss you. We all will, honest! Can't you change your mind? You're a decent bloke! Who's going to take your place when you've gone? Who's going to do the Community Group?'

'That I don't know. I'm sure Julian will manage the group on his own, if he has too.'

'Are you leaving the hospital for good, like?'

'No, actually I'll be joining the teaching staff.'

'What, you're going to be teaching us?'

'No, sorry, Billy. I mean the staff training centre – teaching the staff.' His face crumpled with disdain.

With a luscious sneer he said, 'You'll have your work cut out there. What the hell do you want to be doing with staff? It's us as needs yer!' And wasn't he so right! What the hell was I doing going into staff teaching when I should have been building on this contact? Billy sloped off, much disgruntled.

'Bloody Hell! It's not right you know!'

000

And there I was, daily approaching the establishment with diminishing resolve, and parking the car, while agitating about how I was to survive now that I did not have the support of many of my immediate staff. The isolation was becoming unbearable. And these agitations were supplemented with a fervent, prayerful invocation of spiritual succour! This invocation was not so desperate an aberration as it might have appeared at first sight for, at the time, I was a committed Christian attending a Community Church in the Southport area and the strategy seemed appropriate enough for the circumstances. I was looking for any support, grounded or ethereal, that I could muster to get me through this mire! When I had become so burdened by my conflicting role I resigned myself to approaching the Director of Nursing and asked for a change in position to extricate myself from what was becoming an intolerable psychological withdrawal. It was to be to my inordinate advantage, as events would turn out, that I had already established a fruitful connection with the Director of Nurse Education – a charismatic, mentally and physically sprightly sage, with an Ordination in the Church of England, to boot – for this facilitated the next stage of my career. In the belief that it would be to my own benefit, and to that of the organisation, if I was to pursue my industry within a teaching capacity, my imminent request to be transferred into teaching was accepted by both parties, unreservedly. Within the remaining time as a manager I indulged my contact with the patients as best I could. They, meanwhile, had learned of my imminent departure. On the day I left, Billy Baird sidled up to me in full view of the staff and announced that the patients had something for me.

'It's not much, Steve, but we wanted you to have something to remember us by. We did it between us, like.' A small smiling band had gathered around me and I choked back my rising emotions. Unceremoniously, he handed over a coarsely cut cardboard sheet which had been roughly folded in the middle and which was presented with no envelope. The outside was a sophisticated scholarly scene in a pictorial gloss. Opening it, I found the written scrawls of many of the residents alongside the accompanying comments of their well-wishing. I have never discarded that precious relic.

000

'Steve.' I was being called over by Dave Caldicott having offered my farewells to the residents of the admission unit, also. No sentimentality here! He had seated himself unobtrusively by the exit to the dayroom and it became clear that this was purposeful as I prepared to leave. He beckoned me over with an inclining nod.

'Yes, Dave? Don't tell me, you're handing me a leaving card just like next door?'

'On yer bike, what do you take us for, a bunch of sissies!'

'So you're giving me nothing. That's OK, I'll manage,' I continued, teasing. His attitude altered and he frowned, mischievously.

'Thought you'd like to know something.'

'What's that, then?' expecting some aggrandising flourish for my benefit.

'The Sean affair.' He watched me intently as I drew myself up in anticipation of what must surely be a revelation – for what else could it be?'

'The Sean Walton affair?' I replied, without any guardedness for the time for caring had now passed..

'It did happen. Happened as we said.' He waited upon me.

'Not much I can do now, old son.'

'Well, at least you know. That's all I'm going to say.' And he slunk into a challenging stare as I unlocked my departure for the very last time. I turned, respectfully.

'Bye, Dave.'

'Bye.'

OOO

Throughout my career as a mental health nurse I had never found the necessity to, nor did I believe I had the propensity for, "whistle blowing". As misplaced as this might seem to some I had known precious few colleagues who could own to never having committed some act of indiscretion toward patients and the same principle applied to myself. None of us were blameless. "Let him cast the first stone", was my motto. But since the Sean Walton affair had been dealt with in a full police investigation, and I saw no possibility of the situation being exhumed, I conveyed the small nugget of intelligence to the Director of Nursing, in confidence.

'This is just for information, you understand. Dave Caldicott, one of my patients, has quietly informed me that the "Sean Walton incident" did, in fact, take place as the patients described it.' His response was surprisingly derisive.

'Really! And you believe him?'

'What's he got to lose?'

'I think it is strange that he leaves it so late to make the point just when you are about to depart the hospital. And we must not forget that he has a diagnosis of "psychopath."' He had indeed.

000

On that last day in my capacity as a Nurse Manager within the hospital I sullenly approached the gate lodge hounded by ambivalence as to whether I had made a judicious decision to alter my career path. As I clattered my keys onto the window plate the resident gate lodge Charge Nurse – a normally garrulous and outspoken demagogue – enquired, rather ironically, as to my destination as he understood that he would not be seeing a great deal more of me in the future. With not too much enthusiasm for protracting the contact I furnished him with the fact of joining the teaching staff in the Education Centre. His countenance lost its customary conviviality and was reassembled around a fixed and calculated stare as if he was preparing to take aim then released, from the barrel of his lips, a laconic volley of farewell.

'That's the ticket. Always play to your strengths, I say!'

000

When I came to make the move from a *medium security psychiatric* environment into a *high security* one I could not have anticipated just how much would turn on this single decision. I would be forsaking an establishment that flourished on a healthily varied diet of progressive mental health, coupled with a security regime commensurate with the level of patient risk, and displace it with the staple rations that could only sustain an old-fashioned asylum control of mental disorder. Colleagues had, severally, warned me: 'Trying to make changes, there, will be like ploughing a peat bog.' 'What, exactly, did I think I was going to achieve anyway?' 'It's not the patients that are the problem. Well, they are but no more than you'd expect!' 'If you think you've experienced problems amongst us just wait till you get amongst them!' In short, it was impressed upon me that these establishments were not exactly regaled; that, contrary to a misplaced perception that they held an elevated position in the psychiatric hierarchy, they were bottom of the psychiatric league; that they exemplified institutional resistance to any outsiders who did not conform and to any development that was not done in the interest of the staff? All was to no avail. Hadn't I always managed to introduce some useful ideas wherever I had worked, despite people kicking against the traces? Besides, I had developed in an old, psychiatric institution myself, and knew all the dodges. Why should I be daunted, now? But daunted was precisely what I had been reduced too. I had to review why I had landed in the predicament in which I now wallowed.

Whatever had induced me to pursue a managerial career in the first place? Had I ever rationally weighed its remit and whether I had sufficient qualities to perform it? Did I possess an awareness of my relative strengths and weaknesses in relation to the remit? Perhaps, I would have been more suited to the past, to the era of the hospital Matron which had long since gone, who personified the exemplary; invigilated all ward activity; ruled on performance; wielded autocratic powers over subordinates; and admonished at will according to her personal expectations? But those times of unquestioned autocracy, where organisational management was fairly rudimentary, were far simpler. Among other factors, the increasing organisational complexity, the clinical diversity and specialisation, and the professional accountability of each individual, resulted in the supervisory role of the single Matron becoming expedentially more untenable. Come the early 1970s, a rudimentary nurse management structure was instituted throughout the National Health Service not only to facilitate hospital organisation but to provide an incentivised career structure for nursing staff who had little else to aspire to beyond the confined opportunities of the wards, and the positions of Ward Sister and Charge Nurse. Relative to the tight-knit integration of the Matron era, ward-based "clinical" activity and nursing roles would become distinguished from the overseeing managerial roles, and a kind of schizoid process was set in motion with a separation of powers. However, whereas such bodies as the medical and psychology professions had retained some clinical contact and focus, whatever their level of specialisation, seniority and age, nursing managed to relinquish it altogether as the management tree was ascended. I came to know some individuals who, as their careers progressed, would refer to themselves as professional managers rather than nurses, so much had their focus altered. The plain fact was that if a nurse wished to progress, financially, and in terms of seniority, it frequently meant applying for a managerial role which would split them off from the earlier clinical careers for which they had been trained. For many the transition would be accomplished with little hardship and few regrets.

Some would make distinguished use of their new opportunities and view it as the right vehicle for utilising their creativity.

Then there was the question of why any health agent would want to derive a substantial part of their professional career encased in a psychiatric fortress, working with a dangerous patient class with a low rehabilitative prospect, when working with the general psychiatric population would likely yield more substantial potential outcomes and a greater personal satisfaction, as a consequence? As for myself, it was never answered easily. The rational fragments I could muster never amounted to what could be described as a rounded integrity. As a National Health Service employee I had found myself surprisingly satisfied at working in the public sector, contributing to a public service, which had forestalled the need to be motivated by more profitable private interests. Because the public sector pay did not provide for a home and having no great expectation of earning anything remotely approximating a substantial career salary, I elected to acquire what incremental benefit there was available within the career options before me. I determined that the emerging field of forensic mental health nursing, a derivative of forensic psychiatry, would be the more financially lucrative. Yet, the extent of this pathetic advantage – a mufti clothing allowance plus a financial supplement – showed just how low were our nursing incomes, and consequent expectations, that such piffling subsidies should matter. Not that this precluded a professional interest in the field but, as in the aforementioned instance of promotional opportunities, the motivational thrust was as much economic as it was vocational.

Whether or not 'vocational' could be too strong an emphasis, I had certainly derived an uncommon, occupational interest in the more difficult class of patients. Within the more conventional environments of County mental hospitals I had found myself drawn to the volatile contact with difficult to manage, refractory and aggressive patients. Even within these relatively benign environments, the disturbed hospitalised patient was easily restrained by a multitude of structural, treatment and staffing resources available for the purpose. But my year and a half's spell in the Accident and Emergency Department of a London teaching hospital drew me into contact with innumerable individuals whose swirling psychological chaos erupted among the cosmopolitan streets, seared through the social conventions about them, gathered like uncontrollable barrelling waves, and smashed them through the "casualty" doors like so much psychiatric detritus. These folk were emotionally raw, untreated and often floridly distressed and the hospital facilities were not suited to manage them on even the most temporary of bases. This really did call for the individual skills of professional staff to deal with people who didn't quite fit the usual categories of accident and emergency. In point of fact, even those admitted for taking chemical overdoses were viewed as undeserving, not entitled to the facilities of the more conventionally deserving, those upon whom pathological events had been self-imposed. It was to be dealing with a patient class that many of your colleagues were keen to pass on, get shot of, dispensed with, discharged. I remained attracted to the irregular contact with the distressed, the unpredictable, and the risky. No doubt through these people, I experienced the well known symbiotic phenomena that while helping others you were, also, engaging in self-empowerment and affirming your sense of selfhood. The more I managed to help them, the more I improved the prospect of my own self-efficacy. In raising the professional stakes by working with the very perplexing, unsettling and conflicting demands of much of forensic mental health work I had, unconsciously, of course, raised the possibility of my own efficacy, development and self-aggrandisement. That said, empathy only stretched so far. If the degree of distress spilled into personalised threatening, abusive and violent behaviour, then I was perfectly capable of stepping back and rationalising that it was the patient's underlying personality that was dictating the deliberately obstructive and resistive inconvenience to others, while forgetting to take more account of the overlying disorder. Though, at the time, I was perfectly conscious of ejecting empathy in favour of an expeditious resource to rejection, I would not have been so aware that the patients' needs, as exhibited by their aggression, were beyond my personal level of expertise.

As to the question of whether my earlier professional stance remotely contained a belief that we could seriously help and turn around psychiatric patients with serious forensic histories, the like of which we worked with, I had as nebulous a view as anybody else, I imagined, in the beginning. But, after becoming orientated to the forensic climate – not least that this class of patients have normal pre-morbid personalities until disturbed by their symptoms – it was not long before my green-stick deliberations on the subject calcified into a resolution. This simple resolution was to hold relatively stable despite the trials and disappointments which strained to dislocate and fracture it over the coming years. It was that, even for those patients whose offending approached the atrocious, and almost defied credibility – as also appertained to offenders whose crimes were not linked to mental disorder – there was little or no reason why they should not be entitled to the best mental health care, even if there was little rehabilitative optimism due to the periodic relapses or unremitting symptomatology. Their catastrophic and irreparable crimes, though as causally articulated with mental disorder as a mechanical hinge, might conceivably exclude them from ever acquiring future social or legal approval for re-entering civic community, but this should never dissuade mental health staff from endeavouring to achieve this. The political, media and public consensus, whether or not it included the professional agreement – because, frequently, it did not - was that this extreme class of patients and prisoners would see out their time as terminally forensic, psychiatric and secured. Indeed, if laws had not decreed otherwise, who knew what alternative sanctions would have appertained if the public and journalistic will had held sway – decapitation, electrocution, castration, the fiery furnace – nothing would have been too good for them! A related conviction was that for the remaining class of forensic patients, exhibiting a lower degree of dangerousness, there should be no reason why they should not be afforded the professional optimism of a complete return to the broader populace as was the expectation with the conventionally mentally unwell, or the physically unwell. The decisive variable separating the more extreme category from the less serious group was the degree of dangerousness that their illnesses implied for others and if this was so directly articulated with psychological instability then it could be ameliorated by its effective chemical treatment, and community care package. The issue, therefore, was determining the threshold between a relatively stable, manageable rehabilitation and an unstable, untreatable dangerousness. That was the basic guiding premise, but this could be found wanting in practice since, in individual cases, safe predictions were fallible. For instance, some individuals discharged from the institutional setting with a past history of dangerousness might never commit any dangerous act again. Others, while not repeating that past behaviour, shall we say arson, and who had not given any indication of other deviant preoccupation, might commit a dangerous act of a quite different magnitude, shall we say, a killing. Then there was that devastating category – which created the greatest scepticism about the viability of mental health treatment for forensic patients – who, upon release, perpetuated the very same dangerousness that had caused them to be therapeutically incarcerated in the first place. None of this had dissuaded me from continuing in this explosive field. Indeed, it was the very complexity of these many variables which so engaged my interest and became my overwhelming motivation for staying in this field. Be that as it may, I had now come to reconsider the sense of remaining within a therapeutically defunct, custodial repository at this "Special Hospital" along with the unenviable staff dynamics into which I had become entangled.

From these reflections and the ambivalence that now burdened me I had to shelve the prospective clinical projects I had foreseen for the adolescent unit. I had, perforce, to withdraw from the personal clinical work which I had managed to conjure from the limitations of my official role. The rest of the clinical team would require another nurse manager who would reassemble the group dynamic of the team again. And, as significantly, was my abandoning of the patients whom I had, in no small part, felt that I had needed to give some protection. There was the disconcerting burden of doubting my managerial competence, my interpersonal effectiveness, my resilience in the face of obstacles, my lack of aptitude for conflict resolution in this situation, and my personalization of the opposition I had encountered. And if my resignation had represented a muted conscientious objection to the resistant regime, affixed to this was the conjoint and painful realisation that, in the swirl of my emotions, I was prioritising my own cowardly exit and personal survival. In no small measure I battled over whether I was defaulting on my own professional purpose.

000

I soon established myself in the Nurse Education Department where I had hoped the experience of being ostracised was now behind me, but I was disappointed to have to continue with the seering discomfort of further isolation. For, while an agreeable contingent of the education staff accepted my incorporation into their midst, there was an equally sizeable number that replicated the isolationism meted out by the ward nursing staff. In short, it was clear, for their part, that I bore the mark of a traitor to the cause. So, it was with some relief that I was to spend the majority of my teaching over the next two years in the local School of Nursing, which included a qualification in Teacher Training. During this period, my ongoing interest in research came to the attention of the S.H.S.A. hierarchy and I was rewarded with a secondment to a clinical and academic research team attached to the Institute of Psychiatry in London, in which capacity I spent the ensuing year.

000

In 1990, another "Great Storm" ravaged the British countryside, affecting a wider area, and causing more destruction than had prevailed during the similar event three years earlier. Again, millions of trees were uprooted, and extensive collateral damage was sustained. Forty-seven people on this occasion lost their lives. If we had had any prescience of events closer to home then they would have augured of an accelerated decline in the industrial relations, and treatment provision, within Moss Side Hospital. For later in the same year – a third period of industrial action swirled through the hospital yielding another unprecedented revelation and widespread journalistic coverage and recrimination from outside quarters.

000

That same year, the newly colonising, London based, Special Hospitals Service Authority, who had been charged with running the four "Special Hospitals", had a range of competing priorities to establish not least its authority. It swiftly advanced its centralised proclamations against the waiting indigenous tribes of the dispersed establishments. One of the first of these centralised tasks was to rationalise the previous history of staffing expenditure, one such legacy being the issue of "Assisted Travel Payments". This scheme entitled staff to claim for travel expenditure if their home lay beyond a certain radius from their place of work. It was an open secret that many of the staff maximised this situation by sharing their journeys into work thereby halving their petrol costs. But the Authority needed to lay down a marker that would represent its intentions to bring the service within the administrative boundaries of the National Health Service, while testing its managerial potency and viability. For those employees in the wider NHS, knowledge of this extra subsidy would have amounted to an "expenses scandal" which should never have been allowed to go unchallenged over the years. For the "Special Hospital" staff who had previously enjoyed the preserved rights of civil service status, differential pay, pensions, allowances and disciplinary procedures, quite distinct from the rest of the National Health Service, this amounted to a threat to their occupational rights. The sums were not insubstantial for the staff and would represent an effective cut in salary and they could not be blamed for opposing this financial cutback. Predictably, in a recalcitrant backlash, they resorted to their entrenched default position – industrial action which was perfectly prepared to impinge, directly, on patient care. A good number of the nursing staff had their personal names re-submitted to their professional bodies for engaging in unprofessional conduct. The industrial action, which had directly targeted the quality of patient life – the withholding of personal mail, preventing patients from using the telephones, and refusing to supervise visits from friends and relatives – was now in full swing and took on an even more menacing tone. The staff affiliated to the P.O.A., virtually all the nursing staff, *and* the occupations officers, walked off the job leaving the patients without professional cover on the wards! A "walk-out" as it was called in conflict parlance!

Since the hospital had to be kept running the whole of the hospital's remaining workforce was challenged to place their regular occupations on hold while they accepted a reallocation to ward duties. Nursing managers and the Director of Nursing; medical staff, including the Medical Director; social workers; psychologists; administrators and secretaries; patient education staff; cooks, chefs and domestics; all accepted the responsibility of stepping onto wards and caring for potentially dangerous patients even though many would not have had any remotely appropriate training for the task. The one notable exception, especially inappropriate bearing in mind their own relevant backgrounds, was the entire contingent of hospital-based nurse tutors who steadfastly refused involvement preferring not to run the risk of jeopardising their future relations with nursing colleagues. The remainder of us hadn't thought of that, of course!

It was fun! Truly it was fun! Arriving at a ward not knowing who would constitute the team for the working shift and organising the day in an ad hoc fashion proved to be eminently surmountable. Though the regular routine was largely devastated the patients did not only muck in but guided the rest of us! Whilst they clearly relished the sense of controlled anarchy, they informed us of the basic timetable – morning wakening, meals, medication administration, retiring to bed, etc – while we facilitated the day's basic requirements. Educational, occupational, outside recreational, and rehabilitation trips had had to be suspended. Duty nurse managers were not called upon to monitor the injuries to staff from assaults, or patient seclusions for violence or self-harming behaviour because…there weren't any! There simply weren't any! Not even among the females for whom this had been a daily occurrence. The argument presented by the P.O.A. staff was that the patients were cooperating in a short-term honeymoon with the replacement staff who were reneging on the usual stringent routines, and enjoying all the alternative advantages of a lapsed, liberal and seriously flawed caper. But, maybe, just maybe, the patients were also gleaning some of the attention and responsibility that they required, needed, and appreciated and that they were genuinely grateful for it! We were even able to indulge our therapeutic inclinations without the accompanying glower of admonishing nursing staff. One delightful day, the Chief Nursing Officer, now the Director of Nursing under the S.H.S.A. reorganisation, joined me as part of the team on the adolescent admission ward and accepted my invitation to hold an open forum with the patients. He had already spent part of his earlier career in a Therapeutic Community while I, during a period of recent further training, had also acquired the opportunity to gain clinical experience at two other famous Therapeutic Communities. Everyone piled into the dayroom at the suggestion in what was a party atmosphere, and he and I were in our element!

Chapter 4

Revelations

Back in May 1979, A Yorkshire Television programme, entitled *The Secret Hospital*, exposed the scandalous flagrant abuses, ill-treatment and criminal assault of patients held in the high-security Rampton Hospital by members of the nursing staff. Those accused of these allegations were referred to the Director of Public Prosecutions, whereupon a number of staff were subsequently tried in court, with one sustaining a prison sentence. The exposé triggered a systematic review of the hospital's organisation and facilities, its monitoring of standards of care, its procedures for dealing with complaints, and its strategies for maintaining nurturing links with the outside world. Speedily expediting this, the review was published in 1980, the following year, and urged that the institution should be subjected to increased public scrutiny since the cause of its old-fashioned regime could be assigned to its inward looking isolation from a wider professional network. The "Rampton culture" was overly prescriptive of disciplinary rules, lacked adaptability, and caused unnecessary conformity among the patients, many of whom were adjudged not to be in need of the restrictions of such an institution in any case. Nursing staff were assessed as over-emphasising security and this had predisposed them to "judgemental", "moralistic", and "punitive" attitudes toward patients. The integration of the male and female sexes, staff and patients, was advocated. Individualised treatment programmes were to be designed for each patient, including behavioural modification programmes, and the nursing staff were encouraged to provide much of these at ward level, supported by the input of clinical psychologists. Overall, it was the patients' quality of life which was as acutely advocated as the nursing regime was condemned. Yet, presented into the public domain only eight years prior to my own arrival at Moss Side, it could be argued that it was considered to have no applicability to its sister organisation, Moss Side Hospital. If ever there was evidence of the relative insularity of each of these institutions, then the inability of the remaining "Special Hospitals" to generalise the adverse findings of the Rampton Review to their own circumstances, was surely as indicative as any. But Rampton, at least, had to have learned its lessons.

000

Yet more revelations! By the time the Committee of Inquiry had been proposed, instituted and was fully functional during 1991, the separate establishments of Moss Side and Park Lane – which, in any case, had survived separately alongside each other for nearly two decades – were incorporated under the one mantle of Ashworth Hospital, with their former titles dissolving into history. The Inquiry had been required because, as is so often the case, the public media had managed to gauge the ethical and professional temperature of an institution, and the implications thereof, more effectively than any other body – the institution in question, included. The media on this occasion was a *Cutting Edge* television documentary earlier in the year of 1991, entitled "A Special Hospital". This featured a number of patients' testimonies about their own treatment, and the treatment of others, whilst resident in the hospital. Chief among the allegations, and the Inquiry proceedings, were the events relating to the death of... Sean Walton, the young lad who had unexpectedly died in seclusion on my unit! Discharged patients from the adolescent unit on which I had been the Nurse Manager laid out their criticisms of their treatment at Moss Side.

Deriving their purpose from the T.V. programme the Committee of Inquiry embarked on its pursuit of the veracity of the televised recriminations. Its Terms of Reference were to investigate allegations of improper care and treatment at Ashworth Hospital and to review the complaints procedure afforded to its patients. The Inquiry team, headed by an exceptionally rigorous Chairman, were so thorough in their examination and requirements that they thoroughly embarrassed all parties. The police, pathologists, coroners, clinicians, the hospital authority – people, events, documentation, administration and clinical practices – were scrutinised with a socioscopic obsession, all topped off by their fulsome final report and list of recommendations!

The Committee of Inquiry had much to go on. In the first place, they trawled through the recent history of industrial disputes which had tarnished the reputations, and the patient care, at the "antiquated Moss Side" and the "purpose built Park Lane". Corroborating this were the foregoing incidents of staff intimidation which were roundly

192

aired in their report.

Then, having been furnished with a list of named patients who had offered written complaints about their improper care and treatment, or had these offered on their behalf by other patients, four specific cases were highlighted and pursued: two patients who had resided at the former Moss Side Hospital, and two at the former Park Lane. The first examined the circumstances of a patient found dead in seclusion – my very own Sean Walton. So crucial was this case that it engulfed no less than half the case studies material of the four patients. The second, allegations of extensive, sexual impropriety by a male member of staff toward a young female patient. The third, allegations of physical injury resulting from an assault by nursing staff – the injuries having been photographed. And lastly, the retrospective evaluation of care given to a suicidal patient who, following threats to do so, then proceeded to hang himself. This selection exposed the ranging, inadequate treatment conditions that had congealed around the patient body over the immediately preceding years. Of the individualised counts of complaint with reference to these four primary cases, several were upheld by the Inquiry, thus undermining the veracity of all the original police investigations and findings in relation to the reported incidents, as well as the hasty conclusions of pathologists and coroners and, as importantly, the woefully impoverished internal enquiries made by the Hospital Management Teams.

As part of the inquiry process all staff at Ashworth Hospital had been invited to offer any comment, in writing or anonymously, that expressed their views of patient care and management, in general. What emerged simply shone a super-trooper light on such a deal of nefarious matter that it must have enhanced the justification – if any further was needed – of the Committee and its indefatigable resolve to root out what it concluded as an abominable regime.

And guess what? The instigation of the Inquiry triggered yet another spate of industrial action by the P.O.A. membership!

000

I never volunteered my services to the Committee of Inquiry. I really had nothing to fear from Counsel for the Inquiry as their stance was, unambiguously, to support any positive endeavours unearthed in the hospital. By the same measure it would surely compromise me, at some stage in the proceedings, in respect of the opposition. Hot on the heels of this was the fear of reprisals from the hospital staff as I anticipated that my testimony would be antipathetic to their cause and there was an established history of vengeful action. All this would have been very difficult for me and I have frequently weighed the relative merits of having missed an opportunity to give my informed opinion about the place against the conceivable repercussions of so doing. These repercussions were not inconsiderable.

In the next instance of my reticence, my instinctual response was a concern about the simple matter of being subjected to questioning in such an open and inquisitorial forum, however convicted I felt about the issues. Furthermore, I might have found myself utterly undermined, or indeterminate, by the clever tactics of legal representatives.

Then there might always have been the possibility that I should have been marked as a "whistle blower", a stain which could follow me throughout the remainder of my career. I had observed this phenomenon back in the County hospitals where such individuals were subjected to the lean streaks of defamed reputation and suspicion long after their exposé.

But I could rationalise all of these reservations with the presumption that having been the Nurse Manager of the unit on which Sean Walton had died, I was more or less bound to be required to attend the inquiry process whose venue was a famous Liverpool hotel. For despite my two rest days commencing on the day when Sean Walton was initially secluded, and ending the subsequent day on which he died, so that I was in no position to comment on the precise circumstances involving Sean's demise, I fully anticipated that this fortuitous situation would not prevent me from having to give an account of the general nursing regime that appertained at the time of the death. And what *would* I have considered to be the general context of nursing care on that unit? And then I expected to have to provide an outline of my role and duties at Moss Side Hospital. I had begun to rehearse the answers.

That, although my role had administrative and other managerial components, I marginalised these as much as I was able in favour of freeing up time for a clinical input to the unit, as well. How I had made it my business to model a clinical enthusiasm and innovation, as far as I was able, and also attempted to help nursing staff to develop their professional skills and to work with patients' mental health, emotional and social needs, in equal measure to their antisocial propensities. And could I give a flavour of the staff orientation, their attitude to staff-patient relationships, whether it was a therapeutic atmosphere or an industrious environment? I would, necessarily have been drawn into my accountability for all the ward activity, and procedures, and relationships, but contentiously have to admit that these did not mirror my personal expectations of what should be happening in a contemporary mental hospital. That, in my view, a conservative culture readily condemned the patients' irredeemable criminal pathology with the forcefulness of social taboos with the effect that, once so afflicted, there was little prospect of rehabilitation, or a return to mental health or social order. That the staff seemed to interpret their role as society's wardens, even domineering adults, who performed the function of a failing society when there were adequate opportunities to be positive, temporary models that the lads could have internalised for their future benefit. How, as a consequence, any ward activity tended to be recreational and distracting rather than strictly clinical and therapeutic. I would have played the security card and accepted the need for a staff body with the authority to establish unequivocal boundaries for young men who had proven themselves to lack internal controls in the past but then have to counter this by arguing that this was the only premise upon which the staff seemed to base their work. There was little opportunity for the young patients to acquire those internal controls for themselves, so that, if released, I could not see how they would have benefited from their time on the unit or the hospital. It simply was not an enabling atmosphere that worked with individual needs. For the amount of time that staff spent with patients – several years in most cases – there was ample time for this. What there was, was a one-dimensional, wardened environment that suppressed the patients' potential for any recurrence of their past misdemeanours.

Undoubtedly, there would have been a strong possibility that one Counsel or other would attempt to justify the system, if only rhetorically, and that it existed as the pragmatic answer when faced with the types of patient-difficulties that were apparent? Then would follow a difficult passage as it had to be accepted that, despite their youth, the majority of the patients had committed crimes, not just at the lower level, recidivist law-breaking often associated with young men, but extreme acts which people might think youngsters would be incapable of, and which cast them in a particularly obnoxious and undeserving light. Serious acts, often criminal, most of them involving a severe attack on somebody, often a family member, or threats to kill someone, or range over man-slaughter, arson, stalking, sexual assault and rape, as with any adult. Occasionally, it could be a combination of these. That there remained the residual possibility that they might continue to threaten public safety and property if they were to be returned to live in the general community. I thought it appropriate to then presume that someone would surely proclaim that it was this criminal status of the patient group, rather than their medical status, which was exactly where the due emphasis should be placed, in fact, and how I should have had to argue that this shouldn't be allowed to relegate the significance of the psychiatric issues. A rhetorical step down from this might follow: how this characterisation of antisocial and dangerous conduct would create a professional priority for a strict and disciplined environment, even in the case of adolescent males, which not only secured the current safety of staff and other patients but would better serve these young men to manage their futures without repeating that dangerousness. And I should respond with the conundrum of the day which was that though the "Special Hospitals" were explicitly set up to coral the exceptionally disturbed mentally ill and learning disabled they were also psychiatric hospitals charged with a professional duty of advancing the mental health care of their clients. And that, while the nursing fraternity of the "Special Hospitals" were obliged to keep pace with the broader developments of their profession, my experience on my own Unit, and within the wider hospital, was that professional nursing development was all but subjugated by the emphasis on security, and strict discipline.

I rummaged through the possibilities of further questioning, and my responses, and how I might try to present some justification for the regime to give a more balanced appraisal. How in so many respects it was tied by its history. How nothing else had been expected of the staff over the years. Theirs was a "Special Hospital" provision, with especially dangerous patients, and a special job to do. This was indubitably so but the misplaced, almost grandiose claim, lay like a slough over every therapeutic opportunity of the working day. It couldn't be called an industrious place since most of the patients were off the ward during the day attending either the Education Centre or the Hospital Workshops. Evenings were recreational opportunities with the occasional structured activity put in place. It resulted in an atmosphere which was not at all conducive to truly therapeutic work. The test that I put to myself was, if I had been a patient on this unit do I believe I would have benefited from it? Not only would I most assuredly answer in the negative but I believe I would have emerged with a very vengeful attitude toward society. And I should have had to argue that patients were never credited with their positive behaviour, per se.

Then I might have faced the prospect that, having made a pretty strong indictment of the ward context, I might be called upon to provide some precise examples of what I had tried to change if I was so opposed to the entrenched system. How I might then have spoken of the effort, with the tacit non-acceptance and resistance of the nurses, to start up a weekly community meeting on one of the two wards and that, though this was normally a rigorously monitored and organised strategy from the field of social psychiatry with enormous social and therapeutic potential, we instituted it in an adapted form, making it a voluntary attendance rather than compulsory, and wedged it into the week outside of the regular programme hours with all the potentially hazardous consequences laying in the offing. How the venture took off even though we could not grant permission for the real dynamics of the community to be expressed in a climate where this had always been expressly forbidden. How this severely limited the therapeutic impact for the patients in such a forum since it necessarily had to be watered down to the level of a formalised socialisation gathering. Then, how the unit psychologist and myself had considered finding an alternative reward system that was not so punishing and approaching the Mental Health Act Commission with our concerns. How they proved heartily sympathetic and asked us to defer the issue to the hospital management, which we did, only to have it deferred back to us to find a viable solution which we did not believe was our project, alone, so that, in the end, we were not successful in replacing what was already in place. I could then have summarised the "nursing assessment schedule", and the prospective "introductory course in mental illness", which I had initiated for the benefit of the staff. By these I would have hoped to justify my modest efforts to revise the clinical focus of the unit.

000

In the event, I was to be found present at the Inquiry – by proxy, in effect! The subject of my role on the adolescent unit was introduced by Heinrich, the unit psychologist, who had volunteered his critical opinion of the nursing regime to the Committee of Inquiry. During his own cross examination he had been asked about a former colleague, the psychologist who was hounded out of the hospital for his outspoken critique of the nurses' roles as "jailers and detectives". Hienrich had then referred to me as another example of an individual who had attempted progressive therapeutic changes to the hospital but that I had been forced out by an established and resistant nursing staff who had objected to an outsider's interference. It was then established in this exchange that, though I may have been forced out of the hospital, I had gone on to complete a degree in criminology and been appointed to a notable project, thereby putting this enforced situation to good use. This single intervention precipitated a brief flurry of exchanges on subsequent occasions in which the Counsels for both the Inquiry, and the Prison Officers Association, back-tracked to establish the merit of Heinrich's original intervention.

From the written transcripts of these brief exchanges it was possible to extrapolate what might have transpired if I had actually born the full brunt of the official questioning which I have recreated in the following scenario. Starting off with the Counsel for the Inquiry.

'Mr. Burrow, you have, no doubt, heard the contributions made by other senior members of the clinical team about your personal involvement in the Adolescent Unit and how, in the case of the Consultant Psychiatrist, he believed the nursing care was "reasonably alright" until you arrived on the scene. Then, and only then, he "realised that things had not been alright and things needed improving". Do you accept that?'

'I think the comments were a little disingenuous, actually. He certainly communicated to me his absolute dissatisfaction with the ward regime and nursing input throughout my time on the unit. Those views gave some impetus toward my attempts to change things, of course. And I do not think it requires a Nurse Manager to have to point out the shortfalls of nursing practice – he should have been perfectly capable of assessing that for himself prior to my arrival. The inference is that I had some sort of exceptional expectation which illuminated the nursing shortfall and I do not accept that. However, I do appreciate that, whereas I have now left the wards, people such as himself still have to continue to work alongside the staff and are reluctant to be seen to be openly critical of their immediate colleagues.'

'I see,' says Counsel for the Inquiry. 'And the matter of being forced out, as was proposed by the unit psychologist?'

'Well, as he has said, I became aware of being frozen out by my staff and, because I appreciated that I was making little headway with them and began to feel the stress of it all it seemed in everyone's interests to resign my managerial position particularly if my continued presence might actually be damaging the patients' predicament.'

'You unequivocally agree that you were "frozen out"?'

'It became absolutely clear that many of the staff were not cooperating with me and would only talk to me if I addressed a specific question to them.'

'In general parlance, you were *sent to Coventry*.'

'Exactly.'

'We also understand that your membership of the Royal College of Nursing, compared with the conventional Prison Officers Association, may have considerably contributed to this outsider status and the staff's rejection of your methods?'

'That is impossible to be certain about but I have no doubt that was a relevant background influence, yes.'

With his reputation well established in the transcripts that I read, I would have had no doubt of the stance of Counsel for the P.O.A., who would have taken a long, studied pause, wiped the sweat from the bridge of his nose and rested both knuckles on the table in front of him, before slowly raising his eyes to stare intently at me, his next witness.

'And all of this adolescent deviance, and criminality, was brought together and distributed onto two wards within the unit for which you were responsible. For all these reasons I believe it just wouldn't be possible.'

'It depends what you mean. Obviously, there will be problems with particular individuals or even a couple of people, at any one time, but in terms of a concerted communal action I don't believe that is a true potential, no.'

'What makes you so sure?'

'A number of things, really. Firstly, the majority of the lads are far too suspicious of one another's motives to work in concert with each other. The distrust would extend to an expectation that any planned insurrection would most certainly be betrayed by one of their number. For the betrayer, this would enable them to settle old scores and to gain considerable favour from the nursing staff, particularly. They will also be aware that it might indicate that they are making good progress by acting in a responsible way and hasten their discharge. In any case, as young impressionable people who have often been denied sound family relationships, especially sound father figures, they are keener to receive the attention of older people and the potential source for this is the nursing group. Then there's the various psychological problems which would prevent them from turning the place into a powder keg. The mental illnesses and mental handicaps that they exhibit, both in some instances, would prevent most of them from either planning, focusing on, or carrying through any act of communal defiance. I believe it just wouldn't be possible.'

'What about the patients who are diagnosed as psychopaths of which there are, I understand, quite a number on the Unit? I note you have made no mention of them. Aren't these capable of acting together to effect some serious revolt of some kind about which the nursing staff have to be constantly vigilant?'

'Yes, they certainly have such potential, to a degree. But, it is particularly rare for them to trust one another, in my experience. They are the ones most likely to try to rise to the head of the hierarchy and would simply delight in any opportunity to "shop" a similar individual who they saw as a challenge to their position. So, with the unlikely exception of one or two actually being trustworthy friends, none of them are going to risk confiding a serious plan of insurrection.'

'Are you saying that you could not conceive of a possibility, shall we say, of a member of staff, shall we say a female educational staff member, being taken hostage by two or three patients?'

'Conceivable, yes. Of course, entirely possible, in principle. But that is precisely where we, as mental health nurses, bring our professional responsibilities and skills into the arena, rather than concentrating our efforts on being efficient jailers.'

'Is that what you are accusing your staff of being...efficient jailers? Is that so, Mr. Burrow?'

'Could I put it this way? I certainly think that they place an emphasis on security competencies without a commensurate acknowledgment of their essential professional development.'

'No doubt, they would disagree with you?'

'Probably.'

'No doubt, many of them would say that they had kept up their professional development?'

'In my experience this would fall very short of modern expectations.'

'Really? It is not, perhaps, that you have an unacceptably high expectation of *them*?'

'No, I don't think so, no. I'll give a basic example. This institution was originally commissioned to manage the mentally handicapped patient for which the staff were trained in the field of mental handicap.

Whereas, for some time now, a good many of the admissions come under a remit of mental illness, for which most of the staff are not qualified. They need a professional training or, at least, a significant reorientation in the issues of mental illness.'

'Well, in your capacity of the Unit Manager did you take any relevant steps in correcting what you perceived as a deficit?'

'I certainly did. I had been in negotiation with the Director of Nursing, over some time, about producing a locally administered training in this area and the response was very positive.'

'You didn't think, maybe, that there was sufficient in their original training as mental handicap nurses that was common to both fields, that was readily transferable, so to speak?'

'That may well be for a significant part of their training, yes.'

'So, why are you so sure that this was *not* sufficient?'

'I came to this judgement based on an observation that has already been raised by the unit psychologist. The nurses gave me no indication that they had even a basic knowledge of what we call "behavioural techniques". This was something which you would expect nurses with a qualification in mental handicap, to have.'

'And why do you think they did not have these... behavioural techniques?'

'I can only imagine that it was a result of a rather poor training. Maybe, they were not given any opportunity to undertake this field. After all, their nursing tutors can only teach their students what they, themselves, know. And if they haven't had experience in that field, well, how can they possibly pass it on? They cannot educate what they don't know.'

'You seem to be suggesting that the qualification of the mental handicap nurse is not worth very much?'

'As somebody who has not had that training I would expect to be able to call upon those that have specialised in that field to be able to demonstrate and apply it to their work.'

'I infer from that that you did not believe them to be sufficiently specialised. Is that correct?'

'Like my psychology colleague it was most certainly my impression that they had no real conception of the principles of behaviour modification, for example.'

'Well, how could you be so sure since, as you have admitted, you are not a specialist in this field?'

'I have had the fortunate experience of applying basic behavioural methods to a client group, earlier in my career, and these efforts were supported by a psychologist.'

'Am I to understand that behaviour modification is a psychological model, rather than a nursing skill?'

'Strictly speaking, yes. But, I have checked the 1982 nursing syllabus for nurses of the mentally handicapped and it itemises this model as part of their training.'

'You are sure about that?'

'Categorically.'

'Indeed. Then, in your own case, are you saying that as a mental health nurse you have a comprehensive knowledge of all fields within that speciality?' This would have brought me out in hives, confounded by a long and anguished sweaty pause, while my composure deserted me for some moments, I've no doubt. Clearly disconcerted I think I should have continued, falteringly.

'Of course not. The mental health field is vast and that is why professional up-dating and development should be valued and encouraged so that there is an opportunity to widen our horizons and competencies.'

'Let us turn to a related matter. Would it surprise you to know, Mr. Burrow, that the nurses that I have spoken to did not feel that their contribution to the care of these patients was valued by the rest of the multi-disciplinary team, including yourself?'

'I probably would not be surprised, no.'

'In fact, they site you as being a difficult person to work with and that you continually managed to rub them up the wrong way. What do you think of that assertion?'

'I think that they were not used to a senior nurse having such a direct and active involvement in the clinical area; that they were accustomed to being left alone provided that they operated within acceptable parameters; and that they saw my participation as interference and that I should keep my distance. In short, that I should have behaved as other senior nurses did.'

'But you had to be seen to be different, perhaps, because you needed to prove yourself to all your colleagues because you were an outsider?' This was what I had most feared. Another uncomfortable pause and physical adjustment while I hoped the Inquiry Chairman might extend some refereeing of this barrage. Having to find the emotional resources, let alone answers, while being subjected to a continuous erudite onslaught before a seasoned inquisitor who sought to expose any weakness with the rabid paws of a salivating bear.

'I cannot deny that I wanted to prove that I could make a

substantial contribution to the nursing care, especially since I was an outsider. If I was different it was that I simply did the job that I believed I was hired to do. I did it sincerely. If I had not involved myself as I did then I would have felt that I was not performing my job properly.'

'But there may have been some discrepancy here. Maybe you stepped well outside of your brief?'

'When I was appointed to this manager's position I was appointed by a panel which included two representatives from the Department of Health. The panel appointed me to do a job which they must have believed I could do irrespective of my outsider status, and that would have included my experience of General Management principles – something which the "Special Hospital" applicants would not have had experience of at that time. That panel selected me on the basis of my appropriate, contemporary experience, presumably, and I have never doubted that that experience was entirely relevant to the position. I should not have been expected to down-grade, or dumb-down, that experience because a host organisation had not kept pace with the times.'

'As I was saying, one might form the view, indeed... you have implied as much during your answers, that you did not have much confidence in your staff and you felt that you were providing your staff with an innovative leadership.'

'That was what I believed, yes.'

'Then perhaps you could explain, for the benefit of the Inquiry, why you told one of your staff, Charge Nurse Camper, that you thought the nurses in the hospital were *rubbish*, that they deserved what they would get, and that the hospital was a *dustbin*?' The disconcerting claim would have sunk among the assembly like a plummeting rock-fall while my adversary resumed his graduated assault. 'What sort of leadership would you call that, exactly?'

'Perhaps, there might be some context to this comment provided Mr. Burrow did, indeed, make it, of course?' the Chairman intervened, casting me a rescuing line.

'I hardly think that any context would diminish the seriousness of such a remark, Mr. Chairman,' turning back, to resume hostilities.

'Um, I see your point,' the Chairman concluded, reluctantly, I believe.

'Well, did you make such a remark?' he said, taking up Council's refrain. It would have been the most chilling moment for me but there would have been no point in denying the uncomfortable truth.

'I remember saying such a direct thing to Mr. Camper but in a very specific context, yes. Mr. Camper was one of my Charge Nurses and the remark was made in the confidence of an excellent relationship and rapport between us both. This relationship had extended into the hospital soccer team for it was he who had originally encouraged me to join the team after he had learned that I played the game. Furthermore, the remark emanated from the period in which all the hospital nursing staff were being assessed under the new Clinical Grading process. The staff were bellyaching about being entitled to the best the new grading system could offer whilst, simultaneously, being prepared to take industrial action against their patients of the order of locking them up. I could not justify any improvement in their grading whilst effecting a veritable vigilante course of action. That was part of the context in which the comment was made. But it was offered to someone in whom I had some confidence after having shared with him a number of informal conversations talking about the state of the hospital and its future prospects. It must have been my belief that he would not have taken offence at my views otherwise I'd not have shared them so frankly. On the contrary, I had the impression that he rather enjoyed our deliberations. I am very surprised that he has taken this stance.'

'And that informality that you speak of gave you permission to run down your colleagues in a flagrant denigration of their reputation, did it?' continued the virulent P.O.A. Counsel.

'In the context of our very reasonable relationship I suppose it did, yes. But there is a wider context. The hospital had been involved in no less than three major industrial disputes during the time that I had been a manager with the most extraordinary, and unprecedented, repercussions for patient care, and the administration of the hospital. The industrial relations behaviour in no way accorded with professional health care.'

'So, now, are you saying they did not have the right to take industrial action?'

'Of course they did, in principle. But, their actual action went far beyond what their professional contemporaries would have expected of them. In fact, their actions were unprecedented in this country I am led to believe.'

'Changing circumstances called for innovative reaction, no doubt. Which brings us to another issue which will cast further light on the appropriateness of your appointment, I think. You weren't used to dealing with the P.O.A., in fact, were you?'

'No. Having worked in the N.H.S. throughout my career my personal participation and contact was with public service unions. These have, from time to time, encouraged their membership to take assertive action against management and the government, but never the extreme industrial action which the Prison Officers' Association guided its members into.'

'As I said, you were not accustomed to dealing with the P.O.A. You see, I put it to you, Mr. Burrow, that your personal experience and operational expectations of your staff were, in fact, inappropriate and were more suited to the local hospital from which you hailed?' When such considerations were put before you so abrasively you were compelled to spend some moments weighing their appropriateness, and implications, before regaining sufficient composure. This done, I now wanted to defend myself against this unjustifiable slur.

'It is the hospital's association with the P.O.A. which is not suited to modern health care and I should not be condemned for lauding the expectations of the modern health service, for doing my job, and for doing it in good faith.' Counsel for the P.O.A. now drew back the scimitar ready for a lethal blow.

'Mr. Burrow, I don't see any leadership credibility, under any circumstances, when a manager is so unashamedly prepared to castigate, even humiliate, his subordinates. Such an example of "man-management" leaves a great deal to be desired. The comments are offensive in the extreme. In fact, I put it to you that this might be a proper time and place for you to retract those recriminations. How say you?' What a shocking moment this would have been but I hope my nerve would have held.

'The comments were not a public statement. They were said, in confidence, to one individual whom I had good reason to believe would have retained that confidence.'

'So, you are not retracting your statement.'

'I am not.'

'A good place to end this session, I think,' was the relieving intervention by the Chairman. 'But just before you go, Mr. Burrow, if you would allow me a little indulgence. You will have heard of the several instances in which staff at both Moss Side and Park Lane were subjected to threatening, abusive and intimidating behaviour from their colleagues. In the circumstances one would have suspected that there was a strong likelihood of you also being subjected to like repercussions. Could I ask whether any of these was also your experience?' Indeed, I had frequently considered this very same matter during the interim period since my managerial departure. And despite the high expectations that I held of being treated like some of my colleagues and receiving either abusive mail and telephone calls at work or home, or of sustaining offensive personal interactions about the hospital estate, or of discovering my car tyres or windscreen wipers to be damaged – and of being in a state of reserved readiness that any of these could erupt – not once did I find myself the victim of any of these bullying tactics.

'Much to my own amazement I have never been subjected to any of these aggravations.'

'Then perhaps it was considered sufficient to have "sent you to Coventry" and successfully encouraged you to withdraw from your position.'

000

The revelations contained within the Ashworth Committee of Inquiry Report pronounced on both Moss Side and Park Lane Hospitals, thereby completing a hat-trick of highly critical investigations into "Special Hospitals" in just over ten years. The revelations were to read like a distilled version of an apocalyptic, institutional disintegration. It was as if an isolated band of disillusioned combatants had eventually deserted their own side, given up their avowed purpose, aligned themselves to a renegade leadership, adopted a xenophobic resistance to any outside influence, and came to lose all sense of a civilised perspective. Armed only with the perception that they were surrounded by enemies, even those who by association were of their very own fold, the renegades descended by slow degrees into a state of occupational mutiny! Even the national paper *The Guardian*, in an editorial comment, was moved to suggest that it was difficult to read about the psychological abuse at the hospitals 'without gagging'!

The Inquiry learned that, by the time the third bout of industrial action, so much anxiety had been generated by the customary conflicts and the potential repercussions for their professional futures, that a handful of nursing staff had broken away from the P.O.A. and become affiliated to the Royal College of Nursing for a more professionalised representation of their interests. This had placed them in a most invidious predicament for it was now the duty of the R.C.N. members to turn up for work when the P.O.A. had instructed otherwise, cross

206

the P.O.A. picket lines, and man the hospital wards. Which they did, reaping the vituperative outbursts of their P.O.A. colleagues, in doing so, who now proclaimed their "scab" status. A barrage of intimidating tactics flooded into the hospital consciousness, then the local press. There were incidents of the "scabs" being screamed at and threatened while crossing the picket line; of a female nurse living on the hospital estate having her home daubed with the words "scab" and "bitch", having dog faeces pressed through her letterbox, and having a brick thrown through the window; of a wheel coming off a nurse's moving car; and, following the action, of R.C.N. staff being "sent to Coventry" by their colleagues. In the most extreme example, the local R.C.N. Chairman received a succession of abusive telephone calls and notes, including a threat that his union office door would be kicked in so that he could be dealt with.

An outbreak of "alternative literature", in the form of posters, personalised mail, and an informal magazine representing a most reprehensible series of principles and targeting a wide range of hospital personnel and organisational initiatives, was spawned across the hospital site. Patients were not exempt. One male patient who had undergone neurosurgery with the loss of some brain tissue, and who was referred to by nursing staff as "half-brain", discovered pictures of anatomical brains, and others which abused his physical condition, pined to his door and on the inside of his personal locker. A female psychology staff member was sent abusive documents which attacked her opposition to some staff practices. One example, informed her that she needed a cervical smear test because she was an "interfering cunt" who was due to be "well-fucked". On another poster was scrawled "I will tear your fucking head off you cock-sucking bastard". She was later informed that she would be getting a "fatal stabbing" because she was a "left-wing communist slut". Institutionalised homophobia and racism was also apparent via the literature. British National Party posters, affiliated to the British National Front, promulgated the white race and called for an outlawing of homosexuality and protection from Aids. Some of this was prominently displayed in the hospital's gate lodge. The recently convened Royal College of Nursing received mail which personally threatened its new members and defaced the R.C.N. posters billed around the hospital. What the Inquiry report failed to make much of was the additional circulation of an "Alternative Weekly News" pamphlet. Though written in a brilliantly humorous guise it amounted to a derisive and ridiculing targeting of individual members of senior staff from the nurse managers through to the General Managers, thus revealing a comprehensive disrespect for fellow colleagues.

The Inquiry learned from a crucial group of highly placed professionals which it characterised as "The Ashworth Five" – a Consultant Psychiatrist, three female psychologists, and one female social worker – who brought together an integrated and damning critique of the hospital regime and of their personal difficulties whilst working in the wards to which they were clinically attached. Between them they described in some detail what they considered to be the regularised, psychological abuse of patients by nursing staff. In addition to personal observations they reiterated comments made to them by their patients about specific incidents: of a nurse who informed a patient that he had run over the latter's much loved dog on his way to work; of staff who would drop their cigarette ash down one patient's trousers; of one nurse who submerged a patient's head in the kitchen sink to test their breaking point; of a live snake being sent in a package to a patient; of female patients having been strip-searched by male staff, even when patients had a past history of been sexually abused by males; of patients required to ask for tampons when in the process of having their biological periods; and when a pig's head, replete with thermometer placed in its mouth, was ostentatiously paraded in the staff office window to frighten off a patient who continually pestered for cigarettes. One of the psychologists had particularly aligned herself with the predicament of the female patients, which included many of the self-harmers, who were considered by the staff to be merely attention-seeking. She had openly couched the female self-harming behaviour in terms of attempting to regain some personal initiative in an institutionalised power game which disenfranchised them, forced them to be compliant and docile, and which punished their consequent, and justifiable, opposition, anger and aggression. Female patients were so misunderstood, she posited, that they were infantilised by the staff treatment of them and offered nothing therapeutically productive that might equip them to remain outside of the hospital for long. The use of sexist language was aired by the references to the patients as "girls", "little ones", "perverts", "beasts", "wops", "mess-pots", "slags", "low grades", and "high grades" which was defamatory, abusive and infantilising. The five summarised their submissions as confronting and condemning the incestuous, custom and practice of the nursing regime and for its retributive stance toward the patients which was manifested in a systematic abuse, humiliation and oppression by a concerted contingent of its members. These five were to endure anonymously written threats as their efforts to challenge the repressive status quo, and its "sinister agenda", gathered momentum.

The Committee of Inquiry were, themselves, to conclude after hearing from all the witnesses that the psychological abuse of patients was "evidently a commonplace daily occurrence in Ashworth". The nursing staff were not culpable, alone. What it also deemed as an inexcusable hindrance to therapeutic and cultural progress within Ashworth was the retrograde attitudes of a significant number of the medical staff, Consultant psychiatrists and above, who attempted to rationalise the nursing regime and their own sense of therapeutic pessimism in relation to their work. The Inquiry members took a different view of the patients in a number of respects with the effect of elevating their status as citizens with equal human rights as normal people. In respect of their status as witnesses to the Inquiry patients were considered, in principle, and despite their disabilities, to be as capable of giving reliable and competent accounts of events as any normal person.

Unsurprisingly, the nursing regime was hammered. The qualified nursing staff, most of whom were "Registered Mental Handicap" nurses, were accused of a lack of knowledge of the most basic tenets of mental disorder and even learning disabilities. The nurses showed more aptitude for performing routine duties of a controlling nature and the care planning around patients' needs was found to be superficial and lacking a rationale for the care delivery. It was further acknowledged that the ward staff had been bereft of sufficient leadership as their managers were too office-bound, only maintained outdated, institutional procedures, had failed to provide clinical input, or to audit the quality of nursing care for which they had responsibility. The Director of Nursing was hammered for inspiring so little change during the duration of his watch. This last, I felt, was a very unfortunate conclusion. The Director had chosen to support his nursing staff as much as he was able – a well-intended, but fallacious, choice in the end and he suffered more than his fair share of scapegoating for what was viewed as his managerial contribution to this precarious establishment. His career was over, at least in this format!

Finally, seven members of nursing staff were suspended over

charges of alleged abuse or neglect of patients and faced possible disciplinary charges.

Subsequent to their final Report the Inquiry members, stepping beyond their brief, vehemently advocated an independent review of the "Special Hospitals", if not their closure, because they were irredeemable. This imploring was rejected by the Minister of State, Virginia Bottomley. But the lessons now had to be learned across the "Special Hospital" board.

In just over ten years, all of the country's "Special Hospitals" had sustained the most penetrating of organisational investigations and had been found wanting in most respects.

000

The most disingenuous of all the contributions to this scenario must be attributed to the Prison Officers' Association who, on learning of the findings of the published Inquiry Report in August, 1992 – totalling 90 recommendations – issued a News Release which suspended the current industrial action on account that because it was biting so severely, the patients would be "seriously affected".

Chapter 5

Reconciliation

So, the situation had been reached whereby several notable outside agencies had established the case for a total re-think on the strategic size and role of the "Special Hospitals" since closure did not appear to have been a political option. Who else, after all, could have taken on this hybrid class of clients? The demands for staff development and training, for greater humanity toward patients, for a renewed recognition of their rights, for further reorganisation, and a massive financial injection, engendered raft after raft of changes.

The Committee of Inquiry's recommendations implicitly had the effect of a massive job creation scheme. Firstly, the strong criticism of Ashworth Hospital's contingent of remote nurse managers who gave little support to their ward staff on clinical matters demanded a cultural change in the nature of the nursing leadership. And the Special Hospitals Service Authority obliged with a recruitment of ward-based managers in every single unit across the three hospitals! They were selected from all ethnic groups, and both sexes, and were equally shared between internal staff and those originating from external facilities in order to maximise the cross-fertilisation of ideas. This was the most acute example of the subsidiarity promulgated by the Chief Executive. Only one problem with this. The nursing hierarchy, in taking their eye off the *clinical* ball, elected to send each and every one of these newly recruited leaders onto Management Diploma courses which orientated the ward-based focus toward financial and organisational issues. OK, the Chief Executive was ensuring that he retained a desk free of paperwork but, to my mind, this militated against the more proper emphasis which should have been the "clinical management" of the wards. And so, briefcase adorned, and crisply attired, the staff leadership converted valuable ward areas into paper-bound office space, spent the days recruiting for overtime, and plucking at their abacuses. Meanwhile, the nursing competences lay unattended.

The Inquiry's forceful repudiation of the hospitals' over-prescription of seclusion included a recommendation that patients should not be locked in their rooms during night-time hours. The S.H.S.A. responded with a massive drive to increase staffing numbers so that this could be effected. Now a team of several staff would be allocated to each and every unit during the night shifts to effect a 24-hour, ongoing contact with patients instead of the previous situation of allocating a solitary night-watchman per ward. Theoretically, the organisational momentum was shifting exponentially toward the therapeutic pole of the therapy – security spectrum.

000

I had held relatively senior nursing posts in the "Special Hospitals" over a ten year period, from 1987-1997. Whatever occupational ideals informed these roles, with the passage of time, psychological space, and the benefit of retrospection, I found myself reviewing this catastrophic period of high security mental heath provision and reconfiguring my evaluation of the nursing staff who had come spiralling through this maelstrom. At Moss Side Hospital, the first "Special Hospital" at which I was employed, only nursing staff who had wrestled themselves free of the wards to work in units such as the Rehabilitation Centre seemed to manage to entertain change, development, alternatives, and to enter into a new compact with other disciplines, the patients and, ultimately, themselves. In all other respects there was little psychiatry, or mental health, or therapeutic rehabilitation other than stranded oases of professional activity that hung on despite the constant, reactionary hostilities and outrage of an insulating, institutional culture. It could be argued that the nursing and occupations staff had enjoyed a working class solidarity which invoked the industrial and social history of the Liverpool area and was precipitated by the political and professional managerialism which came to beset it during this era of change. This perpetuated the perception that this was a continuation of the social and industrial reconstruction of the locality by a professional and managerial class. The anticipated sequel was of a fragmentation and marginalisation of their collective identity and solidarity which they found intolerable. The institution could have been figuratively characterised as a vessel in the professional "doldrums" – becalmed in a state of gloomy stagnation lacking any therapeutic winds. But while the vessel idled, the majority crew conspired to invoke the energising forces of mutiny, immune to the threat of the professional gallows and gibbets.

At the particular juncture of "Special Hospital"/high security hospital evolution, during the five year troubles from 1987-1992, the revisionist managerial context began to wrest control from long-established hospital domination and practices. When the Special Hospital Service Authority took control its explicit therapeutic programme was incompatible with, yet incapable of changing, the default setting of the "Special Hospitals", and Moss Side Hospital in particular, with its pre-selected option of the defence of staff rights, and the demotion of patient-rights. It could be argued that not until the Committee of Inquiry had overwritten this with its unprecedented defamation did the default setting change to a defence of patient rights, and the demotion of staff powers. The 1992 Committee of Inquiry had, in the final analysis, wholly condemned the low standards of therapeutic practice that prevailed in Ashworth Hospital and demanded what amounted to a cultural transfusion. In granting them some little slack it was moved to concede that the inadequate medical and managerial leadership in the hospital had left a "power vacuum" which had been readily filled by the Prison Officers' Association which, by its very nature, would elevate security above therapeutic endeavour. This was a minimal concession made not only in the context of contemporary expectations but in the context of the original, beneficent remit of these hospitals so unambiguous affirmed in *Rules for the Guidance of Officers, Attendants, and Servants. Broadmoor Asylum, 1866*: *'Kindness and forbearance are first principles in the care and management of persons of unsound mind; few such persons are beyond their influence. The mischievous will become somewhat less troublesome, the dirty less careless; the irritable and violent often render most essential service to the Attendants who treat them firmly, justly, and kindly.'* This must have been lost to posterity but there had to be sound reasons for defaulting on these purposes.

Put simply the Committee of Inquiry and its findings and recommendations could be said to have constituted the "tipping point" that radically altered the course of "Special Hospital" development. And if this was the critical extra weight that tipped the balance then, by definition, it was not the only factor which brought about change but the single most emphatic of the whole slew of irresistible pressures which finally wrestled the strong arm of Special Hospital resistance to the table. I would argue that it was possible to delineate

213

some causative account for an institution which was so therapeutically moribund – a necrotic limb dangling from the body of the modern national mental health services. An account of numerous and wide-ranging pressures and influences.

In a very real way, the "Special Hospitals" had all been "Secret Hospitals". So exclusive had these organisations developed, with so little contact even with each other, that they saw no reason for learning the lessons of the other's downfalls unless it concerned matters of staff and public safety. The explosive revelations about the others' regimented routines, or concerns about patient care and standards, were not generalised or internalised because the institutional momentum was focused on security, custody and the wardens' role. To this extent they could be accused of an inward-looking, parochial chauvinism that prejudiced their capacity for learning from outside agencies.

All organisations include their historical foundations and it must be accepted that, far from mortifying into oblivion, these will continue to bear influence over the evolution of any enterprise. Organisations for the offending mentally disordered were no exception. The very nomenclature of criminal lunatics, and criminal lunatic asylums, and the legislative basis for institutionalising the field – first in the Criminal Lunatics Act (1800); then the Criminal Lunatics Act (1860), the Broadmoor Act, which sanctioned the building of Broadmoor – heralded what was an exclusive specification from the outset. This early legislative basis drew these institutional origins into the orbit of the criminal justice system where management was vested in the Home Office, ultimately the Home Secretary. Yet this did not entail an inclusion into the penal system. The service to criminal lunatics functioned alongside the Prison Service, but was never integrated with it. Neither was it integrated into the wider hospital provisions for pauper lunatics that was to flourish throughout every county across the land. These were legislated for under quite distinct Parliamentary reforms such as the Madhouse Act, the County Asylum Acts, the Lunacy Acts, the Mental Treatment Act, and the Mental Deficiency Act.

Historically, the field of forensic psychiatry constituted a numerically marginal but politically significant enterprise. From the commencement of nineteenth century Britain, the initial Criminal Lunatics Act (1800) specifically legislated for the institutionalisation of the criminally insane for the first time. Though this "Act for the safe custody of insane persons charged with offences" was a piece of unique legislation, the criminally insane it served had to continue to be admitted to the already existing facility of the Bethlem Royal Hospital in London (popularised as Bedlam). It was not until the Criminal Lunatics Act (1860) – the so-called Broadmoor Act – that direction was made for the construction of Broadmoor Criminal Lunatic Asylum as a dedicated facility for the criminally insane. The inaugural inmate population was an initial tranche of female patients when it opened in 1863, the same year that the Battle of Gettisburg raged in the American Civil War. Along with all the other social dislocations which jostled and destabilised the economic, social and political stability of the period, criminal behaviour was at the forefront with the consequence that the following year saw the enactment of one of the most influential pieces of criminal justice legislation – the Offenders against the Persons Act (1861). This elaborated a wide range of offences abounding at the time which is still operative today.

So, until relatively recently, an operational separation always existed between forensic psychiatry and its generic neighbour, general psychiatry, because they were responsible to different authorities who managed quite separate concerns. One adverse repercussion of this arrangement was that forensic psychiatry came to be viewed as customarily dragging its heels behind generic psychiatry. An early example illustrated the point which was to be proven again and again. The enactment of the Mental Treatment Act (1930) marked a far more enlightened social policy toward the mentally disordered, not least, the removal of its pejorative predecessor the Lunacy Act (1890). The Mental Treatment Act was partly fuelled by the published condemnations of psychiatric conditions pertaining to the Prestwich Asylum in the North of England where a Dr. Montagu Lomax, a Medical Officer at the hospital, decried the inhuman, custodial and anti-therapeutic conditions to which the lunatics were subjected. Among the many recommended improvements was the transformation of professional language that introduced the concepts of "patient" and "hospital" in place of "lunatic" and "asylum". However, this humanising shift did not filter into the operational consciousness of forensic psychiatry until the Criminal Justice Act (1948), nearly twenty years later. Thereupon, the "criminal lunatics" of Broadmoor were re-designated as "Broadmoor patients", and "Broadmoor Criminal Lunatic Asylum" was reclassified as "Broadmoor Institution". This landmark legislation essentially de-criminalised the patient population of Broadmoor.

The term "Special Hospitals" was characterised, as such, under the Mental Health Act (1959) and referred not only to Broadmoor but its sister institutions, at the time, of Rampton Hospital and Moss Side Hospital, thereby constituting three forensic institutions. By the time that the revised Mental Health Act (1983) was enacted, Park Lane Hospital had been added to the elite throng. Under new management from 1989, Moss Side and Park Lane Hospitals were combined into what became Ashworth Hospital. Under these Mental Health Acts, "Special Hospitals" were designated to treat patients who exhibited dangerous, violent or criminal propensities within conditions of special security. Effectively, this facilitated the transfer of a large number of violent patients from ordinary County hospitals under straightforward, civil proceedings, along with those who were necessarily admitted via the criminal courts. And from this unconscionably vague launching pad, with no definition or description of "special security", or whether the ambiguous direction to "treat" referred to just the mental disorder, or also encompassed the anti-social propensities, violent and dangerous behaviour, these institutions were expected to make a fist of a monumentally complex task.

And so it was that this tiny archipelago of motley characteristics was stranded on the borders of other far less ambiguous organisational arrangements that had been secured on behalf of the conventional psychiatric population. It must be argued, therefore, that there was a perception that these were enterprises with a difference, bolstered by a direct political patronage, that marked them out for special consideration from the rest of national health care.

The inclusion of the Prison Officers' Association into the criminal lunatic asylum service in 1939 was no perverse act but an occupational strategy to fit the staff interests and industrial relations of the time. The P.O.A. were retained nevertheless and the governmental bodies did nothing at the time to revoke this insurgence. By the time of the Mental Health Act (1959) this handful of elite hospitals were all being managed by the Ministry of Health and all acquired the title of "Special Hospitals". From then onwards, the Ministry of Health, later to become the Department of Health and Social Security, permitted the hospital staff of the service the employment conditions of civil servants by their direct association with the D.H.S.S. while, simultaneously, expecting the staff to abide by the conditions of the National Health Service. If this duality of employment was not

216

complicated enough, arguably, the most significant historical factor that created the hybrid philosophy of the "Special Hospitals" was the continuing acceptance of P.O.A. staff representation. This triumvirate of authority was counter intuitive to any reasonable sense of integrative development and by continuing the arrangement the D.H.S.S. allowed the competing interests and cross-purposes to gather momentum. The Ministry of Health/D.H.S.S. had, unwittingly, facilitated a leadership vacuum. For its part, the P.O.A. merely did what it considered to be its legal responsibility – to protect the employment interests and rights of its constituent members wherever they were to be located.

Under the Ministry of Health/D.H.S.S. the hospitals would be permitted a self-regulating remit, offered no guidance on inculcating therapeutic objectives, per se, and it was taken for granted that security and control would predominate. Neither was there any centralised stipulation about the nature of a proper complaints procedure let alone one which conferred due reverence to the accusations made by patients against their conditions and treatment. Nor did the Ministry/D.H.S.S. convey anything but a tacit acceptance of the intervention of police involvement when serious allegations were filed against staff members. Conclusively, they were open to the charge of relegating the worthiness of patients' rights and opinions about their management, while elevating the rights of staff, when such distortions had already been considerably adjusted within the National Health Service. Afforded this local control the hospitals fashioned their own guidance to staff. Take the Moss Side staff handbook. While elaborating the legal purpose of the hospitals under the Mental Health Act (1959), it also elected to devise the local treatment goals: to provide "training in social responsibilities and encouraging progress towards higher levels of maturity". Where did this come from? Because nowhere in the Mental Health Acts – the legal basis of care – would this have been found, nor would it have been an explicit aspect of their nurse training. Consequently, for anyone employed at the hospital, this philosophical premise would have formed part of their occupational consciousness, not least because it would have had some intuitive value in the absence of anything avowedly therapeutic. In the same booklet, a somewhat derisory reference was made to the motives that lay behind patients who made complaints against the staff. It categorically stated that the vast majority of patients' complaints in such hospitals were either vexatiously motivated or were ill-founded! Such explicit conjectures – indeed, ill-founded prejudice – would be responsible for distorting what should have been a more beneficent regard for justifiable complaint. And listed among the Hospital Rules, in the same text, was the advice to avoid any emotional involvement by a member of staff with a patient. It had to be said, unfortunately, that this was a lamentable fact for all of us working in mental health in the past but never stated so explicitly. The overwhelming tone of the handbook was the promotion of a lamentable distrust of the patients so just how the staff were to promote "social responsibility" and "maturity" defied credibility.

When the Department of Health and Social Security finally severed the exclusive political linkage and handed over the baton of "Special Hospital" management to the Special Hospitals Service Authority in 1989 it could be said to have abdicated all responsibility for having "queered the pitch". On the surface it may have appeared that the new S.H.S.A. merely confirmed the exceptional elitist status of the "Special Hospitals" that continued to be managed by a separate authority form the rest of the Health Service. But this was a false dawn. The S.H.S.A. were expressly charged with incorporating the service under the general management principles, and conditions of service, of the N.H.S. The staff were losing ground and losing it speedily.

Continuing political influence was by no means limited to the historical link with the Home Office, Ministry of Health, and the D.H.S.S. As late as 1988, Edwina Currie, the Parliamentary Secretary for Health, in outlining the management changes to the "Special Hospitals", said: 'Our first priority is as always the safety of the public.' The message was unambiguous and not exactly surprising for there was always an Achilles Heel in the care of the mentally disordered offender, as was the case with the conventional population of prisoner offenders. Mistakes were politically costly! News of patient escapes and homicides not only made very unwelcome headlines but they impeded liberal objectives and ruined personal reputations. This was no less significant for the forensic mental health team – their mistakes causing an outraged backlash which could mutilate individual careers. If it was to quell fears that irresponsible liberties were to be taken by the new management agenda, Edwina Currie's statement would have done little to engender a relaxation of fears about the patients held in "Special Hospitals". Rather, it would have perpetuated the belief that a security mantle of structural design, technology and procedures was to remain woven into every physical feature, activity, practice, and interpersonal contact over every inch of the Special Hospital estate. In this context, with the use of patients' rooms as night time cells, the protracted isolation of newly admitted patients, and the routine use of corrective isolation, it would help to explain how, during these phases of acute industrial action, the practice of secluding the patients for excessive periods had seemed second nature to the nursing body!

There was also a more diffuse, but arguably no less pertinent, political initiative in the field of prison service development during the 1980s. The growing concern about young male offenders led to the feted announcement by the then Home Secretary, William Whitelaw, of the start of a more punitive regime for this category of criminals. Based on the American "Boot Camps", these "Detention Centres" were to deliver a 'short, sharp shock' via a regime with a militaristic orientation which included marching drill, physical education, outward bound courses, and other challenging activities. Yet again the Special Hospitals, with their P.O.A. links to the Prison Service, would have been acutely aware of this conservative, and heavy-handed experiment in managing offenders.

Consideration should also be given to the region's socio-cultural influences that helped nurture consolidated industrial reaction in the face of the threat of change at Ashworth Hospital. The Liverpool populace had long enjoyed a reputation for industrial disputes. Faced with the uncertainty and reconstruction in many of its private and public services, and in the context of appalling poverty, unemployment and social inequality, there were many notable examples. Historically, the recurrent dockers' strikes, for example, that made the biggest impact in 1889 when 30,000 dockers paralysed the British Empire but brought recognition of their union. In 1989, this was to re-emerge in a six week strike action that lasted longer than anywhere else in the country. In 1911, the Liverpool general transport strike commenced with a walk-out by seaman and which eventually mobilised 70,000 workers. The 1919 Police strike, over an August bank holiday weekend, which generated unprecedented scenes of social unrest in mob violence, looting, and burning. These conflagrations would have formed an inherited, industrial backcloth against which the hospital's current industrial relations would have been compared. But there were more contemporary events to mirror this theme. During the 1960s and 70s, the Labour Party was a broad based church of many hues. One deeply red affiliation was the "Militant Tendency" which impacted on the Labour movement with its convicted socialist stance. By the early 1980s a constitutional schism erupted with the conventional wing of the Labour Party attempting to oust the militants because militant members who had come to dominate Liverpool City Council had orchestrated major resistance to the Conservative government. The effect was to bring major disruption to many of the public services in Liverpool. By 1987, the political fallout was severe enough for the Labour leadership to distance itself from the Militants' objectives and forty-seven Liverpool City Councillors were banned. In turn, Militant withdrew its allegiance to the Labour party because of the lack of representation of the working classes upon which it was based, and because of the capitalist orientation it had come to adopt. The impact of the Liverpool Councillors' insurrection would have been enormous just at the time the hospital was embarking on its own conflagration.

This history of Liverpool's deprivation, poverty and other social ills had also been reified through various pieces of drama of which there were two especially notable examples. The *Blood Brothers* musical, which has managed an extended current London run, recounted 1950s Liverpool society where a child's familial and class upbringing was correlated with very determinate outcomes. The entire story emanated from one working class family's impoverishment and inability to economically manage two further additions to a growing family. It traced the lives of these twin brothers, one of whom was literally given away by his mother at birth to a childless, wealthy couple who was able to pursue a life of advantage and privilege. While he advanced through a homely security, to university, and a subsequent successful political career, his twin brother scrambles among the street gangs, is laid off from his work, is drawn into crime to obtain money, all culminating in a criminal conviction and imprisonment. Upon his release this disadvantaged brother is reunited with his twin with the eventual tragic outcome for both brothers who, simultaneously, die a violent death. My own first viewing of the piece was in Liverpool, itself, during my time at the Moss Side Hospital when it was undergoing a resurgence in the late 1980s.

The second drama, *Boys from the Blackstuff*, was a television drama series, again set in Liverpool, which charted the progress and general decline of five unemployed, working class colleagues whose previous employment had been tarmac laying. Their subsequent paths, most re-employed, was diverse, devious and desperate and completely associated with the ravages of unemployment, the lack of social support, and a belief that there was a concerted North-South economic divide in the country. One particular protagonist, named Yosser, deteriorated into a particular desperation, fruitlessly hunting for a job, losing his wife's company and the custody of his children, and skating on the brink of a mental breakdown. This highly successful series was repeated in 1989 so that its content and sentiments would have been revived among the population of Liverpool... and the staff at the secure hospitals.

On a quite separate personal level, just a small cameo served to acquaint me with the industrial relations awareness of a very intelligent, if outspoken, cleaner employed within Ashworth's Education Centre. Among the many political views she expressed to me was her avowed conclusion that it was shameful that the pay and bonuses due to the hospital's Chief Executive should partly be based on the loss of other employees' jobs arising out of any restructuring, rationalisation, and efficiency savings. And that was just the education department's cleaner!

A more deadly event scarred the Liverpool consciousness during 1989 when ninety-six traveling fans of Liverpool Football club were crushed at one end of Sheffield's Hillsborough Stadium. If this was not bad enough it echoed a similar football tragedy at the Heysel Stadium four years earlier, which involved the Liverpool fraternity again. Of resonance for the Moss Side Hospital staff was that one of the ninety-six was one of their own. And what particular hospital unit had he hailed from? None other than the adolescent unit! The adolescent unit nurses really must have believed the Gods were punishing them!

Also related to the regional focus, was that the area could never have been described, despite its itinerant seafarers and steady Irish immigration, as especially cosmopolitan. Naturally, there were small enclaves of immigrant communities such as the Chinese located around Chinatown but nothing approaching what could amount to an immigrant consolidation or a proliferating cultural diversity that would be expected in most other large conurbations. This was to be reflected in the ethnic makeup of the hospital staff at Ashworth Hospital. In the case of the Park Lane side, some ethnic representation did exist, it had to be said, but for the Moss Side part of the hospital, only a token one or two were to be found. Neither was the hospital able to benefit from the 1970s recruitment into the National Health Service of well-educated, immigrant, student trainees who had hailed from Mauritius, the Caribbean Islands, West Africa, Hong Kong and

Malaysia, as if a closed-shop had excluded such recruitment. Conversely, the County psychiatric hospitals around the country had benefited greatly from this influx and the students went on to develop full-blown careers in the mental health sector. Curiously, not many approached the confines of the "Special Hospitals" up to this point. Inevitably, the lack of ethnic colour and cultural diversity would have necessarily reinforced the entrenched, chauvinistic isolation of the institution and depleted it of one further culturally nurturing ingredient.

000

It is necessary to reiterate, at this point, a handful of contemporary adversities which reinforced the defensive side of the fundamental security-therapy debate and the rationale for prioritising the public safety both from within, and without, the "Special Hospital" provision. The diversion of the mentally disordered offender into an ostensibly hospital environment, and ensuing treatment, far from precluded the possibility of further untrustworthiness, and dangerousness. Written large in the media headlines were a succession of fatal adversities resulting from the release of this category of patients into the community furnished the media and public sensitivity about the wisdom of rehabilitation. Categorically, released mentally disordered offenders, and additional patients under community psychiatric supervision, had inflicted serious assaults and deaths upon the public. Within the hospitals themselves, staff could also become victims of patients' ruses, and assaults which imposed injuries and absenteeism through physical and psychological sickness. In 1988, a Park Lane patient feigned acute appendicitis and was transferred to the local Walton General Hospital where he promptly made good his escape before his eventual capture. In 1990, another Park Lane resident was involved in the homicide of a fellow patient on his own ward, prompting another full scale inquiry. It wasn't even possible for the Inquiry members to discover the precise circumstances in which the killing was effected.

Beyond the premises of Ashworth Special Hospital in 1990, the very same year, an unprecedented, violent riot erupted at Strangeways Prison – now renamed Manchester Prison - not more than about 35 miles distance from the hospital. The explosion of unrest, however justified from the prisoners' viewpoint, caused injuries to 147 staff and 47 prisoners, while one officer and one prisoner died. The debacle, including the rooftop protest, which lasted nearly a month, caused so much damage that it cost £55 million to rebuild the institution. As they were culturally associated with the prison staff through their P.O.A. membership the "Special Hospital" staff would have been more alerted by these events, than most, you would surmise. Unsurprisingly this clutch of disparate adversities, taken together, would undoubtedly have fuelled the ongoing staff scepticism toward the patients within their charge during this defining period of their service's evolution. In light of all these antagonisms there was more reason for the "Special Hospitals" to assume a protective and defensive stance, with the additional back-up of historical custom and practice, than the alternative one which would be laden with unhealthy risk. What right had outsiders to interfere?

For many staff the emerging battle between what they had to perceive, to some degree, as the diametrically opposed realms of therapy and security must have constituted the ultimate in cognitive dissonance. As the psychologist who had been ostracised and hounded from the Moss Side precincts had put it in one of his publications: the staff were faced with the conflicting expectations of jailer and detective verses the therapist and carer. There has to be some merit in appreciating the unconscionable schism in the philosophical ideations of the nursing staff, therefore. How were they to incorporate the competing ideations of a body of institution-centric, local employees, requiring attributes of jailing and detection and allied to the Prison Officers' Association, against the beneficent, client-orientated focus of a modern, networked, nursing profession whose most salient hallmark was to serve the patients' interests? Even if, in principle, these were not incompatible the collage of revelations had suggested otherwise. The tilt toward therapy via the accumulating pressures from health professionals, professional bodies, political guidance, Inquiry condemnations and recommendations, and the radical management reconfiguration, would have been unwarranted intrusions upon this established system. And this system tried to inoculate itself against the slowly infusing virulent strains of change which was slowly invading, resting control, and destroying it.

New therapeutic initiatives were on the agenda such as the provision of a multi-disciplinary team of all professional groups to treat the patients. But, in many other organisations, the whole treatment team was located within the individual units so that each had an integrated and regular contact with each other, each fertilising the others' learning and development, and sharing the same patient files in which to record their notes. In the "Special Hospitals", conversely, the remainder of the non-nursing clinical team retired to office blocks far away from the clinical units. This left the nursing staff, as was the case with the historical County mental hospitals, in sole charge of their areas save for the fleeting visits of other disciplines and visitors. To my mind this gave rise to the metaphor of the units being isolated bunkers on a barren plain from which the nursing staff spied the approaching, intrusive threat of other members of the clinical team and management. More acute therapeutic initiatives were being engineered throughout the N.H.S. via the concepts of "normalisation" and "social role valorisation" of clients with mental health problems and learning disabilities. These reflected the sea-change in perceptions towards such clients who had all but been invalidated by the past institutionalising practices in all the country's psychiatric hospitals where they had, effectively, been locked away from mainstream society. Now the emphasis was on de-institutionalisation and an "open door policy": discharging clients to the community; integrating them into normal society: returning them to the host of social, economic and political roles that they had had removed when disposing of them in mental hospitals; and valuing their place in society whatever the contribution, however limited.

An additional ideational sea-change was the gathering emphasis given to the de-criminalisation of the mentally disordered offender. This had, in fact, been an implicit, legal parameter of the very first Criminal Lunatics Act (1800), where juries were directed to acquit a defendant who, at the time of committing an act of treason, murder, or felony, was adjudged to be found insane. This essential legal plank was later refined in that while acknowledging that the guilty act, the *actus reus*, had been committed by the defendant, by dint of insanity, the necessary guilty intention, the *mens rea*, had been absent. Implicitly, the defendant was no ordinary criminal who harboured an intent to break the law. The Act of 1800 determined that the insane person charged with offences should be given "strict and safe custody" but with "kindness and forbearance". Thereon, the criminal lunatic asylums/"Special Hospitals" did, indeed, maintain a strict and safe custody but it could be argued that with the passage of time the institutional tendency was to over-emphasise the criminal propensities of the patients in their midst without making a sufficient countervailing effort toward their effective treatment.

This increasing emphasis on de-criminalisation was comprehensively reinforced in a landmark *Report of the Committee on*

Mentally Abnormal Offenders, 1975, by the Home Office/Department of Health (called the *Butler Report*). This promoted the diversion of mentally abnormal offenders away from the criminal justice system at every conceivable opportunity, commencing with an initial police arrest where the arresting officer should take cognisance of an individual's signs of mental disorder and engage the services of a Police Surgeon to assess that person's mental state. Prior to a defendant's appearance in Court, such a person should be remanded to a psychiatric facility for a medical assessment of their mental state, to be presented at the subsequent trial. If it was then considered as unreasonable to put the defendant through a trial because of being assessed to be "unfit to plead" because of their mental disability, then they should forgo the rigours of the trial and be removed to hospital until they were considered fit to appear, and plead. If reaching the Criminal Court, the presenting expert information alluding to a defendant's mental disorder should absolve them of legal responsibility for their offences so that the jury should be directed to a verdict of "not guilty on evidence of mental disorder". There were other variations in verdicts along these lines. As significant were the proposals for an integrated network of psychiatric provision to ensure that treatment was available to the offending client: high security "Special Hospitals"; Prison Service health care, a brand new network of medium secure units, and low secure units; and community services; all interlinked with other agencies such as the Probation Service, Social Services, and voluntary services. Of these, the most serious consideration was to be given to the construction of a nationwide network of specialised, medium secure units. These would effect treatment by the whole constituency of mental health professionals – psychiatrists, psychologists, psychotherapists, occupational therapists, social workers, and nursing staff – in a dedicated programme of mental health care for the mentally disordered offender. Lastly, in order to effect the appropriate disposal of clients, as determined by the nature of the offences and the treatment requirements, a raft of new powers were recommended for the hospitals and services that would manage them. To re-iterate, the Report presented a contemporary evaluation of current legal and medical provisions in respect of the mentally disordered offender with recommendations for their comprehensive overhaul and improvement so that the best possible treatment option should be made available to patients wherever they lay in the system.

The year 1990 was to be referred to as a "watershed" in the

approach to mentally disordered offenders because it brought together the observations of a number of agencies which were promoting improved provisions for the mentally disordered offender. Firstly, in the joint Home Office/Department of Health's *Circular 66/90*, there should be a maximum avoidance of the criminal justice system for such clients through "diversion" (transferring defendants to health care facilities), and "discontinuance" (the cessation of criminal proceedings against the mentally disordered). Secondly, the Efficiency Scrutiny of the Prison Medical Service determined that health care contracts should be arranged with local Health Authorities in order to provide the best possible treatment for prisoners. Thirdly, the high incidence of serious, self-injurious incidents in prisons attracted the concerns and recommendations of the Chief Inspector of Prisons in the *Report of a Review of Suicide and Self-harm in Prison Establishments*. Fourthly, the *Woolf Report (Cm 1456)* investigating the causes for the prisoner riot at Strangeway's Prison produced regime change recommendations to improve conditions for prisoners. Lastly, research by Professor Gunn and his colleagues from the Institute of Psychiatry estimated that as many as 1400 sentenced prisoners in the Prison Service might require a transfer to hospital facilities for treatment of their ongoing mental disorder. These disparate, but ultimately related, findings from 1990 had a considerable impact on the perceptions of the needs of the mentally disordered offender.

We weren't finished yet! To add to this, another joint Department of Health/Home Office tome – a *Review of Health and Social Services for Mentally Disordered Offenders and Others requiring similar services (1992)*, was completed which, effectively building on the earlier Butler Report, brought together all the foregoing findings, and advanced the causes of a wide range of client needs that came within the category of the mentally disordered offender. The discrete range of needs were: people with brain injury; the deaf/hearing impaired; substance misusers; sex offenders; the suicidal; children and adolescents; the elderly, and women.

This slew of authoritative initiatives, and the cumulative consolidation of provision, were to have far reaching implications for a "Special Hospital" service which had, until relatively recently, had a virtual monopoly on managing/treating the mentally disordered offender. In light of these, "Special Hospitals" would now have but a residual role among a whole gamut of alternative services and be reserved merely for a hard core of clients who would continue to require a high security environment because they were too dangerous to be transferred to conditions of reduced security. But, far from viewing this as a relegation, it only substantiated and consolidated their primary perception of safeguarding society against the most lethal of the mentally disordered fraternity.

000

Small wonder that when outsiders such as myself, along with the rest of the "Therapy Thespians", came in good faith to fulfil what we believed to be nothing more than our occupational purpose and duty we were perceived to be practicing the dark arts of a liberal and therapeutic subversion of intuitively reasonable practices refined over time, and that these dark arts were only applicable elsewhere. Besides, nobody within their immediate spheres of influence had directly told the staff that new ideas and ways of doing things were required. Who said there should be innovative practices and treatment strategies even if they did apply to other tiers of the forensic mental health hierarchy? Not the D.H.S.S., not Secretaries of State, not local management, certainly not the P.O.A.! So, if the outsiders came with their personal agendas, why should they have been entertained in light of the tried and trusted practices of tradition? What exactly were we outsiders bringing to the table, anyway? Evidence? Evidence that new practices were demonstrably more effective, safer, would guarantee the future safety of the public terrain? Hardly! And even when we took up our positions we were not armed with any guidance from the authorities, ourselves. We were individuals abandoned to make what limited ripples of personal influence we could before the forces of reaction engulfed us. If anything, we also required our own training in how to convert an established institutional culture which recognised the understandable vested interests contained within it.

And what part did I have to play in these changing dynamics during the time that I held the positions of manager, tutor, and researcher at Ashworth Hospital? At the time, I had little conception of "mitigating circumstances" on their behalf though I had a superficial acquaintance with the notion of the paranoid processes which are generated within institutions. However, this was not sufficient to equip me with the means to manage the practicalities. In the beginning, I did my best to work with those few staff who seemed more receptive of change, who appeared better motivated, especially those better placed to implement new ideas. But with so few to work

227

with the project became one of increasing attrition and I focused more and more on those resistant elements, those I considered to be lost causes. Furthermore, I was prepared to be assigned the stigma of unpopularity in order to pursue my objectives. But I had little regard or sympathy for the interests of "institutionalized" staff who had revealed little or no effort to improve themselves over their career and they became a ready target of my own judgements. Neither did I respect the intransigence and hostility toward changes and developments which were rapidly gathering momentum in the national mental health services – developments which I wished to be party to. I had quickly assumed a working premise that two opposing forces were railing within the hospital: the moderates' liberal rehabilitation of the excusable disordered offender verses the hardliners' reactionary punishment of the unforgivable criminal lunatic. It seemed to me that the ideas of therapy and care were interpreted as somewhat feminising attributes, antipathetic to a masculinist culture of discipline and retribution. In terms of the offence backgrounds of the patients in their care this would seem to have been counter-intuitive. Security was deemed the pragmatic, essential ingredient of control rather than the power of the human encounter, through therapeutic relationships, that might provide an alternative, positive model of human relationships which the patients could internalise and enhance their self-control. The treatment and rehabilitation of mentally disordered offenders which, perforce, would require engendering the self-belief that they were not irredeemable monsters, along with similar therapeutic abstractions, would have been off the scale of reason. Professional education had been so limited that the very notion of patient "counseling" was distorted to mean a skilled version of verbal discipline. Consequently, the staff's own semi-professional language I put down to an indigenous slang, and their therapeutic repudiations to a vested folklore, and I was probably not far wrong, in truth. And over time, more and more energy was fuelled by these ideations, and more time was wasted in confronting the opposition, until my motivation gradually deserted me.

When I endured the uncomfortable experience of being one of the individuals who were probably demonised for contributing to the staff's predicament I struggled to contain my own sense of rejection and my flourishing anxiety. My personal psychological withdrawal became inevitable but throughout this difficult time I managed to hold on to a core of beliefs that therapeutic intentions, and patients' rights, must necessarily orientate the staff to a patient centred regime that improved their developmental potential and mental health, and that any staff resistance to these should be decried. But I would readily acknowledge that a better acquaintance of institutional dynamics, and my personal contribution to them, would have been mightily helpful at the time. If that had been the case, who knows what might have transpired. Not much perhaps. I say that because the whole experience of working in this "Special Hospital" accorded me the chance to completely re-evaluate my own professional purposes and role, to stir my conscience, something that may very well not have happened if my career trajectory had run more smoothly, and had not met with such obstacles. More positively, I was then able to pass it on to others as a salutary tale.

There was an even more uncomfortable realisation that my own fight-back may have been derived from more personal considerations. In fact, nothing more than a compulsion to resist anyone who proved himself to be of a particularly belligerent constitution who might have approximated the dogmatic, humiliating and dismissive influences of the early parental authority in my early childhood and adolescence? When I had hunkered down and disposed of my managerial gloves in a spirit of an invigorated defence of my objectives, was this really nothing more than a reliving of old, dormant travails and personal rebellion against my parents? At this level, it begged the question of whether it was ever quite possible to engage in occupational relations – or any other for that matter – without familial personalities and backgrounds encroaching to distort the present. From a psychodynamic point of view, of course, it was never quite possible. So was it ever conceivable to make an informed, objective assessment of any life issue, or circumstance, or any interpersonal encounter, without it being filtered or contaminated by the prejudice of personal disposition and past parental load? Was it not crucial, therefore, to ensure that these projected personal issues and beliefs that could prejudice any aspect of working life should be made a focus of professional development so that when putting voice to a personal stance on an issue it was offered with a more grounded awareness and insight?

Yet another uncomfortable realisation began to fester in my conscience. That there may well have been vested self-interests for those who sought frank therapeutic involvement with patients who required not only a defining of the mental health needs and solutions of patients, but a need to obtain the necessary therapeutic skills. On the one hand, though acquiring these interventions and skills which would enhance and promote our professional effectiveness, and our professional ambitions and advancement, they also afforded us with the plain means of becoming more personally useful than we would be, otherwise. On the other hand, empathising with patients' problems and life dilemmas, and equipping ourselves with the means to help, vicariously aided us in helping ourselves to solve our own conundrums. In short, helping others was to be helping ourselves. These are not exactly unacceptable notions and do not necessarily contaminate therapeutic relations with either colleagues or staff provided there is an awareness of what might be happening between a therapist and patient. Indeed, such issues are the focus of the Jungian school of psychoanalysis which acknowledges the benefit of the "wounded healer" in the therapeutic relationship. It is just such dynamics and potential complications for which the realms of "clinical supervision", and "personal therapy", came to be proposed and introduced into mental health services. These were to enhance the professional integrity of mental health staff who participated in them, though they were not much in vogue at this time for the generic practitioner.

But the Fates had not given up their hold of Broadmoor yet. During the following year, 1989, within eight years of the damning *Rampton Review*, a National Health Service "Health Advisory Service" Report, in fulfillment of its national remit to review and improve hospital and community health care in England and Wales, adjudicated on its inspection of Broadmoor Hospital. Among the many admonishing conclusions was the general ineffectiveness of the treatment measures for its client group: the lack of opportunity afforded for a collaborative pact between patients and therapists in determining the treatment approach – something which was to be expected in most other therapeutic circumstances; the lack of integration between the two patient sexes within the hospital; the over-use of seclusion of the patients; and the lack of any evaluation of any of its treatment methods, including medication. In sustaining the characteristics of a penal institution an endemic conflict had undermined the potential marriage of security and therapy with the consequence that Broadmoor was condemned as a resistant, isolationist, excessively custodial culture which was non-therapeutic. It posited that time was running out for the hospital and that prospective, professionally qualified staff, with more enlightened approaches to mental health care, would not be attracted to such an environment where the emphasis was so uncompromisingly depersonalising and institutionalised. But Broadmoor, at least, had to learn its lessons.

This relatively short Report was no passing ship. It was the final catalyst in the burgeoning demands for a comprehensive change in managerial direction. The civil servants of the D.H.S.S., the intelligent yet distant controllers of the high security Special Hospitals, were to give up the ghost and managerial authority came to be vested in the Special Hospitals Service Authority from 1989.

000

A small token of perversity presented itself in 1988 when the peaked caps of the male staff uniform were completely phased out, by the early 1990s, the complete serge tunic was strategically transformed into contemporary, dark lounge suits. There was a staff reaction to this in the form of – hair, or lack of it! Initially there were conjectures about premature baldness or, maybe, of an epidemic of alopecia but the concerted outbreak of shaved heads that cut across the body of male staff confirmed a more disturbing possibility. Perhaps the staff were compensating for the relative loss of power, authority and status, previously conferred by their officer uniforms and more disciplined regime, by a more fashionable display of physical masculinity! This was a highly personalised recalcitrant symbol of separation from the encroaching management and, doubtless, the increasingly potent patients.

During the 1987-1992 years, a philosophical tsunami swept away the established, staff-centric regime with its "deserving" status, potency, and rights, which placed the patients in an 'undeserving' status, with minimal rights, and reasserted a demand for more purposeful goals toward forensic clients. And whilst these represented a creditable evolution of aims for patients they were not only detrimental to, but incidentally victimising of, the staff of "Special Hospitals". It could be said this conflation of untoward events, accumulating concerns and evidence about the abuse of patients, changing political and professional agendas, the mounting professionalism of nursing and its demands for individual responsibility and accountability, and the fallout from the industrial actions, coalesced into a concerted revision of the "ancient régime" as represented by the prevailing industrial relations. They came to represent an assault upon the nurses' traditional recourse to union protected, group action and whittled away a localised, parochial identity. The resulting P.O.A. inspired grievance and reaction could be characterized as ramping up the maximum reaction possible. Alternatively, or conterminously, the accumulating disturbance among the nursing group *could* be characterised as a self-determining resistant action of a working class faction which defied the ongoing persecution of economic and political bosses and authority.

000

In retrospect, needless to say, I came to conclude that the lamentable behaviour of "Special Hospital" nursing staff over this divisive period had an element of comprehensibility – if not exoneration, exactly – attached to it. That more credence should have been granted for the profuse mitigating circumstances that had accumulated over their evolution – a position toward which, at the time, would have been entirely unpalatable to me. Their history, presenting problems, and the dysfunctional patterns by which they related to changes in management arrangements, other professional staff, and patients were all relevant parts of a cumulative, institutional pathology in the same way that an individual's personal history, symptoms, and patterns of interaction can come to characterise a patient's disorder. It would seem a little egregious that the same excusable consideration should not be vouchsafed to the hospital staff for their professional transgressions that was granted to the patients for their psychological violations. I have found it useful to try to understand the institutional processes and relationships within the Special Hospitals, as they erupted into a kind of pathological disorder, through the psychotherapeutic model of Cognitive Analytic Therapy (C.A.T.) which will be expounded only briefly.

One major theoretical strand of Cognitive Analytic Therapy built upon the psychoanalytic and psychodynamic model of "object relations". "Object relations" theory developed the notion of "object" as a broad description of stimuli and experiences which do not refer to the self, but to someone or something which has relevance for that self, starting from when they were an infant. The theory of object relations grew out of Freud's earlier "drive theory" which posited that an infant's psychological motivation demanded an implicit "object". These drives were predominantly the pleasure-seeking "libidinal" drive, or the "aggressive/destructive" drive associated with painful experience. This was developed by another psychoanalyst, Melanie Klein, whose conception was that an infant's contact with early object experiences were not understood in a visual sense. Accordingly, an individual infant experienced, and acquired, a range of external stimuli which were generally mother-related, such as images of breasts and nipples, along with others such as parents, siblings, food, bathing, bedding, toys and related matter. The theory posited that these "objects" – the objectives of the infant's instinctual drives – then became internalised as inner objects. But these objects could only be construed as they were *experienced* by the infant. So from early on, an infant learned to differentiate a pleasurable "good" object such as a milk-supplying breast to feed its hunger, from an unsatisfactory "bad" object where this breast was not made available on demand if it felt hungry. Similarly, the stimuli of parental threats and prohibitions could also be internalised as "bad" aspects of these people relations. This drive-motivated behaviour of the infant, which necessarily engaged the infant's care-givers into some level of cooperating relations, became "internalised object relations". Gradually, as more and more object (person) relations came to be experienced, internalised, and integrated, a primitive sense of a "self" was developed as the infant learned to differentiate itself as somebody separate from its care-givers, and the relationship between them. From these early interactions, where internal images of a "self" were substantially formed, the effect upon the person, their self-concept, and management of others, could be life-long.

There have been a plethora of "object-relations" refinements since the original psychoanalytic theories which viewed 'object relations' as "people relations" only. Despite this diverse evolution there remained a general unanimity that "object relations" was not now absolutely limited to just people relations. While they included this internal world of relations between the self and others; they were also inclusive of fantasies and perceptions – shall we say of admiration and gratitude, or terror and rejection – which became "representations" of "others"; and also came to refer to anything in life when these became deeply and symbolically connected to powerful object experiences in the inner world. The concurrence within object relations theory, therefore, was that all people carry within them an internal, frequently unconscious, world of relationships that is often more powerful and intrusive than the external world of real people that are encountered in the everyday here and now. Alongside the real interactions with real people in everyday life, individual selves (subjects), also held onto internal mental representations of other people (objects), from their past. Provided these experiences and internalisations were good enough the infant developed an "ego identity" which remained stable over time with an equally stable and appropriate conception of its care-givers. For the infant/child/adult with a "good enough" parenting experience there formed an ability to hold an integrated image of a reliable and consistent parent despite the variance in being good at some times, and not so good at others. For other people who had experienced a more inconsistent and unreliable parenting style, the discrimination of "good" and "bad" became more polarised, than integrated, with the result that there may have formed a "splitting" of an object (parent). So fragile could the infant's image of the object be that this "split" could predominate so that for much of the time the parent could only be held to be either a perfectly good parent, or a perfectly bad one. The fragility of the relation meant that such people were not able to hold onto one unvarying image of the parent as being "good enough", incorporating both good and bad elements, only that the parent could be either one or the other at any given time.

Cognitive Analytic Therapy built on, and radically restated, the theoretical basis of object relations ideas to explain how the self came to be formed in the psychological sense. It came to stress the social formation of the self and mind during early life, positing that this identity was generated through "reciprocal role relations" rather than by instinctual drives. These "reciprocal role relations" were learned in interaction with early care-givers in the process of "care-giving" and "care-receiving" participation. During this experiential process the infant learned not only that he was a subject in relation to other objects but that expectations about that interaction were incorporated into distinct roles. Because the two roles were derived in relation to each other they were said to be reciprocal, having mutual expectations and acknowledgment. As a result, the infant necessarily internalised the values, images, voices, feelings and relational patterns of the parents and immediate family and culture. This process of internalising these reciprocal roles meant that the child acquired an appreciation of both the care-giving role (object), *and* his own care-receiving role (subject), in what were descriptions of "inner parent-inner child" reciprocal role patterns. These reciprocations created not only the individual's sense of self, and an understanding of the "other", they also helped to shape the child's definition of the wider external world. Provided the "other" in this care-giving relationship was competent, enabling, consistent and reliable then the infant / adult learned to be a collaborative, negotiating care-recipient. Over time the internalisation of care-givers, other significant people, and other variable stimuli, enabled the infant/child to acquire a reciprocal role repertoire which appreciated the very roles of the care-givers, themselves. And the over-riding significance for Cognitive Analytic Therapy was how this repertoire was generalised to other relationships in the future and how it guided the self-management of adults. C.A.T. therapists derived these descriptions of reciprocal role patterns from a number of sources. To begin with, the childhood recollections of their clients while in therapy were found to be highly accessible. Then these patterns would have re-emerged in the relational patterns the clients had with other people, including current relationships. Furthermore, these very same reciprocal roles would be evoked, and repeated in the therapeutic relationship between the therapist and the client in what is termed "transference" and "counter-transference".

This interpersonal process could equally be scaled up so that it could be applied to inter-group relations within organisations. In the instance of the organisational world of this "Special Hospital", it would be possible to delineate the internalised, institutional and cultural "object relations" of the nursing staff, though this would not exclude other professional groups, in terms of the "reciprocal role relations". Applying these theoretical principles the nursing staff were the "subjects" – the care-recipients of the various managerial "objects" – or care-givers. In turn, the patients were the "subjects" of the nursing staff "objects". Cognitive Analytic Therapy theory might interpret these institutional relations in the following description of "reciprocal role procedures".

(1) During the early years of relatively harmonious industrial relations it could be said that a somewhat idealised reciprocal role could be represented. The hospital ethos was, in essence, a staff-focused regime, emphasising staff rights and their "deserving" status, all of which conferred a degree of potency; this potency conferred on them the right to marginalise the patients' rights, and to assign to them an "undeserving" status which left them fairly impotent. In these circumstances the managerial bodies, at that time, could be represented as "good objects". In C.A.T. terms, they could be represented in the role of "Idealised Masters" – characterised as paternalistic, controlling, authoritative and protecting toward the hospital staff. In turn, the hospital staff reciprocated in the role of "Dutiful Subordinates" – protected, controlled, and compliant – because their needs and wishes were largely being attended to.

(2) Through the institutional internalisation of both of these roles the staff were able to revert to the role of "Idealised Masters", themselves, and replicate this role in their own reciprocal relations with their patients. In turn, the patients reciprocated with the role of "Dutiful Subordinates". However, this vouchsafed the staff with a relatively unexpurgated sense of entitlement, power, and control which sporadically herniated into what outside bodies would interpret as the abuse of patients.

For clarity, hopefully, these reciprocal relations have been reproduced in the following diagrammatic representation which is a strategic therapeutic tool in Cognitive Analytic Therapy.

(A) Idealised, Harmonious Industrial Relations.

Staff-focused regime = staff status 'deserving'; staff rights and potency; patient status 'undeserving'; patient impotence.

DHSS employers/local managers   Staff

"Controlling Masters"
(paternalistic, authoritative, protecting)
I
I
"Dutiful Subordinates"
(protected, controlled, compliant)

Staff   Patients

(3) However, this particular set of reciprocal roles could not stand alone because the staff did not experience this idealised state continuously. Alongside the more idealistic version of roles of Idealised Masters and Dutiful Subordinates there evolved a strongly contrasted variant. For the region's historical industrial relations conflicts also predisposed the staff to hold a less than idealistic view of their employers, at the same time, inclining them toward an inherent distrust. This, alongside the accumulating concerns and criticisms of their internal operations by the new managers, professional nursing bodies, and Inquiry reports, created a parallel set

of reciprocal role relations based around conflictual industrial relations where the regime was turned on its head, elevating the patient-centredness, their "deserving" status, rights and potency, while the staff status was now held to be "undeserving" and impotent. In this parallel version of reciprocal role relations, the employers, S.H.S.A., professional bodies, and Inquiries, could now be represented as "bad objects". In C.A.T. terms, these "Fault-finding Critics" could be characterised as abandoning, victimising, abusing and contemptuous of the staff, while the staff reciprocated in the role of "Abused Victims" characterised by feelings of being victimised, betrayed, and contemptible. In respect of the more resistant extremes of professional abuse toward the patients, management, and critical professionals in the hospital, the behaviour of the nursing staff climaxed into a grotesque parody of their professional purpose.

(4) Again, through the process of institutional internalisation the staff were able to revert to the role of "fault-finding critics" characterised by being abandoning, victimising, abusing and contemptuous of the patients, while the patients reciprocated in the role of "Abused Victims" characterised by the experience of being victimised, betrayed, and contemptible.

(5) Faced with the widespread rejection and criticism of all those bodies then this would have had the undoubted consequence of eliciting uncertainty and doubts among the nursing staff as to their integrity and legitimacy. There was no doubt that the nursing staff felt that all these internal critics and external authorities had demonised the "Special Hospital" staff for the shortfalls in the service provision and that they received no acknowledgement for having to deal with people whom no other service would entertain. This *demonising* would have been a complementary element to this "fault-finding critics" reciprocal role pattern to which the staff reciprocated with the "victims" role. Again, the internalisation of both roles would have meant that the staff were able to assume the "demonising critics" role themselves and operationalise it against others. Easy targets would have been the perceived betrayal of other staff within their own organisation – notably individual professionals, individual managers, the emerging body of staff converting to the newly formed Royal College of Nursing, and the S.H.S.A. – and outside bodies such as the Mental Health Act Commission, and the Committee of Inquiry. In terms of the two sets of reciprocal role patterns I, personally, would probably have been assigned to both the acceptable idealistic version, and the unacceptable critical version, when first taking up my

managerial post as, initially, the staff might have hoped that I would be partial to protecting and promoting their interests. But as time progressed, I would have been assigned to a betraying, demonising critic. It is difficult to have to accept that I did, in my own small way, contribute to rejecting the integrity of the staff, and being contemptuous of their reaction to contemporary mental health programmes, and my own initiatives, but that was probably the truth of it.

DIAGRAM

(B) Conflictual Industrial Relations.

Patient centred regime = staff status "undeserving"; declining staff potency and rights; patient status "deserving"; increasing patient rights and potency.

SHSA/Inquires/professional bodies   Staff

"Fault-finding Critics"
(abandoning, abusing, victimising, contemptuous, demonising)
I
I
"Pilloried Victims"
(abandoned, victimised, betrayed, contemptible, resistant, demonised)

Staff   Patients

If anything, this was a tale of moral uncertainty. That there existed no definitive consensus about what was considered to be culturally acceptable, or individually acceptable, or professionally acceptable thinking and behaviour in relation to the treatment and management of the mentally disordered offender to the extent that even the founding principles of the enterprise had been frittered away. In this the mandarins of the Home Office, the Board of Control, the Ministry of Health, and Department of Health and Social Security, had historically colluded with this ambivalence of purpose. And in the vacuum left by such moral uncertainty the "Special Hospital" nursing staff assumed a parochial, moral high ground which validated the institution-centric perceptions of their own purpose, at least. Subsequently, this very deliberate parochialism fed into the conviction of all the evolving external authorities that the staff and institutional functions of the "Special Hospitals" had become perverted, irredeemable, and inexcusable. Indeed, that the former gamekeepers had forsaken their purpose and turned poachers! In the unprecedented circumstances of the *group* action by nursing staff when they unjustifiably locked patients into their rooms, on more than one occasion, and walked away from their wards and refused to attend to their duties, they defaulted on their moral sensibilities and occupational task for which they were employed from the public purse. They left the patients to their own devices and were not available to provide the relevant nursing care. They provoked the risk of exacerbating the mental disturbance of the patients, including self-harm, as well as the risk of harm to the relatively untrained staff who were left to assume their roles in their stead. They increased the potential for patients' escapes into the wider community. In short, the abandonment of their professional duties undermined their own integrity since they were clearly prepared to embark on this risk-laden path with all the attendant dangers that it posed to other people. And for these actions many, many dozens of staff were referred to their professional bodies for breaching the Code of Professional Conduct.

Whilst awaiting the outcome of these deliberations the Special Hospital Services Authority instituted Ward Managers for each and every unit throughout the system. And into these posts they recruited a number of those whom they had already referred for unprofessional behaviour but whose professional fate they were still to learn of! What message did this send out? But the governing professional bodies did not hold the staff to account in the final analysis. No action was taken against any of them. No doubt these bodies took into account the cultural environment, and common practices, whereby the nursing staff customarily secluded patients during the nighttime, inferring that seclusion in the context of industrial action was no great departure from the normal practice of locking patients up at night. What message did this send out? Moral uncertainty abounded across the board.

To reiterate, the Inquiry into complaints about Ashworth Hospital came to represent the "tipping point" for radical change in the high security mental hospitals in this country. It did so using the parameter of the basic human rights to which individual members of society are entitled, no matter that they suffered from mental disorders, no matter that they may have offended against the law, no matter that they be confined for other people's safety. Allied to this was the input of mental health workers who provided their expertise to illuminate what should constitute acceptable professional practice and against which the conduct of the nursing staff was finally adjudicated upon. The whole range of staff deviance illustrated that it cannot be taken for granted that individual staff will always abide by common standards of propriety, or professional standards, even legal sanctions. Thus society is faced with the regrettable necessity to continually police individual and institutional responsibility and accountability, and to differentiate these from their liability, and from their excusability.

In the face of sub-cultural variance it is undoubtedly the task of professional bodies to establish, and inculcate, definitive, over-arching aims and values, and set a revived moral compass, to which the many participants of mental health care are committed for the greater good. This is particularly indisputable in the case of organisations which, perforce, are required to be agents of social control, which forensic mental health services undoubtedly are. Yet all institutions, not just health organisations, require external agencies to intrude and to evaluate their internal machinations in order to ensure that there is compliance with appropriate standards. They have to be nurtured with the humanistic ideals that conflate and coagulate along the path of a broader intellectual consensus than their own institutional entrenchment. This is absolutely essential with reference to health organisations where the current emphasis is to focus on the human rights of patients as equally valued citizens. And with regard to mentally disordered clients that their offending behaviour does not condemn them to an eternity of institutional and social exclusion. Ultimately, that whatever the nature of the client's offences, the only acceptable ethical position of mental health professionals is to aim to work alongside clients, using the evidence of proven practices, to effect responsive outcomes, thereby minimising the risk to society, so that those clients should be returned to the social milieu and full citizenship. It is for the forensic process to judge otherwise and there is some moral certainty in that.

Chapter 6

Departures

Having been exposed to these confounding issues since entering the "Special Hospital" arena it had become my contention that in order to fully fulfill their professional obligations the nursing staff needed to be better equipped for their purpose. That they needed to move beyond generic mental health nursing and secure care to becoming actively therapeutic in the spheres of antisocial, dangerous and offending behaviours where these were pertinent characteristics of their clients. By the year of the publication of the Committee of Inquiry Report, 1992, I had taken up a teaching position at Broadmoor Hospital to lead a newly instituted course which prepared nursing staff for working in "controlled environments". The course was a building block in inculcating the message that a suitable balance had to be struck between the opposing domains of therapy and security when managing the mentally disordered offender in whatever establishment they were contained – low security, medium security, high security or Prison Service health care, whether in the public or private sectors. The course had a major shortfall in not specifying what that therapeutic side of the balance was to consist of.

I had the benefit of being able to include first hand research findings from the survey to which I had been seconded toward the end of my spell at Ashworth Hospital. The research title was the "Treatment and Security Needs of Special Hospital Patients". The survey reviewed the "Special Hospital" population at that time which comprised 1700 patients, 20% of which were women. The average length of stay, based on those who had already been discharged, was 8.5 years. As the nurse member of this multi-disciplinary research team I was charged with compiling a quite separate part of the research which was termed "the Nursing Perspective". The most crucial research team result was that by no means all the hospital population were in need of their current "Special Hospital" surroundings. In the case of the clinical teams based in the hospitals, 50% of the patients were deemed not to require maximum security any longer: while in the research team view a lower level of around

35% were not in need of it. All the remaining patients should have been placed in other less stringent facilities from medium security, or locked wards, or open hospital wards, through to the community. Those patients who had to continue to experience a "Special Hospital" disposal should only be subject to a degree of security which was commensurate with the individual risks they posed and should not be subject to a blanket homogeneity of secure conditions. Neither should there be a homogeneity of treatment strategies. This individualisation should be extended to establishing discrete treatment specialisms such as sex offender treatment programmes and specialist wards to help effect this should become operational. These results went some way to strategic decisions about reducing the future capacity of "Special Hospitals", their prospective clinical focus, and the need for additional, alternative, hospital facilities for those patients who did not require high security management.

My own results and conclusions broadly complied with those of the remaining team of psychiatrists and psychologists. A not unsurprising finding was that it was organisationally impossible for a high security environment to be expected to maximise both security and therapy, for all patients, over a broad spectrum of needs, over such a protracted length of stay. As for their own perspective, the nursing staff believed that the institutional regime of high security hospitals, their high perimeter borders, security procedures, and nursing "discipline", were indispensable ingredients for meeting patients' needs and setting them on the road to recovery. The trouble was that there was no evidence to support any of this and that these merely reflected the intuitive, personal convictions of the staff. Though I didn't blame them for this impressionistic account since no evidence existed to either confirm or refute their opinion! In fact, it was difficult to determine quite what the nursing staff achieved in terms of health outputs. My own research findings revealed the many patient deficits and disturbed behaviours which characterised the body of patients – including those who were evaluated as being ready for transfer out of the "Special Hospitals" to lower levels of security - had not been sufficiently addressed during their sojourn in high security. These unaddressed needs would seriously incapacitate them on their return to a changing, and challenging, community. Even for those who could be transferred out to lower security environments, many would continue to require a considerable range of continuing treatment and therapeutic intervention and present considerable challenges to the resident staff of receiving units.

My belief that there was such a potential entity as a specialist "forensic mental health nurse" incorporating incremental skills beyond conventional mental health nursing, caused me to embark on an upgraded "Diploma in Forensic Mental Health Nursing" which was validated by both the Institute of Psychiatry, and the South Bank University. I became the programme leader and ran the course single-handed. Unfortunately, investment in this initiative was not sustained. I received no further teaching resources to enable me to roll out the programme further, and the wider audience of nurses working within controlled environments lost an invaluable opportunity to acquire a forensic accreditation.

A modern mental health care model no longer relied on the traditional view that located the cause of mental disturbance within the individual patient, alone, as an endogenous psychological disease that required only mechanical or chemical manipulation. It had increasingly accepted the causal influences of exogenous factors so that treatment took account of a patient's internal chemistry, and their social integration, and their personal integration. The forensic variation of this extended linear was to take full account of the logical regression which links a succession of criminogenic indicators which reached back into economic, educational and social deprivation; unemployment; substance misuse; then dysfunctional familial backgrounds and child-rearing patterns. This linear sequence would not only help the patients to develop some insight into the direct relationship between their mental disorder and offending, and the more indirect developmental background, but would also assist policy makers in defining social programmes aimed at improving the life chances of certain groups so that they were made less vulnerable to such adverse consequences. Meaning that appropriate parts of criminological science, and the evidence base for assessing and managing dangerousness, also needed to be an inclusive part of the forensic mental health curriculum. Furthermore, in managing the clients with such a complex causal chain to their histories the cumulative security implications of technology, procedures, and staff/patient relationships, should acknowledge and make explicit both the social control function, and the therapy and treatment function, that these served. In keeping with this trend a forensic nursing accreditation would facilitate the acquisition of "forensic nursing competences" in order to apply the same therapeutic principles to their clients' offending pathology, as they were supposed to apply to the psychological pathology. In a word, that they should contribute to identifying, and therapeutically intervening in, those symptoms of mental illness, learning disability, and personality disorder, which evidence had proven to be criminogenic. In short, to manage the articulating linkage between mental disturbance and potential, or actual, offending from both aspects rather than depending on the simplistic justification that to successfully treat the mental disorder was, ipso facto, to treat the attendant offending behaviour. It would not be the purpose of the forensic nurse to find therapeutic solutions to offending behaviours, per se, as in the case of patients transferred from prisons with pre-morbid histories of criminality. This was a remit for other agencies, especially those in criminal justice, but there would be a fine line between therapeutic and penal interventions since there was a need for clinical care packages for offence categories such as aggression and violence, sexual offences, and arson.

In respect of mental disorder, as such, there are no specific psychological symptoms, or psychiatric diagnoses, which are absolutely determinate of an offending outcome. However, patients' ideas, especially delusions – which are generally considered to be fixed beliefs which have no objective foundation in the subject's social reality – may evolve into criminogenic symptoms. This will depend on the material content and strength of the ideation, its overall coherence, the conviction that supports it, and the degree to which it intrudes upon and distresses the individual.

000

My conviction that nurses working in controlled mental health facilities were not being trained in the relevant skills for their particular client group was maintained over the immediate years that followed. The main "modus operandi" for managing the offending, antisocial, or dangerous behaviours remained the generalised use of security technology and security practices, along with appropriate staff-patient relationships, to safely contain the patient class. Otherwise, incorporating therapeutic interventions aimed specifically at enabling clients to develop insights about their offending, and to what extent, and how, their offending was integrated with their mental status and deterioration, remained un-chartered. When I was later to return to the medium security mental health field after departing from the high security establishments this lack of forensic integration was confirmed on the several occasions when I and my colleagues would visit clients being considered for transfer to our unit. For our task was to compile nursing assessments of such patients. On arrival, our visiting assessment teams would be faced with the same "Special Hospital" rationale, time and time again: that the patient no longer required a high security environment because they were a "model patient". That is, that they readily conformed with the daily ward routine without complaint; showed an appropriate level of independence as far as opportunities could be extended; complied with all the hospital requirements for treatment and occupational therapy attendance; displayed few signs of psychological disturbance; and gave little cause for concern about repeating their past offences. All well and good. Looking at the scenario from the perspective of the staff in "Special Hospitals" it was not difficult to appreciate how they had surmised, historically, that assessing their patients' propensity for danger in the future was something which could be extrapolated from the success with which those risks had been managed within their own environment. Having deduced that those risks had reduced within a high security environment, they drew the conclusion that it was time to hand over the patients for other establishments to focus on their particular remits as the patients progressed toward the community. Unfortunately, progress had demanded the converse – that there had to be evidence to show not just that the danger to others had been successfully reduced in a high security institution, but that the risk was so reduced that patients would not present a grave risk to the public if they were to find themselves in the vicinity of the public. I use the following case as an example of what we experienced, simply to illustrate the point, and not to find fault with the particular hospital or staff, per se. This case also stood out in my memory as illuminating the dilemma for all the concerned parties: the relinquishing "Special Hospitals"; the receiving hospitals; and the patient included.

The prospective client-transfer in this case had been enclosed in the precincts of one of the "Special Hospitals" for around a decade and a half, had been allocated to a pre-discharge/rehabilitation ward for some time, and was awaiting a transfer out of the place. His diagnosis fell into the category of a mild learning disability and his offences were of a sex-offending nature. The offences had comprised sexual assaults on teenage girls over a period of time until he was caught, and tried, and admitted to a "Special Hospital". Briefly, his modus operandi was to travel on his local railway network, trap the girls alone in single railway carriages when no other passengers were present, wield a knife at the girls to ensure their compliance but did not actually inflict wounds with the weapon, and threaten the girls not to call for help until he had made good his escape from the vicinity. His sexual acts had been to put his hands on the girls' breasts, on their genital areas, then press his fingers into their vaginas if time made this possible. Reading the details of what he had inflicted upon youthful girls in what they should have confidently predicted to be safe, public space was mightily disturbing. He had perpetrated this pattern not once, but over two separate periods of his life having been discharged from hospital care for an initial set of similar offences, then re-apprehended and sent to this current "Special Hospital" for a second set of like offences. We were permitted access to the patient's personal notes and, as was usual with long-term clients, were confounded by the stack of files and detail at our disposal. We did our best to filter the more salient of the multi-disciplinary records and learned of the conclusions of psychologists and psychotherapists during his initial hospitalisation but we were damn well not going to rove over an abundance of nursing files. The staff could summarise for us.

'How would you describe his current attitudes to his index offences during the time he's been on your unit?' A look of perplexed indifference was returned by the three male members of staff who had invited us into the ward office.

'Perhaps you ought to ask the Consultant that for a better picture but, from our point of view, he's given us no cause for concern and expressed no interest, whatever, in young girls during his entire time on this ward.' It seemed a pretty obvious line of enquiry but we had to ask it.

'Have you asked him? Do you spend any time assessing his current level of interest in young girls, or women for that matter? Has there been any nursing enquiry into his current thinking about his index offences? That's what we're trying to get at, you see.'

'What, you expect us to continually rake over his past with him? We have to help him move on.' Of course they did. 'One thing's for sure, he doesn't need maximum security anymore.'

'Could we ask whether there's been any risk assessment work by the nurses, or other team members, relevant to the patient's past offences?' we continued to probe.

'What risk assessment work?' they replied. 'We don't do risk assessment work in "Special Hospitals", that's your job in the medium security units. How can we do that here when the patients are locked up in a top security joint, miles from anywhere?'

'Ok, if no risk assessment work has been done what other work have the nursing staff done with the patient that convinces you that your patient would be safe in the future?' we followed up.

'All the therapy work has been done with the psychologists, and psychotherapists, and the like. We carry out our nursing duties.'

'Yes, we've read the notes but that work was some years ago, you see. I think the bottom line for us is how do *you* know the patient's safe now?'

'Well, no one can be sure, no matter how many tests you set him to do. But if a bloke's been with us in the hospital for years and not put a foot wrong in all that time, the model patient you might say, he don't deserve to be locked up for the rest of his life does he? He's obviously matured and he's a lot older so the risks must have reduced. He should be given another chance.' Of course there would be some merit in this.

'We understand your difficulties but perhaps there may be indications from the types of T.V. programmes he watches, or choices of newspaper articles, or objects kept in his room, or conversations with other patients, or responses to female staff and visitors with whom he has contact, or comments relayed by visiting family members, etc. Ring any bells for any of you?' It would seem that none of these had been seriously accounted for in making any real assessment of the man's offending propensities. 'In that case, we assume the nursing staff have individual sessions with him – perhaps these have touched on his sex offending in some way?'

'Yeah, we have occasional one-to one meets but he is doing so well there's not much to talk about. He gets on with his life in his own quiet way and we just monitor him, really. To be honest we don't have a great deal of contact day to day and, as we say, the sex-offending work has all been covered in the past.'

'You wouldn't say he had a high profile on the ward, then?'

'You couldn't say that, no.'

'Does he have any rehab trips into the community with the staff?'

'Certainly. Quite regular in fact. Nothing of note has come from them, no concerns from the staff point of view. He's not shown any particular responses to women whilst on the trips, you know. Nothing unusual's been reported back.'

From the patient's point of view, how was he to prove that this regrettable behaviour of his past was no longer a preoccupation? What could he say to help his case? No doubt, if he admitted to any continuing interest in young girls, of whatever degree, he would be sure that we would interpret this as a sure indication of future risk and his chances would be scuppered. If he denied any interest the equal possibility was that we simply would not believe him. How was he to explain himself? Talk about *Hobson's Choice*! Well, he did his best. He appeared before our visiting team neatly turned out, and groomed, and with the air of someone who was long-acquainted with the exercise. I was surprised, frankly, by his powerful build. Having taken stock of this it caused me to be momentarily transported to those scenes where young girls had been accosted by his presence and how intimidating this must have been for them. Asked to tell us why he believed he was ready for a transfer into a medium security unit he made a good fist of the opportunity. But then, he had had plenty of time to rehearse his efforts. It was a delicate enterprise altogether and, from our perspective, it was no easy task framing relevant concerns that were not construed as reflecting a deep scepticism, at one level.

'We apologise if any of this is painful or offensive but, you understand, we have to make some enquiries. So are you OK about answering some questions about what brought you here and how you've progressed?'

'Course.'

'Well then, obviously we know what brought you to this hospital but we would be interested to know if you think there was a reason for you committing your offences?' This seemed a lot more straightforward than asking someone to say what had "motivated" them to commit their offences. Imagine being asked, "what motivated you to commit aggravated sexual assaults upon young girls"? but that was what we were aiming for, of course.

'The reason was that I was not mentally right. My illness was the cause. I couldn't control myself when I was ill.'

'Could there have been any other reasons? You could have done a number of things but you assaulted these girls?'

'Don't know why I did that. I did what I did, but I was unwell at the same time.'

'But after the offences the first time round, and having had some hospital treatment, you must have learned something about how to avoid going down the same path again.' But if he had learned anything he certainly wasn't telling us. An inscrutable pause. 'Perhaps you've learned what to do, and what not to do, from *this* period in hospital?'

'I know I have to keep away from places where I had gone before to meet young girls.' It could be taken for granted that he had gained some sexual satisfaction from what he had done, for his physical assaults had quickly targeted the girls' intimate body areas so we didn't bother enquiring into this.

'Did you get anything else from what you did other than sexual satisfaction?'

'Umm, I don't know what you mean.' It mattered that he didn't understand this especially if he had received some therapy.

'Ok, if you left the sexual stuff out of it, what other things were going through your mind while you were touching these girls?'

'I can't say. It was all a long time ago, you know.'

'So how do you feel, now, about touching those girls in the way that you did?'

'Oh, I definitely know I did wrong and wouldn't do it again because I'm better now. I regret what I did to those girls, I truly do. It was wrong of me and they didn't deserve what happened to them. I realise that now but I couldn't help myself at the time, as I say.'

'Do you blame those girls in any way for your offences?'

'Not really. They were in the wrong place at the wrong time.' Well, that was a good sign. He wasn't denying his own blameworthiness, entirely, and placing it on his victims.

'Those episodes happened some time ago. What's changed? How have you changed do you think?' He was ready, of course.

'I've matured since I came into this hospital. I've grown up. The staff have helped me a lot to see where I went wrong. I don't have any interest in young girls any more. I'm not a risk to young girls anymore, I just know I'm not. I've got other interests in my life.'

'Thank you for that. Perhaps you could tell us what opportunities you have to meet with females in the hospital?' we ventured.

'Not much really. I work in the gardens mostly, see. Mostly male patients who do that work.'

'Do you attend the hospital socials, outings, dances perhaps?'

'Not if I can help it. They're not my cup of tea. I like to come back to the ward after my work, go to my room, listen to my radio, write letters, that sort of thing. I've got a volunteer who regularly writes to me and I write back. Other than what I've said I like to keep myself to myself.'

'The volunteer, would that be a male or female?'

'Female,' he affirmed in a blaze, off-hand fashion. 'I've known her for a long time. I enjoy keeping in contact.'

'So you don't really have much contact with women, at all, other than this volunteer?'

'No, suppose I don't, come to think of it. Don't really have the need. I'm on a male ward with all male staff. Don't get much chance.'

'But from your room window you might see the odd woman passing by?'

'Yeah but I don't think anything of it – just another woman.'

'What about your rehab trips? You have so little contact with females in the hospital and you suddenly find yourself surrounded with womenfolk in the big outdoors. You must be aware of having some thoughts or feelings? Could you say what they might be?'

'Can't say as I have *any*. I see them walking past and just leave it at that.' How realistic this was occurred to all of us but how far could you pursue this without conveying an impression of frank disbelief. He'd mastered the art of staring directly back at his inquisitors as if a sustained alertness and vigilance would prevent him being distracted and being caught off guard. The lack of spontaneously looking from one to another suggested his discomfort in our presence. But maybe that was reading too much into it.

'Don't you miss the company of women in that case? You're missing out aren't you?'

'No. I don't think so. I'm just concentrating on getting out of hospital and leading a normal life again.'

'Would it be a normal life without women in it?' Maybe he had not considered that for there followed the first pregnant pause of the encounter.

'No, I suppose not,' he granted. We allowed a momentary gap in proceedings. Another avenue of our enquiry was to gauge his empathy for his victims.

'The young girls – the victims if we could use that word – whom you encountered during your offences, must have been pretty devastated.' With no pause for reflection, nor any sign of being stunned that I recall, his instant reply was returned in the same level tone.

'I'm sure you're right. I feel very sorry for them. I do really. What happened to them shouldn't have happened.' The impression and impact had been building. The style of his presentation. The immobility, the steady cross of his leg and lack of agitation, the unchanging expression, the lack of nuance of feelings, as if each question was just another hurdle to fly over. He did not, or could not, elaborate further and no sign of disturbed emotions were displayed.

The paucity of words, of regret, of feelings. But would we be justified in concluding that because he displayed no emotion, none resided within him? Did he have empathy for his victims? Was he capable? If he was then to our minds he did not reveal it in any way beyond those few bland words. But this did not mean, either, that he remained a danger to young ladies, or any women, in the future. How could he have helped himself? The most redolent impression was of a guarded individual who vetted every notion that formed in his thoughts, accompanied them with vigilant sentinels as they descended the long stairway to his mouth, where they were reluctantly released to take flight in carefully prescribed words of reassurance.

'What do you imagine the effect has been on their lives?' His concrete style of thinking was to show now.

'I've not heard about any of them all these years so I wouldn't know.'

'Course not. But maybe you've given some thought to what it may have done to their lives? Think of the situations in which they met you?' He couldn't help us. He couldn't help himself. Think of another angle.

'One more question, then, and we'll finish. Do you believe that what you did to those girls was justified in any way?'

'No.' Silly question?

000

How to get inside the head of that perpetrator? What had he got out of that? Not much, presumably. What of the audacity, let alone the criminality? What of the degree of rehearsal: understanding precisely what he was doing, clearly having perpetrated it many times; feeling confident about his chances despite the risks; probably having a prepared repost to any complications; choosing the ground likely to yield his victims; selecting his potential victims; utilising the powerful persuasion of being a respectable grownup, with a mature voice; exploiting youngsters' weaknesses, the lack of vigilance and innocent tendency to trust adults; comprehending the inability to protest and retaliate; and judging the victims' shame in revealing the incident to others? All of these would have been carefully considered, necessary pieces of the modus operandi. What of the complete disregard for the effect on the victims, their thoughts and feelings, the influence on future life and relationships? What right had he to do just as he willed without consideration of these? How could he sexually assault such vulnerable beings who were so ill-equipped to manage the situation. How could an individual embark on the horrible transformation of such an innocent encounter, manipulate it, then fashion it to fulfill selfish intentions whatever the consequences for the recipients! Though the actual event might only have lasted a few minutes into a person's lifetime.

What consequences could be envisaged at the more malign extreme of the sex predator's acts where degrees of physical and sexual violence were perpetrated and where the offences of our "Special Hospital" resident entered the frame? These young post-pubertal ladies faced with an unprecedented nightmare: a powerfully built, older male from whom they would have anticipated to offer a fatherly protection; a stranger who had transformed into a defiling monster threatening harm, insisting on silence, wielding a knife close to them, sliding into their clothes and bodies, accessing their private, intimate areas, and penetrating them with his hands and fingers. How much would the young victims internalise these dreadful, traumatising events? How much relive the stigma and the betrayal? To what extent would they destroy all confidence in unaccompanied public travel, or of developing trusting future emotional relationships, especially with men, or of sexual intimacy. And would they, perforce, adopt a more or less permanent sense of disempowerment, social impotence and victimisation?

I confess, like most of us in the field, I guess, I never attempted to understand the necessity for collecting such details until I began to seriously refashion my nursing role to incorporate the twin ingredients of a "forensic" perspective, and a "therapeutic" perspective. For if any of us in forensic mental health were to become therapeutically effective there was a necessity to take on board a raft of new material and insights about the victims, and the perpetrators, and the exact nature of the offences, and the hazards of delving deeper into the work, along with our own toleration of it. The requirement to hold onto a frame of reference whereby a patient – that is the perpetrator of violence – terrorises, punishes, abuses, hurts and controls another citizen who is victimised, harmed, impotent and crushed. When it became clear that, unless an offender attempted to appreciate their victims' perspective – victim empathy – there could not be any great confidence in the perpetrator's understanding of the terrorising impact of their behaviour on others, or their rehabilitative prospects. Where, in this type of case, the patient carried the label of a paedophile, and became a monster to the victim and to our own imagination. Where an awareness of the interpersonal dynamics in the therapeutic relationship yielded insights of how both helper, and client, could also be drawn into the roles of victim and victimiser!

When we had departed for our return journey, discussed the interview content that we had had with both the staff and the client, and later shared our thoughts with the clinical team, it was our mutual reservations that predominated over any sense of optimism. The "Special Hospital" staff had not the slightest clue whether or not their patient continued to have deviant sexual fantasies, or deviant sexual urges, which might indicate serious concerns about the future risks he posed to society. If he was still having such thoughts then they also had no conception of how he might be dealing with them. He might be managing them very well, in fact. However, the client himself had steadfastly denied any kind of sexual or gender interest. That was problematic, in itself, since there was a generally held opinion that sex offenders found great difficulty in desisting from their deviant preoccupations without considerable assistance from others. Far better that he could have shown some evidence of volunteering his willingness to mix with women, of sharing some view of women, even of retaining some residual interest in younger females – even if deviant thoughts and feeling presided – but which showed that he had managed to refashion them in more appropriate ways. To show us that he had learned, had changed, had found more adaptive ways of managing harmful ideations. Then there was the absence of any emotional remorse over and above the few words of professed guilt. In fact, we dared to conclude that his presentation suggested someone who had not peered very deeply into himself – or had not been helped to do so – and that he probably did not have a profound appreciation of what he had inflicted upon others. All, or any, of these would have been far more realistic but what had he given us to go on? An individual who did his level best to present an untarnished front; who guarded against any female contact, not daring himself the possibility of temptation. A man who was envisaging an unrealistic return to the outside world when he appeared patently unable to sustain any real relationships within a residential setting other than a tenuous, distant, correspondence. How much was the mild learning disability responsible for this relationship shortfall and probable lack of social confidence? There were also those unholy possibilities that he was only too aware of his ongoing distortions, who opted out of normal social contact to avoid the prospect of giving himself away, and that this permitted him time to ruminate on his deviant preoccupations while he awaited the next chance to indulge his fantasies, perhaps? Was this lack of social and emotional integration, in fact, one of the primary risk indicators and that his sexual offences compensated for these? Perhaps, they were his angry and grievous way of taking revenge upon a world from which he felt so excluded and that he knew his age, his well-built frame, and adult voice were powerful weapons for intimidating emotionally vulnerable and physically slight youngsters? It was not merely the explicit, and repeated, dangerousness, or the lack of appreciation of the effect that these violations would leave on the lives of these young innocents, that exercised us. His sex offences were "motivated" not just by distorted sexual relations. It was the underlying inference that his danger lay in his use of dominating and ruthless power relations over young, unprotected women to compensate for his personal and social ineffectiveness, and that his modus operandi would continue until he had achieved some sense of personal viability, that was the crux of the matter and would need to be worked on. As to whether he had any insight into this, even after these years, we seriously doubted. What therapy would be able to exhume was the causal linkage – as undoubtedly there must be to some extent – between his chosen strategies and his familial and social experiences and background.

But the more we reflected on our client's predicament the more certain we were of the paucity of evidence we had to recommend his transfer to our medium security facility for the immediate future until some further therapeutic work had been attempted. How much was he responsible for this predicament? How had he been failed? What should have been attempted with him, to assist him? Was he even able to tolerate the confrontational intrusion that therapy would mean? Some answers should have been available to a prospective receiving mental health unit. Regrettably, we did not accept him as a suitable transfer to a lower level of security and fed back our recommendations about the work that needed to be done to facilitate his progress. This after a time span that reached well into a second decade of "Special Hospital" confinement! The irony was that the patient had not given any clear indication of having defaulted while residing within confinement. Despite this, the system of care had defaulted on his behalf. All this material was grist to my conviction that there was a need for a forensic nurse specialism.

000

For a raft of reasons, to say that the high security forensic mental health process has had an onerous job is to put it mildly. One of the many generalisations which was associated with the "Special Hospitals" and their history was that they were not renowned for effecting therapeutic remedies, and could offer no absolutely confident solutions about their patients' future propensities after discharge. Memorably, one of the former Physician Superintendents of Broadmoor, a Dr. Patrick McGrath, once said of his task that he had learned that a good percentage of his patients could safely be discharged back into the community, but that his only dilemma was selecting the right patients that made up that percentage! In respect of the category of society whom the Department of Health and Social Security had classified as presenting "a grave and immediate danger" to other people, this fact may be nothing if not alarming. This is not to suggest that the medical or para-medical staff wish to be completely risk aversive these days, so that they block the discharge of their patients, or that they fear the fallacy of their own clinical judgements about patient-safety. But they often have the benefit of the Home Office who, as distant civil servants with the guardianship of public safety as their remit, evaluate medical treatment and clinical judgement and continue to play a major role in discharging patients under highly restrictive conditions. As an intelligent, cautious and rational body – who take account of the recommendations of the medical staff treating individual patients – it also requires very clear evidence of the efficacy of the treatment measures, the developing insight that each patient had acquired of their mental disorder and attached risk, as well as an evaluation of the future risk to society if the said patient was to be discharged. It has always offered sound intellectual balances and checks to the clinical judgement of health care agencies.

The professional campaign, the procedural formalities, as well as ethical dilemmas, to attain a social inclusion of some forensic clients reach a monumentally difficult level of complexity in those most severe, and horrific, of instances and made no less easy by their contemporary character. A handful of examples may serve as a valedictory not only to illustrate this point, but to suggest that this exclusive service remains a contemporary and unquestionable necessity in the modern world of health care dealing with those of mental incapacity, however difficult that may be to accept sometimes. They also ring out a warning note about what the past has still to excavate.

Amongst the "Special Hospitals" contemporary notoriety, Beverly Allitt, came to the attention of the world media in 1991. Dubbed the Angel of Death, and a female serial killer, she became another of the more extreme examples of the type of patient dealt with by "Special Hospitals". A State Enrolled Nurse working in a children's ward in Lincolnshire, she was convicted of four children's murders and of injuring five others in 1993, whilst nursing them during her spans of duty in 1991. Some were as young as two months old. She effected these crimes by injecting either insulin or potassium into the youngsters from the ward drug stock. Sentenced to thirteen life sentences for these acts, she also attracted a psychiatric diagnosis of Munchausen's syndrome by proxy, a form of personality disorder which indirectly aims to attract medical attention for themselves by abusing another in their care, and whose subsequent illness they falsify by that abuse. Because of the disorder, Beverly Allitt was directed to serve out her time at Rampton Hospital, rather than a prison, where she still remains. Allitt's case was relatively rare, both because she was a woman who had killed, and because of the diagnosis with which she was ascribed. She was another example of a direct route into the "Special Hospital" system, the Court having decided on a treatment disposal to a high security hospital rather than a punitive disposal into the penal system because of the *mental disorder which characterised her criminal actions at the time they took place.*

In 1992, Rachel Nikkle was murdered on Wimbledon Common in full view of her two-year-old son but remained an unsolved case until the revelation, some years later, that the perpetrator was already residing in Broadmoor. Robert Napper, had been a patient there since 1995 after having admitted to the killings of a Samantha Bisset and her four-year-old daughter, Jazmine, in 1993. On the *grounds of diminished responsibility, on account of his mental disorder of paranoid schizophrenia,* Robert Napper had been diverted into Broadmoor for an indefinite period. In killing the mother he had repeatedly stabbed her body with a knife before moving onto sexually assaulting the daughter and asphyxiating her. At his trial, he had also admitted to a further rape and two attempted rapes of women but he made no mention of what was to be discovered, and proven, in 2008. At a further trial he had then admitted to the preceding killing of Rachel Nikkle the year before the death of Samantha Bisset. Again, accompanied by a young child – her two-year-old son – she was attacked by Napper who had used a knife to launch a sustained attack of forty-nine stab wounds, including slashing her throat. The child was not physically attacked on this occasion. The investigating police concluded that Napper was probably responsible for around one hundred additional attacks on other victims.

But, this lethal excess by no means applies to the overwhelming majority of the patients and it would do all of them an unforgivable discourtesy if their qualitatively different predicaments were not given some airing. Outstanding among this significant portion of the "Special Hospital" patient fraternity there have been notable individuals who, like the aforementioned Broadmoor Surgeon, have utilised their hospital experience to drive their creative abilities, for example. Janet Cresswell was another such one who entered Broadmoor at the relatively late age of forty-five and remained for twenty-seven years for attacking and wounding her psychiatrist with a knife. What could have had provoked similar consequences – an attempt on the life of the Pope! During this extensive spell in the hospital she became an author of books, and a play, and newspaper articles. The play was professionally performed on the London stage. She has since been released and she has also taken to airing her criticism on her treatment and incarceration over that extensive period.

In 1965, a certain Peter Thompson, while exhibiting a severe mental disorder at the time, attacked and injured three young women with a knife. The women, all hitchhikers, had been thumbing a lift and he had stopped and accepted them into his car late one dark evening. He became a prolific correspondent during his Broadmoor sojourn beginning with his personal efforts to secure either his release, or hospital transfer, by garnering the support and sympathy of an impressive list of political dignitaries and other celebrities. Eventually, he also wrote two autobiographical accounts of his Broadmoor years but his sphere of influence extended into the general and after-care of prisoners released from the British prison system. To this end, he became a co-chairman of the Pakenham-Thompson Committee, along with Lord Longford. He further extended himself into other charitable work.

The forensic process can also appear to be a stern and tortuous taskmaster. Later in my career I would have occasion to meet with former patients of the "Special Hospitals" some of whom had attained a greater level of insight about themselves and their illnesses than others, and all had their tales to tell. And tell them they did, very often. The story of one such individual exemplified another exceptional category of patient who can find themselves between a rock and a hard place, as the saying goes. When I met up with him, Stan Cohen was hell bent on advertising his outrage about how the mental health system had been responsible for extending and ruining, rather than rectifying, his life.

Stan had become somewhat obsessed with a young lady and refused to give up hope of continuing a relationship which she had long wanted to terminate. His index offence – wounding with intent to murder – was perpetrated when he was a late teenager and involved an aggravated assault when he stabbed her with a penknife. Two years into his ensuing prison sentence Stan became mentally disordered, with assaults on a member of the prison staff, and another prisoner. The consequence was that he was transferred to a high security hospital.

Stan found hardly a grateful word to say about the so-called "treatment". Though, eventually, he must have progressed satisfactorily through the hospital system in order that he be considered for an external transfer, his more vociferous recollections were reserved for the troubling encounters of the earlier years. He described the callous disregard by the doctors for the adverse side effects which the medication imposed on his entire body. Indeed, despite only being in his sixties when I met him, Stan's speech displayed the involuntary contortions of the mouth and face (called "extra-pyramidal" because of their cumulative nature). The effect of these years of neuroleptic medication seemed to contribute to his prematurely aging presentation. Pale and gangly, with lank grey hair, he did not look a well man by any standards. I could imagine him being an assertive patient – not to say difficult, perhaps – who would not have taken kindly to those who imposed their will and sanctions upon him. Whether by dint of his own belligerent behaviour, or the nurses' abusive actions, or his resistive response to the latter, Stan described a concerted abuse by the nursing staff. Whilst, presumably, resident on the hospital "refractory ward" for aggressive and violent patients, he spoke of being forced into seclusion for two excessively long periods, only receiving a maximum daily period of two hours away from his confinement in a small exercise yard off the ward. This was a virtual solitary confinement. In addition to these he had sporadic run-ins, of a malevolent nature, with a Charge Nurse who had ordered him to clean the ward floors as part of his daily chores. When Stan found himself unable to manage this to the Charge Nurse's satisfaction his medication, with the Doctor's complicity, was doubled, then re-doubled, at subsequent dates. Stan spoke of the situation becoming so intolerable that he eventually attacked the Charge Nurse who, with the assistance of two other nurses, proceeded to beat him up and break his arm in two places. The poor healing progress was to leave his affected arm paralysed for nearly a year. To the best of his knowledge none of these three were subject to any disciplinary process.

He never forgave the system for that change in his circumstances, which transferred him to a "Special", so that long after his sentence had expired he was still residing as a patient without the right of release. The stay within the "Special" had long exceeded the prison term. He spoke of how the hospital patients referred to the nursing staff as "screws", the term normally reserved for prisoners' characterisation of prison officers. He also elaborated on the excessive abuse of medication which had conferred exceptional side effects on his body, the episodes of electro-convulsive therapy, and the ten-fold increase in the time spent in custody as a result of the psychiatric transfer. He left the "Special Hospital" after an inflationary forty years total incarceration when his original prison sentence had been for four years only! A horror story, but one that the criminal justice and mental health systems would be capable of justifying within their ideational terms of reference.

For his part, he was simply outraged that, while he considered his four year conviction to be entirely justifiable, his subsequent decades of enforced psychiatric treatment were entirely unjustifiable. The lack of justice extended to much else besides simply losing his freedom for four decades. This was his story and he was telling of times when enquires and scandals about life in the mental hospitals and their entrenched institutional practices and intolerant values were seeping into the public domain. Bearing in mind that those of us who listened to his complaints accepted that these were his own perceptions of his experience, and that the staff might offer a different view, we were struck by the incisive detail he offered. However, allegations are easy enough to voice but hard to substantiate, especially with the passage of time and, to gain some balance, there is another side which would need to be heard. This would involve an understanding of how Stan's own personality and behaviour, along with his mental disorder, had contributed to his ongoing incarceration over the years and that it was highly unlikely that everybody else was wholly responsible for his predicament. For their part, the hospital authorities, and Home Office, must have conferred and made cautious deliberations about the course of his mental health, and related dangerousness, over the years of his treatment before concluding that he was now a safe individual. And with his freedom the chance presented itself to avail himself of his personal experience of institutional misconduct.

This has to be put into some reasonable context. Institutional denigration of duty in both democratic and authoritarian societies is a widespread phenomenon. There have been notable examples in an international context: the flagrant neglect of deserted children with special needs in Romanian orphanages; the brutalising humiliation and torture of detainees within military installations such as Iraq's Abu Ghraib Detention Centre. And no matter what the specific field, even within the domestic settings of democracies, closed institutions continually seem to lose their way and adulterate their purposes. During the 1960s, many official Inquiries exhumed the unethical and abusive, malpractices towards the psychiatric patients of ordinary County mental hospitals. There was the concerted physical, emotional and sexual abuse by owners, teachers and carers in forty children's homes across North Wales over a twenty year period between the 1970s and 1990s; and the more recent revelations of sexual abuse and torture at the Haut de la Garenne children's home on Guernsey. Militarily, the humiliation, occasional deaths from punishment, and suicides of young British Army recruits, have been exposed. Frequent exposes of Prison Service abuses of inmates have come to light over the years. Even more open institutions have not escaped detection. The evidence of child and adult abuse, and the subsequent cover-up by the Bishopric, over a minimum thirty-year period by Dublin's Catholic priests in both the school and church environments, and the similar findings among the clergy of the USA, have had an even more damning impact because of the consummate human trust that has been exploited by "infallible" doyens. The recent emergence of political, financial irregularities in respect of the expenses for parliamentary members – iconically known as the "expenses scandal" – seem to indicate that the officers of more or less any enterprise can take advantage of their relatively insular organisations in pursuit of self-interest which is strictly contrary to the spirit of their occupational/professional function. The perverse corollary is that it seems to require external agents such as journalistic investigations, or their own internal patients, to re-assess institutional integrity because of the innate tendency to contrive their own latent rules and the incapacity to be competent self-regulators of their manifest purposes.

000

An example of the "internal patient" informant was seeping into our awareness in the year before I departed from the "Special Hospitals". In 1996, a male patient who had escaped from an Ashworth Hospital rehabilitation trip, made contact with the hospital authorities and a Member of Parliament from Amsterdam and so set in motion yet another major inquiry into this complex of high security mental health care. A convicted paedophile in his own right the patient, Stephen Daggett, disclosed the nefarious abuse of privileges that had been afforded to patients assigned to a recently established "Personality Disorder Unit" at Ashworth. Ironically, the management of the unit had adopted a more liberal and therapeutic style, not entirely unrelated to the recommendations of the earlier Committee of Inquiry report. The extent of the patient abuse was wide ranging and shocking: the accumulation of hardcore pornographic literature, drugs and alcohol; the running of an internet business venture; and the presentation of an eight-year-old girl to a convicted paedophile during regular hospital visits! Coincidentally, the security operations of the staff had been so abysmally depleted as to descend to a travesty of a secure mental health service. Very senior staff were forced into resignations. The hospital had taken a strategic risk with the unit and had failed to deliver so that the pendulum continued to swing between the polar extremes of therapy and security looking for an infallible fulcrum.

000

The historical development of the "Special Hospitals", aided and abetted by their political masters, could be said to have become increasingly "risk-aversive", based on the maxim 'better to be safe than sorry'. Their performance would always be pressured by non-clinical constraints and the conceivable incidence of recidivism, particularly of more serious crimes of a sexual or homicidal nature, which had a tendency to rattle unforgivingly through the media pages, and newsreels, and subsequent Inquiries. It was the adverse consequences of these occasional disasters upon which they were judged, not the many successes. The repercussions are many, not least, that it has been many a year since working parties of patients worked on the farm, or the hospital grounds and staff gardens, or meandered through the village of Crowthorne.

There are parallel examples of the hazards of risk assessment in the modern era that attempt to enable the maximum freedom for one group of individuals who pose a risk, whilst balancing this against the potential risks they may present to those who compose their potential victims. Nowhere is this more prevalent than that of Social Workers working in the Child Protection Agency who attempt to manage children deemed to be at risk of their parents and other close care-givers. The present dilemma has been triggered by the case of seventeen-month-old, Baby Peter, whose family was the responsibility of Haringey Social Services, the same authority that had sustained the equally infamous killing of eight-year-old Victoria Climbie. Despite the entire family coming under the close supervision of the Social Work team, and the added input of the GP services, Health Visitors, and Accident and Emergency Departments, the child sustained the most appalling catalogue of brutal injuries which finally directly caused his death and dictated a prison sentence for the three immediate carers involved in his welfare. The very home conditions, alone, were a metaphor for dysfunction and a sordid contemporary lifestyle. More than this, when the past histories of the three carers were unearthed – criminal behaviour, familial violence, arson and drug addiction – it suggested that an inter-generational dysfunction had formed an alternative framework of values and expectations that ran counter to conventional expectations of an integrated family life and sacrosanct child welfare. In other words, the Social Workers were really faced with the whole gamut of social inequalities and deprivation which had constituted the origins of the abusive and fatal repercussions for Baby Peter. Following the death, and criticism of their strategies and judgement, risk aversion had for the foreseeable future to be a pragmatic solution to the professional dilemmas of social workers in the field of Child Protection. Since Baby Peter's death it has been reported by fostering agencies that local authorities have made a record number of referrals and that more children are being removed from parents while the parents are risk-assessed. It has been argued that increased applications for children to be taken into care have also risen because the families are also victims of the current economic recession causing parents to be unable to provide sufficient clothing and general care for their deprived children. Yet again the strategic pendulum swinging between one polar extreme of facilitating maximum freedom and opportunity to clients, to the other of minimising adverse risk-taking, has needed to be guided as much by political, social and journalistic defamation of professionals and their service provision as the professional judgement itself. The price for accepting this position is the detrimental effect on the many for the failings of the few whose social dysfunction should be set against a background of mitigating disadvantage. Such cases mirror those of the mentally disordered offender so that it may be facile to merely blame miscreant clients for their pathological lifestyles, and the Social Workers and the Psychiatrists, for their service shortfalls, when these need to be contextualised within an unequal society where social planning and reform should be as readily pursued.

Similarly, clinical judgement in forensic mental health management, aided by research calculations on risk assessment, could never function totally independently of external opinion formation. But if it was to rely upon it most of the patients would never see the light of day again. Nevertheless, risk aversion has ranked highly on the management agenda and technological confinement has played, what some might say as, an inordinate part in this. Broadmoor, for example, undertook a redevelopment programme with the closure of some wards, a need for updating some of the older accommodation, and an extensive supplementary addition to the residential stock which was finalised in the 1990s. For safety reasons, such as minimising roof-top protests by the more disruptive patients, the new residential blocks comprised ground floor units, only. Contrasted with the thoroughbred ancestry of the original building structure these lacked any architectural pedigree. Protruding out of the side of the original brick stock like a constructional hernia they only benefited, aesthetically, from the undulating ground which rose and dipped around them as well as the backcloth of conifers that leered over the rendered perimeter walls. The walls, in turn, were now topped with a rounded apex on which it was impossible to gain any kind of a purchase either from within or without. Simultaneously, the expansion not only dispensed with the use of, but demolished, the original Main Gate as if it bore a degree of responsibility for a reputation that was considered oppressive, archaic and opaque and had had to pay a price for this. History had become a victim, defaced in favour of technological modernisation.

The new pretender was, now, a glass-panelled reception block with automated doors and no longer referred to as the Main Gate. It included a perambulated forecourt that intentionally projected a more inviting, transparent, and hospitable presentation. The separate vehicular access was, now, an automated gateway to the side of the footway. With the inflationary expansion of structural and technological security, even beyond these measures, it could be said that a security paranoia, and risk aversion, came into vogue. Further precautionary increments such as an additional perimeter wall, small-gauge wire fencing demarcating internal compounds, high vantage flood-lighting poles, C.C.T.V. installations, and X-ray machines in the reception lobby, spread like a technological rash over the entire hospital area. The brand new, continually-manned Control Room, incorporated all these and the acute vision that was afforded enabled a coordinated surveillance that pierced every physical nook, and perused every movement of staff and patient outside of the wards and offices. (The cameras even encroached into some of the wards, in time to come.) Even physical body searches of anyone entering the site could be administered by specially appointed reception staff. Under the guise of a hospital the inner precinct was divided into discreet fenced compounds, whether they be wards, occupational workshops, professional departments, administrative block, educational department, medical or psychological treatment areas, or recreational facilities, all divided by sheets of fencing. With the result that access to any of these demanded an even more monotonous security routine as individuals passed from one area to another, continually unlocking and re-locking gates and doors ensuring that only bona fide personnel passed through these necessary barriers. This maximisation of security infrastructure turned the site into the equivalent of a sterile area uncontaminated by risk and minimising, rather than optimising, the rehabilitative potential for its patients and staff. With the consequence that, if the image of the original Broadmoor could be glamorised as a Napoleonic Fortress, then its current presentation was but a few weapons short of a militarised zone!

What impact must an unambiguously secure zone have upon the working consciousness of the staff if not to reiterate defensive entrenchment, and the untrustworthiness and unremitting dangerousness of their patients? Alternatively, what signs are there that impart the equally valid message that this place is one of therapeutic and rehabilitative space? The message can be nothing less, surely, than that their moral obligation should be weighted toward public protection and a risk-free society? Yet logic dictates that if the dangerous or offending actions of this class of patients are excusable because of mental disorder, if their individual human rights are to be respected, if mental health provision is at all beneficent, then risk-aversion can never be made absolute. The forensic mental health team, however conscientiously they refine their professional practice, however expertly they configure and test their risk assessments on clients' potential dangerousness, cannot do so without taking risks, and cannot wholly obviate risk. The life chances and the rehabilitation potential of the mentally disordered offender within the hospital precinct cannot be accomplished within a sterile area free from all conceivable contaminants even if the remaining residents do comprise a hard core of disorder.

Arguably, the hardest core of mental disorder relates to what is currently termed the "Dangerous and Severe Personality Disordered" clients. This diagnosis carried with it a tagging of a future high risk of seriously harmful offending and consequent danger to the public safety. The new millennium saw the construction of innovative regimes to provide high secure placements for three hundred individuals who had acquired this diagnosis and of the four units, two were established within the Prison estate, and two within the high security mental hospitals: Broadmoor and Rampton. Discussions about the more or less unanimous demonisation of this social category are to be found elsewhere and are always worthy of being revisited. They are worthy of revisitation because, despite constituting a bona fide clinical diagnosis within mental health legislation and medical classifications, this class has always attracted professional pessimism and scepticism. This has extended to the conviction among many that such a disorder is essentially untreatable. What separates the personality disordered category from other mental disorders is the location of the disturbance within the personality itself. And since a disordered personality is a derivative of disturbed psycho-social development, it is essentially a fixed and constant entity, out of which emerge the unsurprising normative transgressions for which they are condemned. Contrasted with this are the majority of other clinical disturbances where individuals' normal pre-morbid personalities, emanating from far less adverse backgrounds, have been fundamentally altered by the onset of a mental disorder.

Now that these D.S.P.D. units have been operational for a handful of years renewed scepticism is emerging about their efficacy and efficiency from leading academics, and clinicians associated with the project. Their provisional conclusion is that both the treatment efficacy, and their economic efficiency, are undermined by two related issues. Firstly, it is the failure of the very personality disordered clients to accept responsibility for themselves, that they can only make progress through their own efforts, and that treatment cannot accomplish this for them. Secondly, that because of medical and nursing input to their treatment, this responsibility is incidentally taken over by them and removed from the clients. But the implication is that this lack of responsibility is more blameworthy, intentional, and a continuing and unbroken stance of perverse choices on the part of the patient for which they should be held to account. The critics' eschewing of medical/nursing intervention, as if it obfuscates the proper allocation of responsibility-taking, also implies that the personality disordered are more capable of discharging this quality than all the remaining people subject to mental disorder. What happened to the equally viable conviction that, due to the developmental distortions, disruptions and disabilities, the personality disordered are "irresponsible", that is, emotionally incapable of assuming full responsibility? And it might as well be said, *because they know no better*! What else could explain the almost inhuman predations of which some are capable at critical times in their lives?

Indubitably, the most high-profile case that sparked the D.S.P.D. initiative was that of one, Michael Stone, whose infamy vouchsafed him a considerable aura when he entered the prison system. Which was where I encountered him in 1997 when I worked in a prison health care wing. At that time he still held the status of a remanded prisoner, charged with serious offences, but awaiting the first of his two subsequent trials. Details of his seemingly inexplicable crime, at least, those of which he was alleged to have committed, had long been in the public domain. The facts of the case were that, on a secluded lane in the heart of the Kent countryside one summer afternoon, Lyn Russell had collected her two daughters, Megan and Josie, from her local school and, along with the family dog, had walked them all home via that lane. At a certain point they were approached by their attacker who tied the three to trees and bludgeoned them with a hammer, including the family dog. All the parties were found dead with the exception of one of the girls, Josie Russell, the sole survivor who was left to her waiting father. The life history and former psychiatric care and treatment of the accused, Michael Stone, became the subject of an independent inquiry with monumental implications for mental health services and the supervision of patients known to have a violent history. For now he faced charges of two counts of murder, and one count of attempted murder, yet no definite forensic evidence existed to link him with the family atrocity. Due to the nature of the crime, and the precaution that he might be vulnerable to self-harm or suicide or attacks by other prisoners, he was located within our wing. Not least, we needed to monitor his ongoing mental health and prevent any significant deterioration. And this was how I came to make personal contact with one who had perpetrated one of the most disturbing crimes of modern times.

Our special remit included a mandatory allocation of Michael Stone to one of the health centre's few open metal gated rooms which afforded full and continuous observation of its occupant. He was never allowed out of this general area except under the most scrupulous supervision and no one, but no one, was permitted to open that gate without the attendance of the prison discipline staff. When I approached him on those first occasions, I must confess to quite some trepidation. But he never gave me, or any of my colleagues, any cause for concern as it transpired. On the contrary, the consensus was that when approached he was always remarkably relaxed and personable, not entirely unknown among people with such histories it has to be said, as if he might just be enjoying his considerable notoriety. But he showed no signs of any mental health disturbance, not even the slightest hint of depression or even of undue preoccupation. All of the staff speculated on his possible culpability. For myself, I set a private objective of trying to determine whether my contact with him might elicit his capacity to commit the heinous crimes that had been laid at his door. We spoke together of his background and contact with mental health services. He particularly made reference to his former psychiatrist, who was the instigator of linking his client's history and behaviour with the crimes and informing the police of such. He was quite convinced, supported by his counsel, that the psychiatrist had acted unprofessionally in breaking the confidentiality principle that enshrines a professional's relationship with a client. I will own to this day not only that it was impossible, despite all my career experience to gauge Stone's involvement, but that I adjudged him not to be capable of it based on our general assessment of our interactions. This was not altogether surprising. For most people are normal people for most of the time whatever perverse potential pulses within the lair of their inner being. Countedamong Stone's deficits, in the final analysis, must have been a damaged emotional sensor which failed to detect, appreciate or identify with the psychic suffering of others, so that he was neither inhibited from reeking that suffering on others himself, nor capable of manifesting a conscience for it.

In 2001, a Home Office research study identified significant risk factors in the backgrounds of people diagnosed with antisocial personality disorder. Among the most prominent were the parental practices and backgrounds to which they were exposed: parents with their own psychiatric difficulties, and parenting shortfalls; and parental practices which involved neglect, poor child supervision, harsh or erratic discipline, and physical and sexual abuse; and a family history of conflict, aggression, and the child's witnessing of violence.

It is in the nature of the beast that any therapeutic optimism ascribed to the seriously mentally disordered should fall prey to crises of confidence and a faltering sense of purpose. Yet, however difficult to deal with, however inconceivable their motivations for serious offending and dangerousness, the Dangerous and Severe Personality Disordered should be entitled to every therapeutic provision which aids their mental health and social habilitation, especially since they were often denied the stable start in life that was readily, and no less deservedly, accessed by most of the population.

Regarding Michael Stone, I decided to rely on the most emphatic lesson I had gleaned from my years in the forensic mental health field. That it is the emergent well being and relative normality of the recovering client, whatever level of psychological disturbance, dangerousness or criminality prevailed during the duration of their illness/disorder, which is one of the most motivating factors for mental health practitioners, enabling us to advocate and proselytize the reintegration of the mentally unwell back into the community wherever conceivable. That is our avowed professional purpose.

000

The end of my career in High Security Mental Health Services was none of my choosing. I had come to be a participant member of a number of forums within Broadmoor Hospital: the Education Committee; the Research Committee: the wider Senior Management Group; the Admissions Panel for referred patients from other facilities; a number of internal investigation teams; and the Advisor to the Director of Nursing. I had written and had published a number of professional articles and book chapters, and created a University Diploma in Forensic Mental Health Studies. But in one of the regular management culls I found my position made redundant.

And as I departed, the seering regret also derived from the Broadmoor siren persisting, every week, smacking the Monday morning air and chilling the community for miles around of a single incident that happened many, many years ago.

A prescient anecdote is said to have persisted among the elite chaps of nearby Wellington College. It told of the expectation that for some among their number their careers would begin at the College, proceed to the Sandhurst Military Academy, move onto the Aldershot Military Barracks, and terminate behind the walls of Broadmoor! Perhaps the siren whines for them?